D1604070

The Life of the Virgin

The Life of the Virgin

Maximus the Confessor

TRANSLATED WITH AN INTRODUCTION
AND NOTES BY

Stephen J. Shoemaker

YALE UNIVERSITY PRESS
NEW HAVEN AND LONDON

For information about this and other Yale University Press publications
please contact:
U.S. Office: sales.press@yale.edu   yalebooks.com
Europe Office: sales@yaleup.co.uk   www.yalebooks.co.uk

Set in Centaur by IDS UK (DataConnection) Ltd
Printed in Great Britain by MPG Books Ltd, Bodmin, Cornwall

Library of Congress Cataloging-in-Publication Data

Maximus, Confessor, Saint, ca. 580-662.
[Life of the Virgin. English]
The life of the Virgin / Maximus the Confessor ; [translated by] Stephen J.
Shoemaker.
p. cm.
ISBN 978-0-300-17504-2 (cl : alk. paper)
1. Mary, Blessed Virgin, Saint—Early works to 1800. I. Shoemaker,
Stephen J., 1968– II. Title.
BT603.M3913 2012
232.91—dc23
2011052967

A catalogue record for this book is available from the British Library.

10 9 8 7 6 5 4 3 2 1

For Paul and Helen Koutouzakis and their family

Ὑπεραγία Θεοτόκε σῶσον ἡμᾶς

CONTENTS

PREFACE AND ACKNOWLEDGEMENTS

This project originated in a conversation with Michel van Esbroeck at his apartment in Louvain-la-Neuve just a few months before his untimely passing. Among the many topics that we discussed during my visit, we shared a mutual astonishment that this fascinating and important *Life of the Virgin* had been almost entirely ignored in scholarship on religion in late antiquity and the early Byzantine Empire. At the time I was working on my contribution to his *Festschrift*, which tragically instead became a memorial volume. This was to become my first study on the *Life of the Virgin*, and encouraged by both our conversation and the incredible richness of the text itself, I decided not only to pursue a series of studies on various aspects of this earliest Marian biography but also one day to produce an English translation of it. For some time this translation lay on the back burner as I worked on other projects instead, but when I suddenly found myself living between Springfield, Oregon, and Washington, DC from 2008 to 2010, the need for a relatively portable research project arose. Thus it was in this period and in these two locations that I completed this translation, and I am particularly grateful to the African and Middle Eastern Reading Room at the Library of Congress and the Dumbarton Oaks Research Library and their respective staffs for providing such superb and welcoming facilities for research. I would especially thank Dumbarton Oaks for the support of a Summer Fellowship in 2009, and also the Oregon Humanities Center at the University of Oregon for a Fellowship during the fall term of 2009. Support from both of these institutions was invaluable for the completion of this project. I would additionally thank all those who offered comments and suggestions in response to presentations on this text at the meetings of the North American Patristics Society, the Society of Biblical Literature, and the American Academy of Religion, and especially at the conference on the "Mother of God in Byzantium: Relics, Icons, and Texts," which convened at Oxford University in August 2006.

With respect to the last I would particularly thank Margaret Mullett, Leslie Brubaker, Mary Cunningham, Dirk Krausmüller, and Niki Tsironis for their helpful comments and questions. I also thank Monica Blanchard of the Catholic University of America, who guided my first steps in Old Georgian by allowing me the privilege of sitting in on her Old Georgian class in spring 1997. This generous and fortuitous opportunity many years ago was, obviously, essential to this project. Finally, I am most grateful to Malcolm Gerratt at Yale University Press for his strong interest in this project and for his help and advice in seeing it through to publication.

INTRODUCTION

The text here translated for the first time into English is the earliest complete biography of the Virgin Mary, a work ascribed unanimously by its manuscript tradition to Maximus the Confessor (580–662), one of the most important theologians of the early Byzantine period. To be sure, this is not the first work to concern itself with the events of Mary's life: in this it is preceded most importantly by the *Protevangelium of James*, a second-century biography of Mary in her youth, from her own miraculous conception until the birth of her son Jesus. Other important precursors also exist in the ancient traditions of Mary's Dormition and Assumption, narratives of the end of her life first composed during the third and fourth centuries, it would appear, if not perhaps even slightly earlier. These works, together with the canonical gospels, form the basic underlying narrative structure for this earliest *Life of the Virgin*, which begins with her own conception, as in the *Protevangelium*, and concludes with her miraculous Dormition and translation from this world. Nevertheless, the present text moves well beyond the skeleton of events witnessed in these earlier sources, offering extended theological and exegetical reflections on their significance and adding many details of Mary's life otherwise unknown from early Christian literature. It is on the whole a highly sophisticated and eloquent piece of literature, worthy of an author of Maximus' stature, and without a doubt it stands as one of the most profound and beautiful Marian writings of the Byzantine tradition.

Perhaps the most remarkable "new" material from the *Life* appears in its surprisingly developed account of Mary's active involvement in her son's ministry and her subsequent leadership of the apostles and the early church following his Ascension. In both instances Mary's representation in a position of spiritual and ecclesiastical authority stands in marked contrast with the tendency to minimize such roles for women in late ancient and early medieval Christianity. Likewise, Mary's active participation in the events of the Crucifixion and her sharing in the sufferings of her son anticipate by several centuries similar imagery found in later texts of the middle Byzantine period and the western high middle ages, raising intriguing questions about the development of devotion to the *Mater dolorosa*. Of course, there is no reason to assume that these supplements to Mary's biography bear any relation to the historical realities of earliest Christianity: indeed, they tell us no more about the "historical Mary" than the earlier apocrypha that were among the *Life*'s sources. Nevertheless, the traditions gathered together in this earliest *Life of the Virgin* are invaluable for the insight they offer into how Christians at the end of antiquity had come to remember the mother of their Lord and how they interpreted her significance in the life of her son and the beginnings of the Christian faith.

Although it was originally written in Greek, this *Life of the Virgin* unfortunately does not survive in the language of its composition but is known only through an Old Georgian translation. On account of the close cultural and political ties between Georgia and the Byzantine Empire, translation from Greek into Georgian was not uncommon during the middle ages, and as a result there are a number of other early Christian writings that, like this primitive Marian biography, survive uniquely in this ancient Caucasian language. Georgia's ecclesiastical unity with Constantinople meant that Georgians were a significant presence in the most important centers of Greek monasticism, and accordingly these communities provided the primary setting for much of this translation activity. The monasteries of Mount Athos in particular were an important site of such cultural exchange, and it is there that this *Life of the Virgin* was translated from Greek into Georgian toward the end of the tenth century.

The translation is the work of Euthymius the Hagiorite, a prolific and skilled translator who was a member and eventually the abbot of the Georgian monastic community on Mount Athos at the Iviron Monastery.[1] During his time on the Holy Mountain Euthymius translated numerous works from Greek into Georgian, including the writings of Gregory of Nazianzus and Maximus the Confessor, as well as works from Georgian into Greek, as in the case of the famous *Balavariani*, a Christianized life of the Buddha that Euthymius translated into Greek as the *Life of Barlaam and Iosaph* (who subsequently became saints in the both the eastern and western churches).[2] From Mount Athos his translation of the *Life of the Virgin* spread quickly to the other centers of Eastern monasticism, as evidenced by manuscripts from monastic libraries at Mount Sinai and in Palestine, and also to the monasteries of Georgia. Altogether, eleven different manuscripts are known, although several of these preserve only a portion of the complete text.[3] Some of the manuscripts show evidence that the *Life of the Virgin* was used for liturgical reading in these monastic communities, and one of the manuscripts, an eleventh-century manuscript from the monastery of Mar Saba near Bethlehem, includes a guide for reading sections of the *Life* on various occasions throughout the church year. In case some readers might be interested in approaching the text in this manner, I have included a translation of this liturgical guide in an appendix following the translation.

This earliest *Life of the Virgin* had been known to specialists on Old Georgian literature since the beginning of the previous century, and yet it long languished in obscurity owing, it would seem, largely to questions about its attribution to Maximus the Confessor. Korneli Kekelidze, the Georgian scholar who first discovered the text, considered the ascription to Maximus spurious, suggesting that the *Life* had been attributed to Maximus only after his death in an effort to rehabilitate his reputation with respect to charges brought against him (falsely) that he had slandered the Virgin Mary by refusing to call her "Theotokos."[4] Nevertheless, Maximus successfully answered this charge at his trial, laying such accusations quickly and completely to rest, and however one might estimate the *Life*'s attribution to Maximus, this detail from the account of his trial hardly seems sufficient to explain the invention of his authorship.[5] In any case, if one were to identify this incident as the attribution's source, then one must accordingly assume that the text was assigned to Maximus not long after the events in question, since by the eighth century it is hard to imagine that Maximus' reputation stood in need of such rehabilitation.

Thankfully, Michel van Esbroeck recognized the importance of this early Marian biography and published a critical edition and French translation in 1986, offering interested readers a chance to judge the text for themselves. In contrast to Kekelidze, van Esbroeck maintained that the manuscript tradition was in fact accurate in its ascription of the text to Maximus. Although van Esbroeck's arguments are well made, they unfortunately do not resolve the matter as decisively as he maintains, and questions surrounding the attribution seemingly remain, as discussed further below. It is nonetheless regrettable that this remarkable text has remained largely overlooked by many specialists on Maximus the Confessor as well as by scholars of late ancient and medieval Christianity more generally, and it is primarily with the aim of remedying this oversight that I offer the present translation, which hopefully will improve access to this pivotal biography of the Virgin.

I have used van Esbroeck's edition as the basis for my translation, although as the large number of emendations signaled in the notes will indicate, there were many imperfections in this edition ranging from simple typographic errors to significant misreadings of the manuscripts. Consequently, it was frequently necessary to supplement the edition through regular comparison with the manuscripts. Unfortunately, I did not have access to the manuscript Tbilisi A-40, which formed the basis of van Esbroeck's edition, and in the main I have assumed that van Esbroeck's readings from this manuscript are correct, except in instances of clear typos or misreadings. Nevertheless, thanks to the United States Library of Congress' expeditions to Mount Sinai and Jerusalem in 1949–50, I was easily able to obtain microfilm reproductions of two early manuscripts from the Jerusalem Patriarchate (MSS Geor 108 and 148), both of which were used by van Esbroeck for his edition, and a third manuscript from Mount Sinai (MS Geor 68), which van Esbroeck noted but failed to include in his edition. In almost every instance there were at least two manuscript witnesses to compare with van Esbroeck's edition in order to determine the best readings, and I have accordingly made numerous corrections to the edition in the notes that also are reflected in the translation. I can only hope that I have not introduced any new errors, and while I have carefully rechecked each of the corrections, in light of their number, it is certainly possible that something has slipped through.

Furthermore, while I have consulted van Esbroeck's translation at every instance in preparing my own, it too is often far from perfect. In many cases, mistakes in the edition have affected the translation; at other points, the translation is overly literal to the point of near unintelligibility; still other problems arise from misunderstandings or the use of older lexical materials. While the present translation no doubt has many problems of its own, it has benefited greatly from van Esbroeck's earlier work and from the advantage of being a second attempt to understand this complex text and its language.[6] In particular, this translation was able to make use of recent advances in Old Georgian lexicography that added many improvements and refinements to the interpretation of the text: in particular, the recent publication of the *Altgeorgisch–deutsches Wörterbuch* (2005) by Zurab Sarjvelaże and Heinz Fähnrich aided this project immeasurably.[7] Equally invaluable was the growing online database of searchable Old Georgian texts prepared for the "Thesaurus Indogermanischer Text- und Sprachmaterialien" (TITUS) hosted by the Institute of Comparative Linguistics at the Johann Wolfgang Goethe-Universität in Frankfurt am Main.[8] This collection of texts was incredibly useful for identifying and clarifying the meaning of rare forms and words that have yet to register in the various lexicons of Old Georgian.[9]

In translating the text, I have tried to reproduce the Old Georgian as faithfully as possible in idiomatic English, without making any effort to aspire to a translation that would possess literary qualities. Such an approach seems desirable inasmuch as this is the first translation of the text into English. Moreover, it is hoped that by staying as close as possible to the style and syntax of the Old Georgian, this will enable comparison with other related texts concerning the life of the Virgin Mary from antiquity and the middle ages. Nevertheless, despite these goals, I have endeavored in every instance to produce a translation that reads fluently, hoping to avoid the pitfalls of hyper-literalism that occasionally affect van Esbroeck's translation. In places where the *Life of the Virgin* cites the Bible, I have translated these passages from the Georgian rather than making use of a standard English translation. One reason for this decision is that at the time of the *Life*'s translation, there was still no standard Georgian translation of the Bible, and the variations present in this text are thus of some historical interest. This is particularly the case given that Euthymius himself was the principal initiator of a process of standardization that would ultimately result in the widespread acceptance of the Athonite revision of the New Testament as the Georgian vulgate after the eleventh century.[10] Equally important is the fact that, like other Byzantine texts, the *Life* refers to the Old Testament in the Septuagint version, which the Eastern Christian tradition recognizes as the inspired and authoritative version (rather than the Hebrew). There are often significant differences between the Septuagint and the Masoretic Hebrew text, and in many instances the interpretations offered by the *Life of the Virgin's* author depend on these variations. The numbering of the Psalms is also different in the two versions, and accordingly I have given references that correspond to the Septuagint's arrangement of this collection. Nevertheless, in rendering these biblical quotations into English I frequently consulted the New Revised Standard Version and the New American Bible translations, as well as the Orthodox Study Bible and the New English Translation of the Septuagint for Old Testament passages, in order to conform these translations as much as possible to familiar English versions. When the *Life of the Virgin's* wording matches the biblical text exactly (or almost exactly), I have indicated this by italicizing these passages. References to biblical texts (as well as the *Protevangelium of James*) are indicated using the system of abbreviations outlined in *The SBL Handbook of Style*.[11]

Maximus the Confessor and the Earliest *Life of the Virgin*

As already noted above, the manuscript tradition unanimously ascribes this earliest Marian biography to Maximus the Confessor. As of yet, however, there is no clear consensus as to whether he may in fact be understood to be its author, and while in many respects the balance of opinion currently seems to lean towards authenticity, the silence of many experts on Maximus regarding this text is cause for some concern. No less of an authority on Maximus than Hans Urs von Balthasar offered enthusiastic and unequivocal support for the *Life's* attribution to Maximus, in a private correspondence with van Esbroeck written in the year before the former's death that now has been published. "What an extraordinary surprise and what a marvelous gift! I thank you with all my heart. I put away everything else and rushed to read the introductions and then the text. It clearly gives us a Maximus, who is entirely new but recognizable, as you have demonstrated, and who is involved in a great tradition—known and unknown—and is much more accessible than in most of his theological works."[12] In light of van Esbroeck's arguments for the text's authenticity, and in the absence of any compelling reason to suspect a forgery, some scholars of Maximus have in fact begun to include the *Life of the Virgin* among the authentic works of Maximus in their studies of his thought.[13] Yet many others have ignored the work entirely, and one wonders if perhaps a sort of "argument from silence" is being made by these authors, who have chosen to ignore a work that they consider inauthentic and, consequently, unworthy of notice.[14] Nevertheless, the *Clavis Patrum Graecorum*, the standard reference work for early Christian theological literature, lists the *Life of the Virgin* among the authentic works of Maximus, as does Angelo di Berardino's *Patrology*, but the issue seemingly remains unsettled.[15] To my knowledge, the only challenge to the *Life*'s authenticity so far has been published by Ermanno Toniolo.[16] Yet Toniolo's case against the *Life*'s authenticity is rather unconvincing, as I have explained in an earlier article, and for the time being the possibility that Maximus is its author must be left open.[17]

One suspects that possibly many scholars of late antiquity (and non-Francophone scholars in particular), even many specialists on Maximus and on Mary, have not yet read this text, which despite van Esbroeck's edition and translation has not been readily accessible. It is thus hoped that this translation will open the text up to broader consideration of questions concerning both its authorship and its significance. While I certainly do not consider myself qualified to judge the authenticity of this attribution, which ultimately must be decided by experts on Maximus, the matter unquestionably demands more serious consideration than it has yet received. It is indeed somewhat troubling that many Maximus scholars seem not to have even acknowledged the existence of this text in their publications. The *Life of the Virgin* needs to be carefully examined for possible connections with the themes of Maximus' theology, although one must bear in mind that this would probably be his earliest work and also that very little is known about the first forty-five years of his life.[18] And even if many of the characteristic ideas of the mature Maximus are not fully evident or developed in this text, one should also take into consideration the significant difference in genre between this biography of the Virgin and Maximus' more explicitly theological writings. Jean-Claude Larchet in particular has taken some significant first steps in this direction, and his initial soundings show signs of promise for situating the *Life of the Virgin* within Maximus' corpus.[19] Yet it would be most helpful to learn from those who seem to reject the *Life*'s attribution to Maximus why exactly they believe that it could not have been written by him, or lacking that, at least a persuasive motive for someone to have forged the attribution. In the absence of any such contravening evidence, it is not at all clear why the ascription to Maximus given by the manuscript tradition should simply be ignored, resulting in the *Life*'s silent quarantine from the canon of his writings. To the contrary, it would seem that in such circumstances we should at least initially give the attribution the benefit of the doubt.

One certainly should not discount *prima facie* the possibility that a great theologian of Maximus' stature might have authored a major work of hagiography such as this. After all, Athanasius of Alexandria and his *Life of Antony* offered weighty precedent for the inclusion of sacred biography in the oeuvre of any serious theologian. Although Maximus is not otherwise known to have written any hagiographical works, the silence that envelops the first forty-five years of his life certainly invites the possibility that he may have produced something of this nature (indeed, something at all) during this period, before turning in his later years to the rarified and recondite subjects for which he is more famous. Yet more importantly, it seems that Maximus was closely linked to an influential circle of writers who highly valued the production of hagiographical works. As much is clear, for instance, from his close relationship with Sophronius of Jerusalem, who was his spiritual mentor. Sophronius was himself the author of an *Account of the Miracles of Sts. Cyrus and John*, the patron saints of a major healing shrine near Alexandria, as well as a *Life of St. John the Almsgiver*, bishop of Alexandria from 606 to 616, which he wrote together with his close friend John Moschus. John Moschus is, of course, the author of the famous *Spiritual Meadow*, a collection of edifying tales based on his travels with Sophronius among the monks of Egypt and Palestine during the late sixth and early seventh centuries. Likewise, John the Almsgiver himself, who was a friend of both Sophronius and John Moschus, was also a noted hagiographer.[20]

This coterie of Christian scholars, to which Maximus was connected through his relationship with Sophronius, placed a premium on the composition of hagiographical writings. The great Bollandist scholar Hippolyte Delehaye singles out Sophronius and John Moschus, together with their associates John the Almsgiver and Leontius of Neapolis, as "a group of hagiographers who merit special attention," while Alexander Kazhdan identifies them as the greatest hagiographers of their age.[21] Indeed, the seventh century was in general, as Claudia Rapp notes, a period that saw numerous influential church leaders turn to composition of hagiography.[22] In this era, the writing of sacred biographies was highly prized and often placed on equal footing with the production of learned theological treatises. As John Moschus himself explains, writing to Sophronius, "the virtuous life and habitual piety do not merely consist of studying divinity; not only of thinking on an elevated plain about things as they are here and now. It must also include the description in writing of the way of life of others."[23] Maximus himself surely must have been influenced by the importance that his contemporaries and close associates placed on writing hagiography. This is all the more so given that Maximus' connection to Sophronius and his intellectual circle now appears to run much deeper than previously had been thought: there is in fact considerable evidence indicating that Maximus grew up in the monasteries of Palestine under Sophronius' tutelage. In this case Sophronius and John Moschus and others of their company must have had a profound influence on his intellectual development, and in light of the emphasis that they placed on the production of hagiography, one might almost expect that Maximus would have authored a hagiographical text such as the *Life of the Virgin*.

Maximus' close relationship with Sophronius is quite certain, and Maximus himself describes Sophronius as his master, father, and teacher in his letters.[24] Nevertheless, the length of their association and the context in which they first came to be acquainted has become a matter of some debate. There are in fact two very different biographies of Maximus that have come down to us, a highly stylized Greek biography composed in the tenth century that was long our only source, and now also a Syriac biography that seems to have been composed not long after Maximus' death.[25] According to Maximus' Greek biography, he was born to noble parents in Constantinople and as a young man served as an official at Heraclius' court, eventually rising to become head of the Imperial Chancellery. Not long thereafter, however, Maximus renounced the world and entered a monastic community just outside of Constantinople. Then in 626, when the Persians laid siege to Constantinople, Maximus fled along with other members of his monastic community, eventually settling in North Africa around 630, where he met Sophronius who had similarly fled from Jerusalem in the face of the Persian advance. Although Sophronius and Maximus quickly became close friends, according to this narrative they spent little more than three years together in North Africa before Sophronius was called back to Jerusalem in 634 where he had been elected the city's new Patriarch. Thus following the Greek account, Maximus and Sophronius seemingly only had contact for a few years during this period of exile, at a time when Maximus himself was already in his early fifties.

The Syriac biography tells a very different story, however, and is of a very different character. In contrast to the encomiastic quality of his Greek biography, this Syriac account of Maximus' life was composed by one of his theological opponents, George of Resh'aina, a Monothelite theologian of the seventh century who accordingly casts Maximus in a decidedly negative light. Nevertheless, despite its hostile tone, the Syriac biography offers concrete details about Maximus' early life from a contemporary source that would appear to be highly credible. The only problem is that the Syriac *Life* contradicts the Greek narrative at almost every point. According to this text, Maximus was born not in Constantinople but near Lake Tiberias in Palestine to humble parents. When orphaned as a boy of ten years, Maximus entered into the ancient Palestinian monastic community of St. Chariton (the "Palaia Lavra"), where he began his life as a monk. There his brilliance soon attracted the attention of the older Sophronius, and the two began a lifelong friendship grounded in shared theological convictions that would later be tested in the Monothelite controversy.

The two accounts obviously cannot both be true, and despite its openly hostile tone, one is generally inclined to favor the version of the

Syriac *Life* in light of its contemporary witness (the manuscript that preserves this *Life* is itself from the seventh or eighth century). This is particularly the case in matters where there is no obvious reason to suspect polemical distortion, such as, for instance, Maximus' birth in Palestine rather than Constantinople, his entry into the monastery of St. Chariton as a young man, and his longstanding and presumably formative relationship with the elder Sophronius. The value of the Syriac *Life* is heightened further in light of the fact that the tenth-century author of the Greek biography appears to have had almost no information concerning the early years of Maximus' life and instead has simply paraphrased information from the biography of Theodore the Studite, the eighth-century reformer of the Studios monastery in which the author lived.[26] Thus on the whole, it seems increasingly likely that the basic "facts" of the Syriac *Life* present a more plausible account of Maximus' early life and his relationship with Sophronius.[27] Consequently it would appear that the relationship between Maximus and Sophronius—and presumably the latter's broader intellectual circle as well—reached back much farther than a brief encounter in North Africa during the 630s, as the Greek narrative suggests. This certainly makes better sense of the relationship that Maximus describes with Sophronius in his letters and particularly his indication in *Letter 8*, written in 632, that he and Sophronius had been friends already for a considerable amount of time by then.[28] Indeed, the evidence of the Syriac *Life* seems to indicate that this group of scholars would have had a formative influence on Maximus, and accordingly one would suppose that he likely shared their high regard for the production of hagiographies. Such an intellectual milieu thus very strongly invites the possibility that Maximus would have authored a major work of hagiography such as this biography of the Virgin Mary.

In view, then, of Maximus' apparent formation in the company of Sophronius and his connection to this distinguished group of hagiographers, perhaps the *Life of Mary of Egypt*, which tradition assigns to Sophronius, offers an apt point of comparison for reflection on the authorship of this *Life of the Virgin*. Although the *Life of Mary of Egypt* is certainly not equivalent in terms of length and complexity, its attribution, like that of the *Life of the Virgin* (or so it would seem), has occasionally been questioned. For reasons that are not always entirely clear, several more recent scholars have disputed Sophronius' authorship of the text.[29] Nevertheless, the tendency of scholarship from the past century appears to favor the *Life of Mary of Egypt*'s ascription to Sophronius. There are admittedly—in contrast to the *Life of the Virgin*—a number of manuscripts that transmit this narrative anonymously, but the majority of the manuscripts in fact assign the text to Sophronius, as does John of Damascus.[30] Accordingly, such distinguished scholars as Karl Krumbacher, Hippolyte Delehaye, and Derwas Chitty (among others) have judged the work authentic.[31] Thus, despite some minor anomalies in its transmission and some stylistic differences from other writings by Sophronius, a number of scholars accept the attribution given by the *Life of Mary of Egypt*'s manuscript tradition. Yet perhaps more importantly, the question of Sophronius' authorship has been the subject of significant debate, and both possibilities have been deliberated from opposing points of view. One would hope that at the very least this *Life of the Virgin* attributed to Maximus might receive similar consideration.

Moreover, if some might possibly object that the recondite learning of Maximus' *Ambigua* is absent from this narrative, or even that the (relatively) more straightforward theological reflections of the *Centuries* are not sufficiently evident, it is worth noting that the *Life of Mary of Egypt*—and the *Miracles of Cyrus and John*—are similarly lacking in such "intellectual sophistication," and yet surely this does not mean that Sophronius, Maximus' mentor, could not be their author. Indeed, the hagiographic genre has its own conventions of discourse, and the simple fact that "Maximus" does not rise to the heights of theological abstraction in the *Life of the Virgin* that we have come to expect from him elsewhere is no reason to reject its authenticity. We should, it would seem, expect to find instead, as von Balthasar does, "a Maximus, who is entirely new but recognizable, . . . and is much more accessible than in most of his theological works." And most certainly we should not hold a prejudice that such effusive and "simple" devotion to the Virgin Mary as is evident in this *Life* is somehow beneath a great mind such as Maximus. This is all the more so if, as seems likely, this work belongs to an earlier phase in his career, sometime before he approached the relatively advanced age of fifty, when he began to author the various other writings that we count among the Maximian corpus. Moreover, the fact that this work has not survived in Greek certainly should not count against it; its absence is readily explained by its adaptation in the more recent Marian texts discussed below that have displaced it. Indeed, the *Life*'s extensive influence on subsequent Marian literature in the Byzantine tradition suggests that it was likely received as the work of an authoritative figure. Consequently it seems that this *Life of the Virgin* should be afforded serious consideration as a potentially authentic work of Maximus the Confessor. While experts on Maximus may ultimately find good reasons to reject the attribution, the ascription of the manuscript tradition needs to be seriously considered, and this text certainly should not be preemptively marginalized from Maximus' literary corpus before persuasive arguments for its exclusion have been presented.

In any case, regardless of its authorship, this *Life of the Virgin* is widely recognized as the earliest complete biography of the Virgin Mary, and as will be seen in the following section, it was most likely composed during the seventh century by someone quite familiar with the distinctive Marian traditions of Palestine and Constantinople. Its use by George of Nicomedia as the basis for his mid-ninth-century homilies on the Passion ensures that it was written sometime before the beginning of the ninth century at the very latest.[32] Thus even if Maximus was not the *Life*'s author, this text remains essential for understanding the formation of Marian piety during the early Christian period and the transmission of these beliefs and practices to the medieval church. Uncertainties regarding its authorship certainly should not preclude its study and interpretation by scholars of late ancient and medieval Christianity. In its own right this oldest Marian biography merits thoroughgoing study within the broader context of late ancient and medieval Christianity. Nevertheless, the question of the *Life*'s authorship of course remains important, particularly with respect to the authority that this text will command in Christian theological discourse. And while modern experts on Maximus may dispute the *Life*'s attribution, it is worth recalling, at least for Orthodox theologians, that the holy fathers of Mount Athos, Mount Sinai, and the Judean desert seem to have recognized its authenticity.

INTRODUCTION

The Earliest *Life of the Virgin* and the Byzantine Marian Tradition

Prior to van Esbroeck's publication of this new *Life of the Virgin*, it was widely thought that the earliest complete biography of Mary was the work of a certain Epiphanius the Monk, written sometime between 783 and 813.[33] Although Epiphanius' much briefer *Life of the Virgin* shows no evidence of any dependence on the Maximus *Life of the Virgin*, the latter is widely acknowledged as earlier,[34] and comparison of the sources used by each author indicates the Maximus *Life*'s priority. Epiphanius relates that his sources were the *Protevangelium of James*, the homilies on the Dormition by John of Thessalonica and Andrew of Crete, and the *Transitus Mariae* of Ps.-John the Theologian.[35] Epiphanius' rather terse *Life* does not venture far beyond these sources, which clearly mark it as a work of the late eighth century at the earliest, particularly inasmuch as Andrew of Crete's homilies were themselves written only during the first half of the eighth century. Moreover, Epiphanius' use of the Dormition narratives from John of Thessalonica's homily and the Ps.-John *Transitus* reflects the emerging quasi-canonical status of these two texts at around the same time. From the eighth century onward, these two Dormition narratives began to dominate the conversation about the end of Mary's life in the Greek world, edging out the competition so that many of the earliest narratives, which were originally composed in Greek, now survive primarily in Syriac, Georgian, Ethiopic, Coptic, Irish, and Latin translations.[36] Accordingly, Epiphanius' sources show remarkable consistency with development of Marian literature at the end of the eighth century, thus confirming the composition of his *Life of the Virgin* sometime around the year 800.

By contrast, the Maximus *Life of the Virgin* identifies its sources as the writings of the New Testament and the "holy and deeply devout Fathers," among whom it specifically names "Gregory of Neocaesarea the Thaumaturge, the great Athanasius of Alexandria, the blessed Gregory of Nyssa, and Dionysius the Areopagite, and others similar to their virtue."[37] In the case of the first two figures, the *Life*'s author is possibly referring to any of several pseudonymous Marian homilies

14

from the fourth, fifth, and sixth centuries that were attributed to Gregory the Thaumaturge and Athanasius,[38] while Dionysius is explicitly invoked in the *Life*'s penultimate section, which cites the famous reference to the Virgin's Dormition from the *Divine Names*.[39] The Maximus *Life* additionally notes that it has made use of "some things from apocryphal writings" that are "true and without error" and have been "accepted and confirmed by the above-mentioned Fathers." Here Gregory of Nyssa's favorable citation of the *Protevangelium* in his *Homily on the Nativity* is invoked as affording patristic warrant for such use of early Christian apocrypha.[40] Yet in addition to the *Protevangelium*, the Maximus *Life* makes liberal use of the various early Dormition apocrypha, although interestingly enough it forcefully rejects the *Infancy Gospel of Thomas*. Against this work it adamantly insists that Christ did not work any miracles between his arrival in Nazareth and his baptism, railing that "the book that is called *The Infancy of Christ* is not to be received, but it is alien to the order of the Church and contrary to what the holy evangelists have said and an adversary of truth that was composed by some foolish men and storytellers."[41]

The sources identified by the Maximus *Life of the Virgin* are certainly consistent with its production sometime during the seventh century. More importantly, however, the manner in which its author has used these sources and others as well strongly indicates the biography's composition in this century. Indeed, just as Epiphanius' sources exemplify the development of Marian traditions in the Byzantine world at the close of the eighth century, so the Maximus *Life of the Virgin* reflects the state of Marian literature during the seventh century with remarkable consistency. Such connections are particularly evident in the *Life*'s account of the Virgin's Dormition and Assumption, in large part because this was the one area of Mary's biography that had attracted considerable attention in late antiquity, prior to the composition of this earliest *Life of the Virgin*. In fact, the *Life of the Virgin* itself offers one of the most interesting and important late ancient narratives of the Virgin's Dormition. Here for the first time the diverse accounts of the ancient Dormition apocrypha have been woven together into a composite narrative of Mary's departure from this world that represents the full panoply of traditions in circulation at the beginning of the seventh century.[42]

The various sources used in compiling this Dormition narrative are particularly revealing. For instance, the author has clearly used a version of the "Six Books" Dormition apocryphon, the earliest exemplar of one of the two main literary traditions, the so-called "Bethlehem" Dormition traditions. Although this narrative was originally written in Greek, most likely sometime before the middle of the fourth century, it is no longer extant in Greek and instead is known primarily through several early Syriac translations.[43] The Six Books apocryphon's disappearance from Greek is largely explained by its displacement in the early middle ages through an epitome, the *Transitus Mariae* of Ps.-John the Theologian mentioned above in relation to Epiphanius' *Life of the Virgin*. The Ps-John *Transitus* is in fact a précis of the Six Books that appears to have been produced sometime during the sixth century, presumably out of concerns for liturgical efficiency. Before long it supplanted the Six Books in Greek to become the "canonical" version of the Bethlehem Dormition traditions in the Byzantine church, and its use by Epiphanius reflects this newly ascendant status.[44] Nevertheless, the Maximus *Life of the Virgin* does not show any awareness of the Ps.-John *Transitus* and depends instead on the earlier, more complete account given in the Six Books apocryphon, the first of several signs indicating its likely composition in the seventh century. Indeed, on the whole this section of the *Life of the Virgin* seems to rely directly on the earliest Dormition apocrypha for much of its information, giving the sense of an author who is pulling these traditions together for the first time from these rather disparate sources.

With respect to the other major literary tradition of the Virgin's Dormition, the so-called "Palm of the Tree of Life" narratives, the *Life of the Virgin* again appears to have made direct use of the early apocryphal sources.[45] Such incorporation of apocryphal traditions stands in marked contrast, for instance, to the Dormition homilies of Ps.-Modestus of Jerusalem and Andrew of Crete from the early eighth century. Both authors deliberately eschew the early apocrypha, maintaining—quite incredibly—that they could not find any other accounts of the Virgin's Dormition as they were preparing their own.[46] Yet most importantly, this earliest *Life of the Virgin* shows no awareness of the early seventh-century homily on the Dormition by John of Thessalonica. John's homily reflects a self-conscious effort to theologically sanitize the rather heterodox accounts of Mary's Dormition found in the early apocrypha from the Palm tradition, and as such it quickly displaced the much more doctrinally problematic narratives that were its direct sources. Like the Ps.-John *Transitus*, this text soon became the "canonical" version of the Palm Dormition traditions shortly after its production, again as evidenced in part by its use in Epiphanius' *Life of the Virgin*.[47] And Epiphanius was not alone in this. While Ps.-Modestus and Andrew of Crete both largely ignored the narrative details of Mary's departure from this world, other contemporary writers who chose to relate the events of Mary's death and burial did so on the basis of John of Thessalonica's homily. The eighth-century homilies on the Dormition by Germanus of Constantinople, John of Damascus, and Cosmas Vestitor all depend on John of Thessalonica's homily for their accounts of the Virgin's Dormition.[48] This earliest *Life of the Virgin* thus stands out sharply against this pattern of eighth-century Marian literature in its independence and apparent ignorance of John of Thessalonica's homily and its direct use of the ancient apocrypha. This difference would appear to signal its composition sometime before the ascendency and prevalence of this Dormition narrative during the eighth century. Indeed, the *Life*'s recourse to apocryphal sources for its knowledge of the end of Mary's life seems to indicate its production in circumstances very similar to those that John of Thessalonica himself faced when composing his homily on the Dormition, a quality suggesting the *Life*'s composition in roughly the same era.

There are also other important signs that this *Life of the Virgin* is a product of the seventh century. For instance, its sharp polemic against the *Infancy Gospel of Thomas* suggests this era. One might rightly question why a biography of the Virgin Mary would bother to condemn so vehemently this early Christian apocryphon and its account of the young Jesus' often mischievous miracles. The answer would seem to lie in certain early collections of apocrypha that were circulating in Greek during the fifth and sixth centuries but have survived only in Syriac translation in several manuscripts from the same period. These early anthologies brought together early Christian apocrypha relating events from the life of Mary, seemingly in a step toward assembling a kind of proto-biography of the Virgin. The earliest of these collections, a fifth-century Syriac manuscript, juxtaposes the *Protevangelium of James* with the Six Books apocryphon, thus combining in one volume the earliest Christian traditions of Mary's birth and death.[49] Yet two sixth-century Syriac manuscripts add to this sketch of Mary's life the *Infancy Gospel of Thomas*, presumably including this early Christian apocryphon as the only available source of information about the life of the Holy Family prior to Jesus' ministry.[50]

Although these early initiatives in Marian biography survive only in Syriac, it is almost certain that in late antiquity similar anthologies of Marian apocrypha were circulating in Greek. As much is indicated in particular by the so-called *Tübingen Theosophy*, an apologetic text composed around 500, whose contents are now known only from a later Byzantine epitome.[51] This summary indicates that the *Theosophy*'s author made use of several apocryphal texts, including a work identified as "the birth and assumption of our Lady the immaculate Theotokos."[52] Most likely, this title refers to apocryphal collections such as these that were circulating in Greek as well as in Syriac translation by the end of the fifth century. These important precursors in the field of Marian biography most likely explain the *Life of the Virgin*'s hostility toward the *Infancy Gospel of Thomas*. It would seem that the *Life*'s author was familiar with these collections, and his explicit rejection of "the book that is called the *Infancy of Christ*" seems to reflect an awareness that others before him had recently proposed its inclusion to fill out the gaps in Mary's biography. This reference coupled with the *Life*'s frequent use of the *Protevangelium* and the Six Books Dormition apocryphon as sources further indicates that the author likely knew of these earlier "proto-*Lives*" of the Virgin, offering additional evidence of its probable composition in the seventh century.

The traditions of the Virgin's relics in Constantinople that conclude the *Life*'s treatment of the Dormition also seem to reflect a seventh-century context. The *Life* employs a widely circulated variant of the early Dormition traditions, the "late apostle" tradition, to bridge its narrative of Mary's departure from this world with its subsequent account of the various items of clothing that she left behind as relics. According to the late apostle tradition, one of the apostles was providentially delayed while making his miraculous journey to Jerusalem in order to attend the Virgin's funeral. When he finally arrived, Mary had already been buried, and he pleaded with his comrades to reopen the tomb so that he could venerate her holy remains one last time. Upon opening the tomb, the apostles were astonished to discover that Mary's body had disappeared, leaving behind only her funeral garments, her burial wrappings and shroud, items that later would become important Marian relics.[53] The *Life's* author knew at least two different versions of this story, which had begun to circulate in the sixth century, once again revealing the great diversity of early traditions with which the author was confronted. His failure to present a harmonized version of these accounts is further indication that he was filtering through the "raw data" of the early traditions, in sharp contrast to the Marian writings of the eighth and subsequent centuries which present more homogenized accounts dependent on more recent sources.[54]

This quality is equally apparent in the *Life's* treatment of the Virgin's sacred girdle at the church of Chalkoprateia: its brief notice of this item seemingly marks the earliest witness to this important Constantinopolitan relic. Moreover, the *Life's* rather abrupt and terse mention of this relic appears to reflect its composition at a time before traditions about this relic had developed significantly.[55] By contrast, however, the traditions regarding Constantinople's other great Marian relic, the Virgin's garment at the church of Blachernai, were already highly developed by the seventh century. Accordingly, comparison with traditions relating to Blachernai's relic further aid in dating this *Life of the Virgin*, and these strengthen its connection to the seventh century. Indeed, the text's editor, Michel van Esbroeck, saw in these traditions an anchor that could securely tie this biography to the early seventh century and thus to Maximus. Van Esbroeck identified very close literary relations between the *Life's* account of this relic's discovery and a nearly identical version found in a homily composed by Theodore Synkellos shortly after the Avar siege of Constantinople in 619.[56] There is no question that there is some sort of literary dependence between these two texts. Van Esbroeck believed that Theodore had used the *Life of the Virgin's* account, thereby necessitating the latter's composition sometime during the first decades of the seventh century.[57] Van Esbroeck is certainly right that the alternative, the *Life's* dependence on Theodore's homily, is highly unlikely. Nevertheless, it would appear instead that both authors have in fact made use of an earlier source that described the legendary discovery of this relic by Galbius and Candidus. Thus, while the literary relations between these two texts unfortunately cannot secure the *Life*'s composition to the first decades of the seventh century, this connection nevertheless appears to indicate its production within the same literary milieu as Theodore's homily, which we can safely assume places this *Life of the Virgin* sometime during the seventh century, and most likely in the first half of that century.[58]

Furthermore, the range of sources engaged in this final section of the *Life of the Virgin* suggest, if not Maximus, then someone who had a very similar résumé. Its mixture of traditions reflects the work of someone well versed in both Palestinian and Constantinopolitan traditions concerning the end of Mary's life and her relics. The *Life*'s link with Constantinople is unmistakably signaled by its focus on the relics of her girdle and garment and its account of the latter's invention by Galbius and Candidus. These traditions are distinctive to the culture of the imperial capital, where these relics were housed, and there is no evidence of their circulation beyond Constantinople and its environs for several centuries.[59] Therefore the author must have been a resident of Constantinople at some point, where he would have picked up the version of the Galbius and Candidus legend that the *Life* shares with Theodore Synkellos' early seventh-century homily. Yet this primitive biography is also steeped in the ancient traditions of Mary's Dormition, which seem to have originated in Palestine in close connection with the emerging veneration of the Virgin's tomb and the early Marian liturgies of late ancient Jerusalem.[60] In fact, prior to this earliest *Life of the Virgin*, there is no clear evidence for circulation of the early Dormition narratives in Constantinople, which seems to have focused instead on the distinctive traditions associated with its own Marian relics.

Likewise the late apostle traditions, which present a rival account of the Virgin's clothing relics and their origin, most likely originated in Palestine in close association with traditions of her tomb and burial there.[61] One of the earliest sources to record this tradition is the *Euthymiac History*, a sixth-century *Life* of Euthymius (d. 473), the founder of coenobitic monasticism in Palestine. Although the complete work is now lost, its account of the late apostle tradition and the discovery of the Virgin's empty tomb survives primarily through a citation in John of Damascus' eighth-century homilies on the Dormition.[62] Could it be that this early and influential narrative is perhaps the written account of the late apostle tradition to which the *Life of the Virgin*'s author refers?[63] Such a possibility presents tantalizing evidence of a connection to the world of Palestinian monasticism. The *Life*'s reference to Ps.-Dionysius also seems to indicate the author's familiarity with the culture of Palestinian monasticism, the context in which these theological traditions developed during the early sixth century. Indeed, as is well known, Maximus himself played a key role in the early interpretation and reception of this literary corpus, and in this Maximus was particularly dependent on the earlier work of the Palestinian monastic theologian John of Scythopolis, who in the mid-sixth century was the first to identify the passage in question from the *Divine Names* as a reference to Mary's Dormition.[64] All of this suggests an author who, like Maximus, would have been very familiar with the Marian traditions of Palestine and could have combined these effectively with the Marian traditions of Constantinople. The resulting product achieves the first merger of the Marian relic traditions from the Byzantine capital with the traditions of Mary's Dormition that had been circulating in the provinces for centuries by this point, a notable achievement in its own right.

Nevertheless, regardless of whoever its author may have been, the composition of this biography of the Virgin sometime before the ninth century is in any case certain. Its use by George of Nicomedia in composing his mid-ninth-century homilies on the Passion assures its production during the eighth century at the absolute latest, even though the seventh century is clearly a much better fit.[65] Moreover, the tenth-century *Lives of the Virgin* by John the Geometer and Symeon the Metaphrast both depend heavily on this first Marian biography.[66] All three of these Middle Byzantine Marian texts present lightly redacted versions of their earlier source. It is primarily through its revision in these more recent works that the traditions of this earliest *Life of the Virgin* exercised a decisive influence on the subsequent Byzantine tradition. Both George of Nicomedia's homilies and Symeon the Metaphrast's *Life* circulated widely, especially in monastic settings. As a result, this primitive account of the Virgin Mary's life has left an indelible imprint on the Marian traditions of the Eastern Church even up to the present day. As much is evident, for instance, in the Marian laments from the *Life*'s Passion narrative, much of whose imagery and rhetoric continue to echo clearly—in some instances almost verbatim—in the hymns of the Eastern Orthodox services for Holy Friday and the burial service of the Lord at the matins of Holy Saturday.[67] Nevertheless, the full extent of this *Life of the Virgin*'s impact on the later Byzantine tradition still remains to be explored. Its absence from Greek has unfortunately made its importance easy to overlook, and yet it is almost certainly a direct consequence of this very influence that the earliest *Life of the Virgin* has not survived in the language of its composition: it was displaced by the more recent biographies of Mary that it inspired.

Mary in the Life and Mission of Her Son

Among the most remarkable features of this primitive Marian biography is the manner in which it writes the Virgin into her son's ministry, the events of the Passion, and even the foundation of the early church, in each instance placing her in very prominent roles. In fact, the *Life of the Virgin* brings Mary and other women from the early Christian movement to the fore at seemingly every opportunity.[68] Particularly in its section on Jesus' public ministry, the *Life* makes numerous expansions on the canonical gospels that are (to my knowledge) unprecedented in Christian apocryphal literature. Although the origins of these traditions are not entirely clear, and they may simply be the work of the *Life*'s author, it is certainly possible that they reflect now lost apocryphal traditions about Mary that once circulated in late antiquity. During Christ's ministry, Mary remains constantly at her son's side and is portrayed as having a uniquely authoritative knowledge of his teachings. She is identified as the leader of those women who followed Christ, and occasionally they are named as being Mary's, rather than Christ's, disciples. Even at the Last Supper, the Virgin takes charge of the female disciples during the sacred meal, serving in a parallel fashion to her son at the institution of this sacrament.

The Virgin also plays a central role in the events of the Passion, to which she is the unique witness: when all of the other disciples flee, Mary alone remains constantly with her son from his arrest through his burial and Resurrection. Consequently, Mary is the main authority for most of what the gospel writers report about the final day of Jesus' life, and their collective testimony is said to depend on what the Virgin had taught them. Although a handful of Christ's followers are present for the Crucifixion itself, as indicated in the canonical gospels, eventually they flee in terror, leaving Mary alone to bury her son. Enlisting Joseph of Arimathea's help, she secures the body from Pilate, and together with Nicodemus, they place him in the tomb. These others soon depart, however, and Mary alone keeps a constant vigil at the grave. There she beholds the Resurrection itself, unlike Mary of Magdala and the other myrrh-bearing women, who merely find an empty tomb, and the Virgin, rather than the Magdalene, is the first to preach the good news of the Resurrection to her son's disciples. Yet the Virgin's true role in all of this was deliberately suppressed by the gospel writers, the *Life* explains, "so that no one would take it as reason for disbelief that the vision of the Resurrection was reported by the mother."[69] Thanks to the success of their strategy, the *Life*'s author could finally set the record straight.

Mary's leadership role continues even after her son's Ascension, as she assumes a position of authority within the early church, directing the apostles in their prayers and their preaching. Although she initially sets off with John to serve in the mission field, she is turned back by a divine command to "lead the believing people and direct the church in Jerusalem with James the brother of the Lord who was appointed as bishop there."[70] Leadership of the nascent church thus remains within Christ's family, as it is shared by his mother and his "brother," who direct the church in tandem. But his mother in particular is singled out as the one who directs the apostles in their ministries, offering them spiritual guidance as well as teaching them how and what they should preach. Mary's maternal bond with Jesus and her unique understanding of Christ's person and teaching endow her with an unparalleled authority according to this Marian vision of Christianity's origins. In this way the *Life* brings into focus Mary's motherly relationship with her son, a theme often characterized as belonging only to later centuries.

For several decades now, scholars of medieval religion have routinely maintained that such emphasis on Mary's maternal aspect and the affectionate bond between her and her son first emerged only during the ninth century in the Christian East, and even later in the West, toward the end of the eleventh century. Moreover, this "new" maternal image of the Virgin is closely linked with a distinctive style of spirituality also said to have emerged around this same time, often known as "affective piety." Following largely on the influential work of Richard Southern, scholarship on the history of medieval spirituality has posited a dramatic shift in the patterns of devotion that took place in Western Europe during the later eleventh century.[71] In this age, pious reflection suddenly turned to contemplate, with increasing fervor, the excruciating pains endured by Christ in the Crucifixion, inviting the faithful to share mentally in the torment and sorrow. Whereas previously representations of the crucified Christ, both literary and visual, had portrayed him as a regal and triumphant figure who almost passionlessly vanquished death, from the eleventh century onward a different image of Christ as vulnerable and pitiful began to proliferate in the West. The art and literature of this era encourage an emotional, sympathetic response to Christ's suffering, thus eliciting the name "affective piety" or "affective devotion" for this movement in modern scholarship. Very much at the center of this new mentality stood the Virgin Mary, whose unique witness to the events of the Passion provided medieval writers with a compelling perspective from which to relate the horrors of the Crucifixion. Thus, as this mode of piety flourished across the high middle ages, Mary's lamentations at the cross emerged as one of the primary vehicles of affective devotion to the sufferings of Christ. Mary's maternal affection for her suffering son became the model for other Christians as they sought to contemplate Christ's unbearable torments at the Crucifixion.[72]

It is widely held that such affective spirituality first emerged only during the middle of the eleventh century, when this new style of piety burst rather abruptly onto the scene. Nevertheless, it is now apparent that the tradition of Mary's compassionate sorrows at the foot of the cross had reached its "mature" medieval form already at the end of late antiquity, as evidenced in this *Life of the Virgin*. All the characteristic features of high medieval affective piety are on display in this early

Byzantine text: its Passion narrative is suffused with emotion, empha-
sizing Mary's maternal bond with her son; she is filled with yearning for
her son and longs to die in his place; the wounds and sufferings of
Christ are described in graphic detail; Mary suffers unbearable agony
as she beholds the horrors of the Crucifixion, drenching the earth with
her tears; she shares fully in her son's Passion, even to the extent that
her own sufferings surpass those of her son. Moreover, the narrative
directs its audience to contemplate these events in their own hearts, "to
consider the sword's piercing into the heart of the blessed mother at
that moment, and how she suffered with him in everything and suffered
even more."[73] Thus the audience is invited to share mentally in the
sufferings of Christ and his mother, a hallmark of medieval affective
piety. On the whole, it is a surprisingly early appearance of what had
been widely thought to be a much more recent development in Christian
devotion. Accordingly, one wonders if perhaps there may have been
some influence coming from the East that sparked these ideas in the
West. While Anselm of Canterbury and others coming after him
who advanced this "new" style of piety certainly may have "reinvented
the wheel," as it were, the possibility of influence from the Byzantine
tradition seems insufficiently explored.[74]

In its emphasis on Mary's central role in the events of the Passion,
the *Life of the Virgin* frequently describes Mary in terms that many modern
Roman Catholic theologians have understood as indicating her status
as *Coredemptrix*, that is, "Coredeemer" with her son. Indeed, anyone
searching for evidence of such a belief will likely find much useful material in this late ancient text. In an influential article published roughly
fifty years ago, Jean Galot identified John the Geometer's tenth-century
Life of the Virgin as the earliest witness to belief in Mary's coredemption.
In particular, Galot adduced Mary's compassion at the cross as the
primary evidence that John's biography envisions her in this role: her
active participation in her son's sufferings indicates her cooperative
involvement in the redemption of humanity.[75] Yet insofar as John's *Life
of the Virgin* largely reproduces the Passion sequence from this late ancient
Life of the Virgin, the traditions in question may now be assigned in all
likelihood to the seventh century. Nearly all of Galot's key passages
occur in this earliest *Life*, which clearly was their origin.

Nonetheless, it is not at all clear that either of these two Marian biographies actually presents the Virgin as *Coredemptrix* in the manner that Galot has proposed. Absent Anselm's scholastic logic of Christ's atonement through means of propitiatory sacrifice and satisfaction, it is hard to understand how Mary is deserving of such an exalted honor. Only if Christ's suffering and sacrifice offer expiation for humanity's infinite debt or guilt before the Father would it make sense to impute any role in human redemption to Mary's compassion, that is, her co-suffering.[76] Indeed, contemporary advocates of Mary's status as *Coredemptix* base their fundamental arguments on her sufferings at Calvary, maintaining that since Christ's sufferings on the cross are the source of redemption, and Mary shared fully in his sufferings, therefore she merits a participatory role in the work of salvation accomplished by her son.[77] In this way, according to the doctrine's advocates, "she co-operated in the Objective Redemption in a unique way that entitles her to be called Co-redemptrix,"[78] so that "they [i.e., Mary and Christ] work jointly and directly for the *ransoming* of mankind from the slavery and death of sin, paying with their suffering and death on Calvary the prices of the ransom (the *passion* for Christ, the *compassion* for Mary), meriting in such wise the acquisition of redemptive grace for the entire human family, past, present and future."[79]

Nevertheless, not only had Anselm's novel explanation of the atonement yet to be invented when this *Life of the Virgin* was composed, Anselm's rationale is altogether foreign to the thinking of the Greek Fathers.[80] Galot himself recognized as much (and Sandro Sticca after him), a problem that he seeks to address through special pleading, maintaining that it is thus all the more remarkable that John the Geometer would impute such significance to the events of the Passion and Mary's role therein, according to an Anselmian logic that is somehow assumed to be implicit.[81] Yet this focus on the events of the Passion and Mary's sharing in her son's suffering in no way indicates any prescient anticipation of Anselm's satisfaction theory or Mary's involvement in the redemptive process, particularly in the context of tenth-century—let alone seventh-century—Greek theology.[82] No less problematic from this perspective is the *Life*'s peculiar remark that at the time of the Crucifixion Mary was "still ignorant of the mystery of the

Passion,"[83] which seems to imply that she did not fully understand the divine economy of Christ's Passion. Advocates of Mary's coredemption maintain to the contrary that she understood completely the salvific work of her son's suffering and her own participation in it. They further assert that Mary participated in his sacrificial work as the one who offered her son up, fully consenting to his sacrifice, yet it is hard to envision the anguished mother portrayed in this *Life of the Virgin* as willingly offering up her son.[84]

Most importantly, however, in view of the more "incarnational" understanding of salvation that pervades Greek theology from the very earliest Christian centuries up until the present, it is extremely difficult to conceive how Mary's suffering in this earliest *Life of the Virgin* (as well as in John the Geometer's *Life*) could possibly be interpreted as coredemptive. From Irenaeus and Athanasius onward, Greek theology has understood the redemptive process principally through the events of the Incarnation as a whole rather than the sacrifice of the Crucifixion uniquely. As H. E. W. Turner rightly observes of the Patristic era, "the whole Incarnation is seen by the Fathers as involved in the decisive act of our Redemption," and there is little concern with identifying the precise moment of its accomplishment.[85] It is through God's joining Godself to the Creation and to the human race that both are again made whole and restored to God. The guiding principle is not one of retributive justice, in which a penalty must somehow be exacted to satisfy a debt owed to God; rather the transformation of human nature and victory over the cosmic powers that hold it captive to sin and death are the prevailing themes.[86] Human nature is healed by the Immortal One's condescension to unite with the human race in the Incarnation, allowing the recreation, the recapitulation, as Irenaeus calls it, of humankind. Thus is humanity, and indeed the cosmos itself, enabled again to participate in God Godself and to become like God through the process of Deification, or Theosis.[87]

Of course it has long been rather commonplace to characterize this Patristic and Eastern Orthodox understanding of salvation as somehow centered on payment of a "ransom" to Satan (owing largely to the influence of Anselm, it would seem).[88] While some of the Fathers do indeed employ such language (following 1 Tim 2.6), one should not make the mistake of overemphasizing this theme as being somehow definitive of Patristic (and Eastern) Soteriology. For instance, while Gregory of Nyssa articulates a version of the "ransom theory" in its classic form, Gregory of Nazianzus explicitly renounces the idea that Christ was offered as a ransom to the devil.[89] The notion of a "ransom" is thus best understood in this context as a metaphorical concept—one among many—adopted from the New Testament, which signifies not an actual transaction or payment of something owed to the devil but rather is meant to indicate humanity's liberation from the domination of sin and death (and the devil) that was consequent to the Fall.[90] Far more important—and constant—in Eastern Christian soteriology is the notion of ultimate unification with God that is made possible through the act of Incarnation, rather than any compensation due to the devil or, in the case of Anselm, the satisfaction of a debt that God must collect through the suffering and sacrifice of the Crucifixion.[91]

Such emphasis on the Incarnation as the cause of salvation and related focus on Deification indeed figure prominently in the earliest *Life of the Virgin*, particularly in those sections where it reflects (at some length) on the Annunciation, the Visitation, and the Nativity. The *Life of the Virgin* repeatedly identifies the Incarnation as the destruction of the curse that held humanity captive.[92] The fruit of the Virgin's womb, and not a propitiatory sacrifice, has "dispelled the curse that came upon us from the fruit of disobedience."[93] Victory over the cosmic powers and their grip of sin and death was achieved through the Incarnation, so that "when the Son of God came by the will of the Father and put on flesh by the Holy Spirit and the Virgin Mary, he shattered the pride and haughty arrogance of the demons and cast them down from the thrones of their tyranny. . . . Thus he has destroyed the invisible and proud demonic enemies, and also the ungodly princes and kings persecuting the faithful. And he has crushed them and cast them down from their tyranny and rendered their plans vain."[94] Likewise, according to the *Life* it was at the Nativity that "the dividing wall of the fortified bulwark was torn down, and the irreconcilable animosity was destroyed, and peace and joy spread to creation: God became a human being, and heaven and earth were joined."[95]

It is true, it must be noted, that in one instance this *Life of the Virgin* could appear to make reference to certain aspects of the traditional

ransom theory, at Mary's betrothal, where it is explained that her
betrothal to Joseph was ordained in order to confuse the devil. "But this
was also an act of divine Providence ordained from above so that, just
as the Lord and king of all things himself concealed the unapproachable brilliance of his divinity in the flesh in order that the prince of
darkness would not be able to recognize him, so also the virginity of his
mother in the state of betrothal was concealing, so that no one could
know by whom or at what time his Incarnation took place, so that he
could thus ensnare the apostate enemy by the form of his humanity,
because that one knew that he would come into the world through a
virgin from the words of Isaiah and other prophets."[96] While there is
no mention here of any transaction between God and the devil, the
notion of Christ disguising his divinity certainly evokes particular
elements of the traditional ransom theory. Nevertheless, this passage
also makes clear that God's Incarnation was the snare that vanquished
Satan and moreover that the point of this disguise was apparently so
that "the prince of darkness" would not think to treat the incarnate
God any differently from the other human beings under his dominion.
Presumably, if Satan recognized Christ as God, then he would not have
attempted to bring death upon him so that life itself could destroy
death by death.

Of course, there are certain elements of the Maximus *Life* that
could suggest something like Galot's interpretation of Mary as
Coredemptrix in his reading of John the Geometer's *Life*. As already noted,
for instance, this *Life of the Virgin* lavishes considerable attention on the
suffering of both Christ and his mother at the Crucifixion, seeming to
underscore its importance. Nevertheless, on the one hand this focus is
itself innovative, bearing witness to a new development in Christian
devotion for which there is little previous evidence. This move in a relatively new direction is indeed something of a departure from the prior
tradition, whose significance admittedly is not yet fully understood. Yet
on the other hand, the Crucifixion itself can hardly be said to be a new
theme in Christian literature and thought, and there is even some limited
precedent for reflection on Mary's involvement in the trials of the
Crucifixion.[97] Moreover, although the Greek Fathers by and large saw
the Incarnation as a whole, rather than the Crucifixion uniquely, as the

cause of salvation, this certainly does not mean that they regarded the Crucifixion as unimportant or ignored its significance: far from it. The Passion was indeed central in their thought as the culmination of the divine economy through which death was vanquished by death, even if it did not possess the singular importance that it would later acquire for Anselm and much of the subsequent Western tradition. The Maximus *Life of the Virgin* holds consistently to this eastern tradition of soteriology, and despite its seemingly unprecedented focus on the details of the Passion as seen through the Virgin's tearful eyes, it does not ascribe redemptive activity to either her son's or her own suffering. One should additionally note that the *Life* elsewhere emphasizes Mary's full participation—in an explicitly similar fashion—in the sufferings of the apostles and the earliest Christian martyrs.[98] Such Marian "compassion" certainly is not coredemptive in the sense that many Roman Catholic theologians have proposed, and more importantly it suggests that her related sharing in Christ's sufferings is not indicative of unique cooperation in the act of redemption through her travails at the Crucifixion. Rather, the emphasis would instead appear to be on her generally compassionate nature rather than her coredemptive sufferings.

The *Life* does, however, twice refer to the idea of Christ's "sacrifice," once at the institution of the Eucharist, where "he sacrificed himself as a priest and was sacrificed," and again near the biography's conclusion where Mary is described as "a second offering of our nature to the Father after the first one who was himself sacrificed one time on behalf of all."[99] The latter passage is the more striking, particularly for its reference to Mary in relation to the broader theme of Christ's sacrifice, identifying her as a "second offering of our nature to the Father." Here perhaps more than anywhere else the *Life* comes closest to suggesting something that could possibly be taken to indicate Mary's coredemption. But a closer look at the immediate context finds such an interpretation improbable. The setting is Mary's "ascension and translation," that is her Assumption, and it is through these events, and not her compassion at the cross, that a "second offering of our nature" has been presented to the Father: as the *Life* elsewhere writes of her bodily Assumption, "thus our nature was raised up to heaven in the eternal kingdom not only by her son but also by the immaculate mother."[100]

Accordingly, Mary's coredemption in the sense that it is commonly expressed seems very far from view here. The passage does not relate her participation in the redemptive sufferings of her son. Rather, her bodily presence in Heaven has, like her son's Resurrection and Ascension, again brought our nature to dwell in its restored state as an offering in the presence of the Father. It is thus the second of many similar such offerings that presumably will follow as human beings ultimately offer their renewed nature to the Father through Deification and final union with God.[101]

Indeed, a little later in the same section the *Life* describes Mary as a "divine gift to humanity and offering from humanity to God."[102] Here again the broader context is also Mary's Assumption, although the logic also partly seems to invoke understanding of the Incarnation as involving the parallel movements of a gift from God to humanity that makes possible humanity's return to God in Deification, in this case achieved in advance through the Virgin's Assumption. In another passage, from the section on Mary's Dormition, the *Life* remarks that just before her soul went forth from her body Mary "made an offering for the entire world and for every soul that calls upon the Lord and calls to mind the name of his mother."[103] Yet here the offering is unmistakably one of her intercessions with her son. Finally, the opening section of the *Life* describes Mary during her childhood in the Temple as "an offering to God," here indicating, it would seem, her special dedication and consecration to God.[104] In each case, then, the *Life*'s occasional references to Mary's "offering" to God are very far removed from the Roman Catholic view of Mary as *Coredemptrix* through her active participation in the redemptive sacrifice and sufferings of her son. In similar fashion, when the *Life* elsewhere refers to Mary twice as our "ransom," there is equally no sense of her as a Coredeemer: in one instance the language is directly borrowed from the Akathist hymn, while the other identifies her body as "the ransom of our nature," a dignity that her body receives on account of its role in the Incarnation, not the Crucifixion.[105]

As for the reference in this passage to Christ's sacrifice "one time on behalf of all," it should be clear that the notion of Christ's Passion as a sacrifice is certainly one with strong biblical precedent that is not at all foreign to the writings of the Greek Fathers.[106] The same can also be said for the *Life*'s earlier description of Christ as one who sacrificed himself and was sacrificed, a notion derived particularly from Hebrews 9 and 10, here invoked in the context of the Last Supper. Following such imagery from the scriptures, the early Church Fathers often describe Christ's death on the cross as a redemptive sacrifice. Yet like the image of a ransom, the use of such language is seemingly not to be taken literally. It is, as many scholars of patristic soteriology have observed, one among many different metaphors used to express Christ's work of salvation, all of which are important and no one of which alone is seen as sufficient to capture the fullness of this mystery. By contrast, Anselm and much of the subsequent western tradition have in part broken with the polyphony of patristic (and biblical) soteriological discourse to focus squarely on a single metaphor, that of propitiatory sacrifice, largely to the exclusion of the others.[107]

Furthermore, it is important to note that according to the early Church Fathers, this "sacrifice" is not, as the Anselmian tradition would have it, an offering to God the Father, whose justice and honor required the discharge of an infinite debt that humanity owed and God's nature could not overlook.[108] Such thinking would seem to constrain God in a way that was (and is) foreign to the Greek mind, forcing on God a particular course of action. Rather, as Peter Bouteneff notes, "when the Fathers did speak of a 'recipient' of the sacrifice, they spoke metaphorically: the debt was paid *to our condition* (in the words of Leo of Rome), or, as St Basil the Great has it in his liturgical anaphora, 'He gave himself as a ransom *to death*,' so that Christ's death makes 'a path to the resurrection of the dead.'" It is, then, not a payment owed to the devil or the satisfaction of God's justice but a sacrifice that "overcomes a condition best described as captivity to death or sin."[109] Moreover, it bears repeating that the Greek Fathers understood the sacrifice of the Crucifixion not as a singularly redemptive act but instead primarily as the culmination of the Incarnation, in which the Immortal God finally vanquishes death by death.[110] It is the logical completion of God's salvation of humanity through the Incarnation, a concept also evident in the *Life of the Virgin*, which identifies the Passion and Resurrection not with the destruction of the curse but instead as "the completion of the divine economy."[111]

Thus, when evaluated according to the theology of both the text itself and its broader historical milieu, any direct role that Mary might play in the process of salvation would appear to be limited to her Divine Maternity. To be sure, Mary plays a vital and unique role in the restoration of humanity to God through her assent to the Incarnation at the Annunciation. Without her consent, the saving work of God's Incarnation could not have taken place. Presumably, the Greek Fathers and Orthodox theologians alike would have no trouble agreeing with such a position. Yet according to the terms defined by Catholic theology, Mary's willing participation in the Incarnation involves her only in the "Subjective Redemption" rather than the "Objective Redemption" of humanity. The Subjective Redemption consists in the "co-operative activity of the faithful in spreading the fruits of the Redemption," or "the application of the redemptive grace to individual souls, . . . to be distributed to each man who desires to be saved and to be made holy," and in this sense all pious Christians are active in the redemptive process as "coredeemers."[112] Yet this is altogether different from the position advocated by supporters of Mary's coredemption, who ascribe to Mary an active role in the process of Objective Redemption, that is "the acquisition of grace accomplished universally" for the salvation of humanity.[113] Within this theological framework, Mary's role in the Incarnation does not achieve this; only her sufferings and sacrifice at the Crucifixion involve her in acquisition of universal grace.[114] And as René Laurentin and Galot have both demonstrated, in the western tradition the title *Coredemptrix* has been reserved for Mary exclusively in relation to her participation in the Objective Redemption of humanity.[115]

It is perhaps also worth mentioning in this context that on several occasions the *Life of the Virgin* identifies Mary as a "mediator," a title that might suggest to advocates of her coredemption the closely related notion of Mary's unique role as *"Mediatrix"* of divine Grace in conjunction with her son. According to this dogmatic position, the Virgin Mary, because of her unique participation in the redemptive process at the Crucifixion, also "shares in the one mediation of Christ *in distributing to the People of God* the 'gifts of eternal salvation' obtained from the cross (cf. Jn 19.26). Because Mary is Coredemptrix with the Redeemer, she is also Mediatrix of Graces with the Mediator."[116] Yet inasmuch as Mary's elevation to *Mediatrix* is contingent on her alleged status as *Coredemptrix*, it hardly seems possible from a historical perspective that the *Life of the Virgin* envisions such an exalted position for the Virgin so that she could be understood as distributing the Grace of redemption equally with her son.[117] Indeed, advocates of Mary's unique status as *Mediatrix* identify her allegedly singular role as *Coredemptrix* in the acquisition of Grace as the one thing that distinguishes her from other potential mediators or intercessors with Christ: she plays a direct role in distributing the universal Grace that was obtained through her own cooperation.[118] It is true that a number of Greek Marian texts describe Mary as a mediator, but generally these seem to have in view either the idea of Mary's special role of intercession with her son or her role in the Incarnation as one who mediates between the divine and the human through her Divine Maternity.[119] In any case, it is quite clear that the *Life of the Virgin*'s use of the term "mediator" for Mary does not present her as directly involved in the distribution of saving Grace to the faithful. Rather, in each instance where Mary is named a mediator, either her intercession is explicitly invoked in conjunction with her mediation or an intercessory meaning is clear from the context.[120] Thus, while Mary is envisioned as a uniquely positioned intercessor, her mediation is dependent on her son's concession to her pleas, and she does not distribute the Grace of salvation equally with him.

Consequently, it would seem that only by anachronistically importing Anselm's innovative understanding of the atonement, as Galot and Sticca have quite candidly done, can Mary's compassion at the Crucifixion be understood as playing any role in the process of redemption, thereby meriting for her the title *Coredemptrix* (or for that matter, *Mediatrix*). While such an interpretive move is perhaps entirely appropriate within the context of Roman Catholic dogmatics,[121] it is not likely to persuade either many modern historians or many Eastern Christians that this seventh-century *Life of the Virgin* (particularly if it is thought to be by Maximus!) or its tenth-century revision by John the Geometer presents Mary as *Coredemptrix*. To be sure, once this powerful image of Mary's compassion came into contact with Anselm's juridical, satisfaction theory of the atonement, it was bound to take on different shades of meaning. Yet within the theological context in which both of these *Lives* were produced, it is extremely difficult to imagine that Mary's compassion could possibly have been understood as implying her status as *Coredemptrix*. To the contrary, the profoundly incarnational soteriology of both this earliest *Life of the Virgin* and the Greek theological tradition more broadly invites, indeed even necessitates, a rather different interpretation of Mary's suffering at the cross from what is suggested by many advocates of her coredemption. What significance this representation of the Virgin might have had within its earliest historical and theological context still remains to be seen, inasmuch we have not yet begun to explore this new form of piety within its early Byzantine milieu. It would appear, however, that the primary significance of Mary's compassion in this setting will be found principally in the realm of devotion rather than dogmatics, and previous interpretations of George of Nicomedia's ninth-century recycling of this imagery of Mary's compassion at the cross would seem to suggest as much.[122]

CHAPTER 1

BIRTH AND CHILDHOOD[1]

The praise and glory, laud and honor of our all-holy, incorruptible, and most blessed queen, the Theotokos and ever-virgin Mary, and the story of her immaculate and blessed life from birth until the Dormition written by our blessed father Maximus the Philosopher and Confessor.

Kyrie eleison.

I Hear this, all you nations, and take heed, all you inhabitants of the earth (cf. Isa 34.1)! Come all believers and gather all lovers of God, kings of the earth and all peoples, princes and all judges of the earth, boys and girls, the old with the young, every tongue and every soul, let us hymn, praise, and glorify the all-holy, immaculate, and most blessed Theotokos and ever-virgin Mary,

the throne of the king more exalted than the cherubim and seraphim,

the mother of Christ our God,

the city of God of which glorious things are spoken (cf. Ps 86.3),[2]

chosen before the ages by the ineffable forethought of God,

the temple of the Holy Spirit,

the source of the living water,

the Paradise of the tree of life,

the growing vine from which drink of immortality was brought forth,

the river of the living water,

the ark that contained the uncontainable,

the urn of gold that received the manna of immortality (cf. Heb
  9.4),
the unsown valley[3] that sprouted forth[4] the wheat of life,
the flower of virginity, full of the perfume of grace,
the lily of divine beauty,
the virgin and mother from whom was born the lamb of God who
  takes away the sins of the world,
the treasure house of our salvation that is more exalted than all the
  powers of heaven.

All nations that have received the preaching of the gospel, raise your
hands and praise her with voices of joy, with sweet words, with clear
voices, with loud voices, for it is the duty of every tongue and every
nature of humankind to glorify and praise the one from whom our
salvation came to be. But how could this be? For it is fitting that, when
the creator and God of all wanted to come among humankind, as the
blessed and all-praised one was found worthy and her inheritance
divinely graced, *her beauty pleased the king* (Ps 44.12), and he saw fit to dwell
within her. So now we who wish[5] to prepare this praise of her, let us
receive a tongue that is worthy and a mind sufficiently eloquent for her
glory and praise. But there is no one among the human race who is able
to praise and glorify the holy Theotokos worthily and fittingly, not even
if the myriads of tongues were brought together, and even if all the
nations of humanity came together, they would not be able to attain the
worthiness of her praise and glory. Nevertheless, since it is not possible
to be worthy of undertaking the task of her great glorification, we will,
according to our ability, show eagerness to laud and praise the mother
of God, our hope and refuge. For just as her gracious son and God
does not expect the highest ability from anyone, so his all-holy mother
will receive[6] this offering of praise according to our feeble ability with
mercy, as is befitting her sweetness.

2 Let us relate, then, with the grace and assistance of the all-holy
   Theotokos, whence she appeared, and who her parents were, and
how her upbringing and immaculate conduct were, and what great glorification was accomplished in her from her birth until her Dormition,
because her grace and assistance have given us sufficient ability and

speech to open our mouth. Nevertheless, if we should say something about her king and son according to our ability, it would not be inappropriate, because all glory and praise are his, for the blessing and glory of his immaculate mother are from him and by him. Now, then, everything that we will relate and make known is trustworthy and reliable, true testimonies taken from the assembly of the pious: first of all, from the holy evangelists and apostles; then from the holy and deeply devout Fathers, whose words are full of all wisdom and were written by the grace of the Holy Spirit, and their works are beautiful and virtuous. These are Gregory of Neocaesarea the Thaumaturge, the great Athanasius of Alexandria, the blessed Gregory of Nyssa, and Dionysius the Areopagite, and others similar to them in virtue. And if we say some things from the apocryphal writings, this is true and without error, and it is what has been accepted and confirmed by the above-mentioned Fathers. For so the blessed Gregory of Nyssa says, "I have read in an apocryphal book that the father of the all-holy Virgin Mary was renowned for his observance of the Law and was famous for his charity."[7]

3 He was named Joachim from the tribe of David, the king and prophet, and his spouse was Anna. And he was childless until old age, because his wife was barren. Nevertheless, according to the Law of Moses, an honor was afforded to women who gave birth that was not given to the childless (cf. *Protev* 1.7). Now, then, Joachim and Anna were esteemed and honored in deed and word, because they were known to be from the lineage of Judah and David and the succession of kings. And ultimately the tribes of Judah and Levi were united; that is to say, the royal and the priestly tribes were mixed, for so it is written concerning Joachim and Joseph, to whom the holy Virgin was betrothed. Although he was called from the house and the tribe of David according to the nearer side (cf. Luke 1.25), both sides nevertheless became one, the one by nature, which was from David, and the other through the Law, which were the Levites. So the blessed Anna was also an obedient branch from this tribe, and she foretold that the king born from their child would be a high priest as God and human being. But on account of the Law of Moses and the reproach of senseless people, childlessness greatly distressed the honorable and glorious parents of the Virgin when

they were wanting a child to be born from them to eliminate not only their own reproach but that of the whole world and to lead it up to a higher glory (cf. *Protev* 1.5–6, 1.9–10, 2.6–7). Then the blessed Anna, like the first Anna, the mother of Samuel, went to the Temple, and she prayed to the creator of all things to give her the fruit of childbirth so that she would dedicate to him as a gift what had been given by him (cf. 1 Sam 1.1–11; *Protev* 2.9, 4.2). So also the worthy Joachim was not negligent, but he asked God to loose the bonds of their childlessness.

4 The gracious and abundantly generous king looked upon the prayer of the righteous, and he sent forth the good news to both of them (cf. *Protev* 4). First he informed Joachim while he was standing in prayer in the Temple. He heard a voice from on high that said, "You will receive[8] a child who will be a glory not only for you but for the whole world." He made Joachim's good news known to the blessed Anna, but she did not cease from her prayer to God with ardent tears. The news came to her from God in the garden where she was offering prayers and supplications to God (cf. *Protev* 3). The angel of God came to her and said, "God has heard your prayer, and you will give birth to the cause of joy, and you will name her Mary, through whom the salvation of the entire world will come into being" (cf. *Protev* 4.1). And with the annunciation the conception began, and from the barren Anna was born Mary the illuminator of all, for so her name Mary is translated as "illuminator."[9] Then the honorable parents of the blessed and holy child had great joy, and Joachim prepared a great feast, and he invited all his relatives, the learned and the unlearned (cf. *Protev* 6.6), and they all glorified God, who had brought them a wonderful miracle, so that the reproach of Anna turned into the greatest glory. She is the gate of the gate of God and the beginning of her life and glorious deeds. From this point on it is fitting that we should elevate our discourse concerning her exalted mysteries and the glories by her grace, intercession, and assistance, for she is the cause and provider of every good thing.

5 When she had passed the age of nursing, she who for our sake took care to nurse Christ our God from birth, and she was three years old, her blessed parents brought the Temple of God to the Temple

(cf. *Protev* 7.2). And they dedicated her as an offering to God, as promised before her birth, and they brought her there with glory and honor, as was fitting. Many virgins went before her and accompanied her with brilliant lamps, as the king and prophet, the forefather of the immaculate Virgin, foretold and said from the beginning, *"they brought virgins to the king, and after this, her friends brought her"* (Ps 44.15), for the prophet said this, before the Presentation, about the virgins who went and accompanied her. And this prophecy is to be understood not only as about them, but also about the virgin souls subsequently following her path, whom she called her friends. And even if they all are imperfect in friendship and resemblance to her, the souls of the saints are nevertheless called her friends by the grace and goodness of her child the Lord, as the king and creator of all did not himself consider it inappropriate to call his brothers pleasing and friends.[10] For in fact all the souls of the just, who by a life of purity are enabled to become even his friends, will be made worthy by her intercession, and by grace they are brought to her king and son and led into the heavenly Holy of Holies, where, as her son entered in as a forerunner on our behalf, according to the word of the apostle Paul (cf. Heb 9.12), so also the all-holy mother of the Lord entered into the heavenly resting place before all, and the other souls of the saints are led there subsequently by her intercession.

6 Of course, I am eager to describe the later deeds of the divinely adorned Virgin, but my mind does not wish to pass by the words of the blessed prophet David. So let us recall a little further above, and let us understand what prophecy the glorious king and prophet brings forth concerning his blessed queen and daughter and the mother of God. For in the forty-fourth[11] psalm he speaks first about her king and son, as he relates that the Holy Spirit gave the images of his glory: the two-fold beauty of his appearance (cf. Ps 44.3–4),[12] and the effusion of grace from his lips (cf. Ps 44.3), and the excess[13] of Wisdom, and the anointing with joy (cf. Ps 44.8), and the armament of power, the arc of the bow, the girding of the sword to his loins (cf. Ps 44.5–6), the rod of Providence, and the rod of power (cf. Ps 44.7), that were portending the form of his Incarnation, in which he truly calls them to peace and justice, and his complete victory in everything, his triumph and his

eternal reign. Nevertheless, he completed such beautiful prophecies about our Lord Jesus Christ, and immediately he also declared the adornments of his holy mother. And even if some have interpreted these words as being about the Church, there is nevertheless nothing at all that impedes understanding them as being about the holy Theotokos. For words spoken by the Holy Spirit should not be understood only in one way but in many ways, for they are a treasure house of good things. And those Fathers who have interpreted these words as about the Church have spoken well, and likewise understanding the prophecy as being about the holy Theotokos is true and without error.

7 Behold, then, how beautifully he foretells not only about the Presentation in the Temple,[14] but also about her other spiritual goodness and beauty. *The queen stood at your right* (Ps 44.10). This statement foretells her Presentation in the Temple and her location to the right of the altar in the Holy of Holies, which is truly regarded as being to the right of God. Then he relates the adornment of her virtues, how very beautiful she was, and that *she was adorned with a gold-woven robe* of very many colors,[15] *and dressed with diverse adornment* (Ps 44.10).[16] For he said all of this regarding her spiritual adornment: although he says *"gold-woven,"* all of her many-hued virtues are nevertheless foretold, which individually are beautiful and magnificent. But when they are added to each other and united, as they were collected in the blessed soul of the immaculate Virgin, their surpassing beauty is even greater. That is why he says *"with diverse adornment,"* that is to say an adornment of good works and godly thoughts in complete accord with the will of God her savior. As the vault of heaven that appears in the clouds is one in substance and name, and multi-colored and ornate in appearance, so also the immaculate Virgin was from a young age diversely adorned with ineffable adornments of virtue. And as she grew in age, the adornment of virtues increased greatly. And that is why *the king desired her beauty* (Ps 44.12), and he dwelt within her.

8 But how good and appropriate are the following words: *Hear, O daughter, and incline your ear* (Ps 44.11). Hear the first proclamations of the prophets by the Holy Spirit about you and also the new stories

of your parents, their barrenness and old age, their prayers and supplications, and their good news about your birth sent by God, and your unexpected and wonderful birth by his grace. And behold your Presentation now in the Temple, your dwelling in it with honor,[17] and your wonderful nurturing in the Holy of Holies, where[18] the High Priests enter once each year (cf. Lev 16). Behold your wonderful nourishment and the even more wonderful bearer of your nourishment (cf. *Protev* 8.1); incline your ear and prepare yourself to receive the Annunciation, the glorious greeting and the seedless conception of the Word of God. And your thoughts are no longer with the Jews and the house of your fathers. *Forget your people and the house of your father* (Ps 44.11) and everything of this world, and put on new thoughts and a firm hope, and so *the king desired your beauty* (Ps 44.12), and you will be worthy to be called in truth his mother. But he adorned his prophecy even more and foretold her sending forth and her entreaty by the rich. For this reason he said, *"the rich of the people will seek your favor"* (Ps 44.13). And then many nobles and dignitaries of the people gathered together for her Presentation in the Temple, and also now the rich who are full of divine goodness entreat her and glorify her in the Spirit.

9 But so that one would compare her deeds with each other and see in the external honor the higher and more glorious interior honor, for this reason he said, *"all glory of the daughter of the king is within"* (Ps 44.14). Her virtues reveal not only inner riches but also incomprehensible graces of the Holy Spirit whose abundance and beauty are inexpressible. For this reason, as a symbol of their unity and diversity, she received the golden tassels. *She is adorned with golden tassels and clothed in many colors* (Ps 44.14),[19] because as they appear separately in their individuality and are all united in the garment, whose fringe[20] they are, so also the graces and virtues dwelling in the blessed Virgin are also many and are all conferred and prepared by one Holy Spirit. In this way the Presentation of the Virgin in the Temple took place, involving so much more than we could grasp with a feeble mind and describe with a stuttering tongue. But what was the nature of her life in the Temple, and what was the ladder of her wonders?[21] This ladder of heaven raises us up, for after

her new and wonderful Presentation in the Temple, her presence in the Temple became more new[22] and more wonderful, and her nourishment more wonderful, and the development of her mind greater, because her nourishment was from above, and it was given by the hand of an archangel (cf. *Protev* 8.1). And the discipline and knowledge of her soul developed with the growth of her body, and the teaching of perfection was given to her by her nurturing angel, but even more I say by the grace of the Holy Trinity. And so she grew in stature[23] and grace, as the evangelist says of her son (Luke 2.52), so that the growth of her stature corresponded to the nourishment with which she was nourished, and her spiritual discipline to the teaching[24] that was given to her by the grace of God and the co-protection of the archangel, for so it was also fitting for the one who was destined to contain in her womb the uncontainable nature of God, that her every deed was surpassing nature.

10 That is why Scripture says of her bodily forms and disciplines that they were all wonderful, praised, and glorious. For she loved learning and was an excellent student: she was an expert in every good subject and filled with understanding[25] of the divine Scriptures and with all wisdom, because she was to become the mother of the Word and Wisdom of God. She was clever with words and had a pleasant voice, as it is written, *"she opened her mouth with wisdom and imposed order on her speech"* (Prov 31.25), for these words of Solomon were also spoken about her, and also the following, *"she is clothed in her strength and beauty"* (Prov 31.26), by the grace and power that was born from her, and she is dressed in beauty. She is dressed in strength and has been clothed by the one who became incarnate from her. She is dressed in beauty and clothed with power, and the following words were also appropriately spoken about her, *"she was happy in the last days"* (Prov 31.26), for as the queen of all, she holds authority over all things, and from one end of the earth to the other end, all things submit to her and glorify her, for she reigns with her son and king and will reign especially in the last days when the end and conclusion of this fleeting world will take place. And she will reign with her good and sweet son in an unending and incomprehensible reign.

11 It is, then, good and most fitting to call these sayings to mind successively. *Many daughters have acquired* spiritual or material *riches; many have attained power. But you have surpassed* them in nature and knowledge, *and you have been exalted above them all* by divine grace and by the supernatural birth (Prov 31.29). Although these testimonies of the Scriptures have delayed us a little from the narrative of her life, they have nevertheless been mentioned well and fittingly for her glorification and for the benefit of the pious. But let us return to the initial plan of the discourse, for as she is in every way more exalted and glorified than all human beings, so also the manner and conduct of her life were unmatched. She was blessed by all[26] and was full of all grace, and I will say even further that she was supremely worthy of every grace, intelligent with respect to images and words, a scrutinizer of divine visions, completely removed from restlessness, wrath, and gossip, beautiful in soul and body and ordinary in measure of stature, full of every goodness and every good deed. Nevertheless, she was in this way holy by nature and truly a virgin to the point that not even the slightest desire of any passion that would be corrupting of spiritual holiness ever came upon her.[27]

12 But more than anyone else, her holy soul was full of benevolence and compassion, and in this way she was more than anyone else an imitator of her good and benevolent son, having a tranquil and humble mind with such an abundance of virtue and excess of grace. Truly she was the queen exalted above every nature in word and deed and thought, for she was to become the mother of the true king of all things who then became poor and *was humbled* for our sake *unto death by death on a cross* (Phil 2.8). So she, the blessed and glorious ever-Virgin, was also poor and humble in spirit, according to the blessing spoken by the Lord (cf. Matt 5.3). She was obedient to the priests, a respectful servant and respected by all, for she was a child of divine grace and also the parent of the king of angels and of humanity. So then after childhood the power of God overshadowed her and adorned her spiritually and bodily with every adornment of virtue, as *with golden tassels in many colors* (Ps 44.14). With such comportment and such qualities, then, she was present in the Temple[28] of God truly as a

divine offering and spiritual image and eloquent expression,[29] frightful to demons and the desire of angels—but I will say more—wonderful and terrifying to the angels, but virtuous and chosen by the Father, Son, and Holy Spirit.

13 On account of which the blessed David and other prophets proclaimed her from the beginning as *the mountain*[30] *of God, the fertile mountain, mountain on which it pleased God to dwell* (Ps 67.16–17), *the city of God about which glorious things are spoken* (Ps 86.3), *the ark of holiness,*[31] *resting place of the Lord* (Ps 131.8), and *Zion which was pleasing, and he chose to dwell there* (Ps 131.13), the throne of God and his chariot which thousands of angelic powers lead with ineffable splendor (cf. Ps 67.18), the inviolate garden, the living fountain (cf. Cant 4.12, 15),[32] the sealed book (cf. Isa 29.11), about which all books foretell, in which the unwritable Word is written, without beginning and without end, the king's couch with sixty strong men surrounding it (cf. Cant 3.7), who are the foretelling words of his holy Scriptures, the lampstand of gold, the royal scepter that blossomed beautifully, the urn holding the divine manna, the table of the bread of life, the tablets of the true Law, the ark covered[33] on all sides with gold (cf. Heb 9.2–4) by the grace of the Holy Spirit, which contained the uncontainable conqueror of all creatures. Thus, with such comportment and qualities pleasing to God, the all-blessed Virgin was present in the Temple, and she grew in stature and virtue beyond comprehension. Who could describe in detail her ministries and prayers and adornments with every good work, which she showed at a young age, because as all of her deeds were beyond comprehension, so also all of her life was exalted beyond nature, and because it was commensurate with her becoming the queen of all things and the mother of the Lord and king of all things, because she had been chosen by the Father and prepared by the Holy Spirit to contain in her womb the only-begotten Son and Word of God who is inseparable from them and to become the cause of the Incarnation and his dwelling among human beings. So even if, as I say, it is vast and impossible to describe exhaustively all of the glorious works and godly deeds that she accomplished during her childhood in the Temple, nevertheless I will mention the one that is greater than all, the gift of her many ministries and petitions.

14 And after a little while, when she was nearing twelve years old there was a precursor and foreshadowing of her Annunciation. She was adorned with all wisdom and righteousness, with fasting and prayer, with humility and tranquility, with fear and love of God. One day, at midnight, she was standing right in front of the doors of the sanctuary and offering prayers and supplications to God with a merciful and holy heart. Then behold—an event great and tremendous to hear—a great light shone forth in the Temple, so brilliant that in it the brightness of the visible sun became small and dark. And she heard a voice from the sanctuary that said, "Mary, from you my Son will be born." When the blessed Mary heard this, neither was she frightened or afraid on account of her youth, nor did she become proud from excessive joy, and she did not tell anyone else, nor did any[34] change occur in her behavior or thinking, but she was amazed at the utterance, as was appropriate. Nevertheless, she concealed in her heart this truly great mystery that was ordained before the ages and unknown even to the angels until she saw the fulfillment of the providential mysteries in her, when Christ the king was born from her, and he carried out the divine economy of his life among human beings, and he rose from the dead and ascended into heaven.

15 After this the holy Virgin reached a greater age, and she became twelve years old, which was the time of marriage according to the rule of the Law (cf. *Protev* 8.2). Nevertheless, the priests were[35] not able to carry this out on account of her dedication, for they were afraid to expel from the Temple this one who had been an offering to God, because it seemed abominable to give over to the yoke of marriage one who had been entrusted to God, who had been ordained to be in service to the yoke of God alone. But the rule of the Law of Moses also prohibited a young woman who had reached this age from being continually present in the Temple. There was then much consideration among them concerning the matter, in order to determine what was best. Then God sent into their hearts a legitimate and suitable idea that would fulfill the rule of the Law and avoid marriage. And they decided to hand her over in betrothal, but not in marriage, to a man not ready for marriage but old and elderly and accomplished in the perfection of virtues, so that he would be a zealous guardian of her virginity. But this was also an act of divine Providence ordained from above so that, just as the Lord and king of all things himself concealed the unapproachable brilliance (cf. 1 Tim 6.16) of his divinity in the flesh in order that the prince of darkness would not be able to recognize[36] him, so also the virginity of his mother in the state of betrothal was concealing, so that no one could know by whom or at what time his Incarnation took place,[37] so that he could thus ensnare the apostate enemy by the form of his humanity, because that one knew that he would come into the world through a virgin from the words of Isaiah and other prophets.

16 When the priests were making this deliberation, they did not trust themselves to select such a godly man, but they assigned everything to the Providence of God, as Moses did before when many were contending for the office of the high priesthood. He entrusted the judgment of this matter to God, and he brought the rods of the tribes into the Tabernacle and by them made known the will of God through the flowering of the rod (cf. Num 17.8). And again later on, Peter and the other apostles found the one who filled the traitor's place through prayer and casting of lots (cf. Acts 1.26). So also then the high priest and the priests stood in prayer and supplication to God, at the instruction of the great Zechariah, the father of John the Baptist, who held the office of the high priesthood at that time. And he was a witness to the godly life and the incomprehensible ministry that were fulfilled by the most blessed Virgin. When she was living in the Temple, Zechariah was a relative of the holy Virgin, not only because he was from the same tribe, on account of the union of the royal and priestly tribes, but also through his wife Elizabeth, not only because it is indicated by other writings that Mary and Elizabeth were the children of two sisters, but the words of the archangel also confirm it, as it is written in the holy gospel, *"And behold, your kinswoman Elizabeth"* (Luke 1.36). So at that time God placed an idea in Zechariah's mind, and he took twelve rods of elderly and honorable old men who were related[38] to the holy Virgin, and he placed them in the sanctuary of the Temple. And he himself stood with the other priests in prayer and supplication to God with ardent tears, and they asked to be persuaded by a miracle that it is appropriate for someone to receive the Virgin. The Lord gave an excellent sign, and Joseph's rod blossomed and became fruitful as Aaron's before it, and so by the Providence of God and by the deliberation of the priests Joseph received from Zechariah the immaculate Virgin as a guardian and her caregiver and a servant of the mystery that is great and wonderful beyond all comprehension.

17 And Joseph was then more than seventy years old, so that no one could raise any suspicions whatsoever of marriage. And he was poor and lacking in material possessions, so that in his house was raised, according to bodily stature, the one who became poor for our sakes in order to enrich us with his divinity. Joseph was a carpenter by trade, more famous in this craft than all other carpenters, because he was going to be a servant to the true craftsman, the creator and architect of all creatures. But just as Joseph was famous at that time for his trade, so was he also for his virtue, his piety, and his good works: among those of his age[39] he was the greatest, except for the parents of the Virgin. And why is it necessary to say more about him to whose righteousness God himself has borne witness? All the men of his tribe also bore witness.[40] The evangelist Matthew bears witness: *"Joseph was a just man"* (Matt 1.19). When Joseph received the holy Virgin, he led her forth from Jerusalem and Zion to Galilee, to the city of Nazareth, for behold, it was as a sign of the glorious mystery that the Word of God, the king and creator of all things, came to us from the invisible and highest Jerusalem, and from the ineffable and inexpressible[41] glories and the royal thrones.

18 Nevertheless, Joseph led the holy Virgin Mary forth according to his own type,[42] as the queen and leader of his house, and he appointed her over his daughters. As it is written concerning the first Joseph, "Pharaoh *appointed him as lord of his house and ruler over all of his possessions"* (Ps 104.21; cf. Gen 41.40), so also this Joseph appointed the Virgin Mary as the leader and teacher and ruler of all the members of his family, *to instruct them as himself* so that she *would make* his daughters *wise,* as the prophet says (Ps 104.22). Although they were older, Mary was distinguished by the grace of the Holy Spirit. But as the blessed and all-holy one was a treasure house of all virtue, so she also possessed meekness, tranquility, and humility especially. And most of the time she remained at the house and was devoted to prayer and supplication to God with great fasting and labor. Nevertheless, after she went forth from the Temple, a few days later the dedication feast of Tabernacles and the resting of the Ark drew near (cf. 1 Kings 8; 2 Chron. 7; Gen 8.4?). And it was the seventh month after the first month, as is the rule regarding the number of months according to the Hebrews. And the great high priest Zechariah entered the Holy of Holies to cense with the censer, according to the custom, and the birth of John was announced to him (cf. Luke 1.8–23), because thus it was fitting that the lampstand should come before the light, the dawn before the sun, the voice before the word (cf. Matt 1.3; John 1.1), the friend before the bridegroom (cf. John 3.29), and the knight before the king. It was fitting that the less amazing wonder, conception by the barren, should precede the more amazing, the seedless conception by the Virgin, as the archangel confirms and says with the statement, *"Behold, Elizabeth, your kinswoman, also has conceived a son"* (Luke 1.36).

CHAPTER 2

THE ANNUNCIATION

19 And in the sixth month after Elizabeth's conception the archangel Gabriel was sent by God to the city of Nazareth, to the house of Joseph, and he announced to the Virgin Mary the glorious and wonderful Annunciation, ineffable and incomprehensible, the foundation and beginning of all good things. And when, how, and where did the Annunciation take place? The virgin was fasting and standing in prayer near a fountain (cf. *Protev* 11.1), because she conceived the fountain of life (cf. Ps 35.10). It was in the first month, when God also created the whole world, in order to show us that now he renews the old world again. It was the first day of the week, which is Sunday, on which day he dispelled the primeval darkness and created the primordial light, and on which day the glorious Resurrection of her king and son from the grave took place, along with the resurrection of our nature, and not only was it the first day but the first hour, according to the saying of the prophet, *"God will help her in the morning"* (Ps 45.6)

20 Such then were the words of the archangel, and how full they were with mystery: *"Rejoice, favored one!"* (Luke 1.28). *"Rejoice"* was spoken for the destruction of the original sadness and the harsh judgment, and on account of the new grace that now has been given to human understanding, and *"favored one"* because of the Virgin's wealth of virtue and the grace that had come upon her. And like a dowry this first thing was the engagement of the immortal bridegroom and the destruction of the original curse that came upon us through the disobedience and error of our original mother, and instead of woeful sadness, the gift of eternal joy, and the second thing was an indication of the wealth of the unwedded bride: both of these things the archangel proclaimed. Then he added, *"the Lord is with you"* (Luke 1.28). This is the entire wealth of the king; it is the fulfillment of his promise. The Word of God himself, by the word beyond all words, entered into the womb of the holy Virgin. He united himself with humanity not through seed but by the power of the Most High and the coming of the Holy Spirit. He himself was the one who united and the one who was united: he united the two natures in one hypostasis and was united with human nature by grace. He built the temple of his flesh himself as he saw fit. Nevertheless, these same words, *"the Lord is with you,"* were also the destruction and annihilation of the primordial curse that had been placed on women: for man had been appointed the lord of woman, and woman's recourse to man had been commanded (cf. Gen 3.16b). And childbirth was established with pain and affliction because of the original disobedience (cf. Gen 3.16a):[1] as the prophet bears witness, *"as when the pain of childbirth arrives at the time of birth, she cries out from the pain"* (Isa 26.17). In this way, then, there was no end to the servitude and pain and affliction of women. But when the archangel said to the holy Virgin, *"the Lord is with you,"* all the debts of affliction were erased. *"The lord is with you,"* and there is no longer the lordship of man over you, nor the pain of childbirth, for truly she alone is a virgin exalted above all virgins, a virgin ever immaculate: before birth, in birth, and after birth. And not only was the grace of perpetual virginity given to her, but from that time forward she became the foundation of virginity for other women, and by her the ability was given to women who wish to be virgins. Before this, women were not able to be virgins, but the beloved and most-blessed, ever-virgin Theotokos Mary became the foundation and cause of virginity for women who desire it, for in fact she also became the cause and source of every good thing for men and women, the glorious and all-holy mother of the Lord and God and our savior Jesus Christ, the ornament of human nature, the song and joy of the angels, intercessor for humanity and aid to all the faithful.

21 But how complete and concise is the conclusion of the angel's address: *"blessed are you among women"* (Luke 1.28), that is to say, more than all women, for these women were made worthy of blessing by you, as is man by your son, and even more the natures of both men and women are blessed by both, by you and your son. And as men and women were punished with the curse, the pain, and affliction from both

Adam and Eve, so also joy and blessings were spread forth over all by you and your son. But consider the holy Virgin's intelligent character and her words full of wisdom. She clearly did not resist and was not incredulous, nor did she naively accept the message right away. But at the same time she surpassed Isaiah in blind and unwarranted obedience (cf. Isa 6.8), and also Zechariah in immeasurable skepticism (cf. Zech 1.9, 1.19, 1.21, 2.2, etc.): she held to the middle way and *was greatly troubled,*" as was appropriate. She was not greatly troubled by the archangel's appearance, for she had become accustomed to his appearance many times when he brought her nourishment in the Temple, but by the words that she heard. For this reason the evangelist also explained and said, *"she was greatly troubled by the saying and considered what sort of greeting this might be"* (Luke 1.29), for at the moment she was still unaware of the depth of the mystery, and she trembled at this communion of the divine nature with the human and considered how this might be. But the wondrous messenger Gabriel, although he did not speak with the Virgin, he nevertheless, as if reading the thoughts of her mind, perceived the deliberation in her mind. Not only did he dispel her fear, but he also spread forth joy, and he explained the indescribable birth and said to her, *"Fear not, Mary, for you have found favor with God"* (Luke 1.30). The favor that she had found was the honor and name of Theotokos, for this she was called, and in truth she became the Theotokos. She in fact found great favor with God, for she became the mother of his only-begotten Son. Oh favor exalted beyond all favors, which the mind cannot fathom, which language cannot describe!

22 Now, then, let us consider and examine the glory of the unwedded bride and the dowry of her virginity. Let us ponder what the archangel revealed briefly and clearly: *"Behold, you will conceive and bear a son, and you will call his name Jesus"* (Luke 1.31). *"Behold, you will conceive,"* so that in that moment, with that word he informed her about the wondrous conception. *"And you will bear a son and call his name Jesus,"* because his Father is not on the earth: in his human birth he is without a father, as he is without a mother in his eternal birth. And that is why *you will give birth* without a father *and call his name Jesus,* which means "Savior," because you will experience nothing of the maternal conditions and pains, but as conception was given to you without seed, so also his birth will be without corruption and without pain, and it will be for the salvation of the whole world, and this act will be made known by the name. *"He will be great and will be called the Son of the Most High"* (Luke 1.32) with respect to his human nature. He said this because in his divinity he is exalted beyond every glory, but concerning his human nature he said *"he will be great and will be called the Son of the Most High,"* not only because of the hypostatic union, but also because of the call from on high and because of the confirmation by wondrous deeds. *"For you will call him Jesus."* Nevertheless, later on the Father will call him from heaven[2] *"beloved son"* (Matt 3.17), and when he begins to accomplish innumerable miracles, it will be known by all the wise that he is the Son of the Most High. *"And the Lord God will give him the throne of his father David"* (Luke 1.32). And he spoke this also concerning his humanity, because with that he began preaching the gospel and receiving those who believe in his name, who call him the throne of David and the house of Jacob. *"And he will reign over the house of Jacob forever; and of his kingdom there will be no end"* (Luke 1.33). He speaks of the unending reign not only on account of his divinity but also on account of his humanity, because with respect to both natures there is no end to his reign, and he will reign over those who received[3] his reign with faith. Now he will reign over those who believed in his word, but at the end of all things, when all things will be subjected to him, as the holy apostle Paul says, he must reign until his enemies have been placed under his feet, *because he has put all things in subjection under his feet. When all things are subjected to him, then he will himself be subjected to the one who put all things in subjection to him* (I Cor 15.27-8), God the Father, because he called him to submit to the deliberate subjection of our nature, for he assumes the labors of our victory.

23 But consider the wisdom of the blessed and all-holy Virgin and her excessive love of virginity. She believed the archangel's message but was astonished by the matter. That is why she answered and said, *"How can this be, for I have not known a man* (Luke 1.34), nor is this possible, because I have been consecrated immaculately to God, and without a man conception is not possible." For this was her fear and distress: that he related the loss of her virginity, which was steadfast in her heart, to remain in virginity until she died, as is reported to us by the writings of the pious Fathers. For she was completely unfamiliar not only with the affairs of marriage but also with the desire of lust, as she was trained from the beginning in complete holiness and purity of soul and body. And no desire of passion at all had come into her heart and mind, and in this regard she was greater and more exalted than all human nature. That is why her beauty was pleasing to the king and creator of all things (cf. Ps 44.12), who sees thoughts and *who scrutinizes hearts and reins* (Ps 7.10). And he made his dwelling place holy, and he saw fit to dwell in her and be clothed in our nature from her. That is why her herald and messenger of the ineffable mystery resolved her astonishment, and he explained the ineffable birth, as the blessed evangelist Luke says, *"The Holy Spirit will come upon you, and the power of the Most High[4] will overshadow you* (Luke 1.35). You say, *'how can this be, for I have not known a man?'* But there is no need for a man in this matter, for your affairs are not like those of other women, just as the affairs of the child that will be born from you also will not be similar to those of other human children, who are conceived in their mother's womb and born in sin. Nevertheless, your conception will not be the destruction of virginity, but above all it will be a seal and guardian of purity and a nurturer of holiness. For *the Holy Spirit will come upon* you to prepare and adorn you as the bride worthy of the Lord, and to sanctify from the beginning your holy body and soul adorned with godly virtues. And immediately your immortal bridegroom and son, who is *the power of the Most High, will overshadow you*, for Christ is the power of God and the Wisdom of God. He will overshadow you himself and will build within you the temple of his all-holy body. And the immaterial and bodiless one will put on[5] from you bodily[6] and material flesh. The power and brilliance of the Father will overshadow you in essence, and the Word of the Father will become incarnate from you. The invisible God will appear visible as a human being, and the Son of God the Father will become and will be called your son, and your son will be called the son of the Most High, and your virginity will remain uncorrupted and intact."

24 "O wonderful and glorious events! O ineffable and incomprehensible mysteries! Nevertheless, even if the image and likeness of your wonderful[7] conception and incomprehensible birthing are not found in this world except in lesser miracles, believe in this exalted thing and consider that the one born from you will be called holy and the son of the Most High, who is able to do whatever he wishes. *And behold, Elizabeth your kinswoman has also conceived a son in her old age, and this is the sixth month for her who was called barren. For nothing is impossible with God* (Luke 1.36–37), but all that he wishes is realized in actuality in an instant." And again consider[8] intellectually the extent of the blessed Virgin's wisdom and the steadfastness of her holiness. So long as there was some question concerning a man according to the order of nature, she would not admit the conception but said: *"How can this be, for I have not known a man* (Luke 1.34). Although you are an archangel and have announced supernatural mysteries to me, it is nevertheless not possible that I have joined with a man so that the conception of which you speak could take place." But once the archangel revealed the coming of the Holy Spirit and the overshadowing of the power of the Most High, she rejoiced and believed that nothing is impossible with God. She became neither proud nor haughty in her thinking, but she put on the greatest humility and meekness. And Mary said reverently, *"Behold, the handmaid of the Lord; be it unto me according to your word." And the angel departed from her* (Luke 1.38), for when he accomplished the task that had been assigned to him, he was amazed at the beauty of her virginity. Nevertheless, the holy Virgin had to hide this great secret in her heart, for she was full of wisdom as the mother of Wisdom, and she did not reveal the angel's message to Joseph or anyone else in those days. That is why some of the Fathers interpret the words that the evangelist spoke concerning Joseph, that he did not know this until she gave birth to her first-born son (cf. Matt 1.18–24), as meaning that he did not know about her mystery or the angel's Annunciation or the supernatural conception. For if he knew this, how did he raise inappropriate doubt that her conception seemed shameful to him? How did he decide to divorce her quietly until he saw the angel's dream? And again, at the birth of the Lord, the miracles were made manifest: the proclamation to the shepherds and the arrival of the Magi by the guidance of the star. Afterwards, the blessed Virgin revealed the archangel's Annunciation. Nevertheless, at the time when the archangel made the Annunciation, no one knew, but she went forth to her kinswoman Elizabeth, whom she imitated in virtuous deeds, so that she would know that the words of the angel spoken about Elizabeth were true, that she had also conceived a child.

25 When she reached Elizabeth's house and Elizabeth heard[9] the voice of her greeting, suddenly the voice of the Word, the lamp of the light, the prophet[10] of mercy looked up from his mother's womb and heard the voice of her greeting, and stirring in the womb he showed a form of greeting and reverence for the king who was to be born (cf. Luke 1.41), who was going to be baptized by him, in order to show that he was going to be a prophet, the Forerunner and the Baptist. That is why his mother also proclaimed the mother of the Lord, *and she cried out with a great voice and said, "Blessed are you among women, and blessed is the fruit of your womb! And why has it happened to me that the mother of my Lord should come to me? For behold, when the voice of your greeting came to my ears, the child in my womb leaped for joy. And blessed is she who believed that there would be a fulfillment of what was spoken to her by the Lord"* (Luke 1.42–45). After this, she explained everything about herself to the mother of the Lord, the punishment of barrenness and the priesthood of her husband Zechariah, and the annunciation by the angel while censing with the censer, and his muteness, which, although it did not allow Zechariah to speak, nevertheless was explained to Elizabeth by her husband in writing (cf. Luke 1.7–23). But Elizabeth's words to the Virgin were truly revealed to her by the Holy Spirit, as the holy gospel says, *"Elizabeth was filled with the Holy Spirit, and she cried out with a great voice and said, 'Blessed are you among women, and blessed is the fruit of your womb'"* (Luke 1.41–42). For it was revealed to her by the Holy Spirit that Mary's conception was seedless[11] and without a man. That is why she called him the fruit of her womb, for the substance of his holy body was from her womb alone and not from a foreign seed. *"Blessed is the fruit of your womb,"* because he is the true fruit, the nourishment[12] of the world, as David bears witness: *"All look to you to give them nourishment in due season. You give it to them, and they are nourished. You raise[13] your hand and fill all with the sweetness of your will"* (Ps 144.15–16).[14] And then he himself also gave us spiritual nourishment, his precious and all-holy body and blood. Truly is the fruit of your womb blessed, O immaculate Virgin, which dispelled the curse that came upon us from the fruit of disobedience. This fruit cast us out of Paradise, but that blessed fruit from your womb has opened the gate of Paradise, and even more has led us to heaven and calls us to the inheritance of the Kingdom of Heaven.[15]

26 *Blessed are you among women, and blessed is the fruit of your womb!* For the fruits of other women were under the curse from the original sin of Adam and Eve, and by carnal marriage and the corruption of sin they entered into the world. But the fruit of your womb alone is blessed, for he was conceived neither by the seed of a man nor by the corruption of sin, but without seed and in incorruption he put on flesh from you. And *he committed no sin at all*, and *no guile was found in his mouth* (1 Pet 2.22). And not only is he blessed and sinless, but by the grace of his divinity, he gave blessedness to the nature of humanity, which had been punished by the curse, and the most-blessed Lamb of God took away the sins of the world. Then the wonderful Mary, adorned with every grace, as she surpassed nature in every aspect, being a mother and a virgin, so also here, as she was a cause of prophecy for others, she herself thus spoke words[16] full of prophecy, full of grace and prayer and theology, for she was full of the Holy Spirit, as the evangelist informs us: *"Mary said, 'My soul magnifies the Lord, and my spirit rejoices in God my Savior, for he has regarded the lowliness of his handmaiden. Behold, from now on every generation will call me blessed'"* (Luke 1.46–48). Her soul was filled with all humility, meekness, and fear of God, and that is why God her Savior had regard for her: as it is said by the prophet, *"to whom will I have regard but to the humble, the meek, and the one who trembles before my words?"* (Isa 66.2). Thus he found Mary blessed and had regard for her, and he saw that there was no one like her among the human race. For this reason he saw fit to dwell in her, and from her he took on a human body and came to seek the lost. And the Most High made the cause of his Incarnation holy and made the dwelling place of his divinity blessed among every generation. With these words the blessed mother of Christ confirmed the words spoken by Elizabeth about her[17] and the archangel's announcements that were spoken by the Lord: as she says, *"blessed is she who believed that there would be a fulfillment of what was spoken to her by the Lord"* (Luke 1.45), for those things that the archangel announced were spoken by the Lord, by whom he had been sent.

27 That is why the one who had received grace offered thanks to the Lord and glorified his holy name and called herself humble and handmaiden. She said prophetically, *"from now on every generation will call me blessed"* (Luke 1.48). Truly the hosts of angels and generations of humanity call her blessed, and those who do not call her blessed and do not glorify her, they are not reckoned among humanity, but they are children of perdition and the portion of the devil. Nevertheless, every generation of true human beings calls her blessed and glorifies her and has her as a helper and intercessor with the Lord. And the words that follow are filled with such grace and wisdom: *"For the Mighty One has done great things for me, and holy is his name. And his mercy is on those who fear him from generation to generation"* (Luke 1.49–50). His name and his mercy are his only-begotten Son, whom he sent out of mercy toward those who fear him to become incarnate[18] from the holy Virgin and to have compassion on the forlorn and to seek the lost. But how is it said that the Son is the name of the Father? Because the Father is known by the Son, as the Lord himself said, *"I have manifested your name to humanity"* (John 17.6). *He has shown strength with his arm* (Luke 1.51), that is to say by his Son, for he is called the arm of God (cf. Isa 53.1; John 12.38), as he is called the *power of God and Wisdom* (1 Cor 1.24), and the image of power (cf. Heb 1.3), the immutable seal (cf. John 6.27), the right hand of the Most High (cf. Ps 76.11). So he is called the arm of God, and through him God the Father *has scattered the proud in the thoughts of their hearts. He has cast down the mighty from their thrones* (Luke 1.51–52), those who were the princes of the world, the evil demons who because of the original disobedience and excessive sin ruled over the human race and constrained them with force by sins and transgressions.

28 Nevertheless, when the Son of God came by the will of the Father and put on flesh by the Holy Spirit and the Virgin Mary, he shattered[19] the pride and haughty arrogance of the demons and cast them down from the thrones of their tyranny, and *"he has cast them into chains of darkness and given them over to torment,"* as the apostle Peter says (2 Pet 2.4).[20] Thus has he destroyed the invisible and proud demonic enemies, and also the ungodly princes and kings persecuting the faithful. And he has crushed them and cast them down from their tyranny and rendered their plans vain. *He has exalted the lowly; he has filled the hungry with good things, and the rich he has sent away empty* (Luke 1.52–53). These undistinguished and poor fishermen, lowly and uneducated, unknown and scorned by men, he has exalted them in word and in deed and has made them the teachers and apostles of the entire world, to the extent that their voice has gone forth to the whole world and their words to the ends of the earth. And he has made them honored by kings and princes and among countless people. And he gave them the Kingdom of Heaven and made them blessed on earth and also in eternity. Truly he has exalted the humble and blessed apostles with boundless exaltation. He filled with good things the hungry peoples of the gentiles, who were hungry for the word of God, uneducated and imperceptive, through the preaching of the apostles. He filled them with the good teaching of the Holy Spirit and comprehension of the divine mysteries.

29 But those rich in the vain and empty wisdom of the world, the proud and arrogant, he has sent away empty, as it is written, *"I will destroy the wisdom of the wise, and the learning of the learned I will abolish"* (Isa 29.14). *He has helped his servant Israel in remembrance of his mercy, as he said to our father Abraham and to his descendants forever* (Luke 1.54–55). He has helped his servant Israel, those who believed in his word, and by his only-begotten Son they have been made worthy of becoming children of God, and they have become the mind beholding God, for thus is Israel translated, "the mind beholding God."[21] And they are the descendants of Abraham, and in them is fulfilled the oath that he swore to our father Abraham, in Christ as the first born who became incarnate for us, and by him[22] in all who believe in his holy name and are made children of God by him: as the evangelist and theologian John says, *"To all who received him, he gave power to become children of God"* (John 1.12). For as the apostle Paul says, *"not all who are from Israel are Israel, nor are all descendants of Abraham his children, but 'Through Isaac will your descendants be named.' This means that it is not the children of the flesh who are the children of God, but the children of the promise are reckoned as descendants"* (Rom 9.6–8), who have believed the word of the Lord and have been baptized in the name of the Father and the Son and the Holy Spirit, be they Jew or gentile, and have become

Christian and been taught the fulfillment of the Lord's teaching. They are called Israel and the servant of God, and in them are fulfilled the words of the holy Theotokos, *"He has helped his servant Israel in remembrance of his mercy." And Mary remained in the house of Elizabeth for three months, and she returned to her home* (Luke 1.56), because after the death of the holy Virgin's blessed parents, she saw Elizabeth in the place of her mother. That is why when she received the Annunciation from Gabriel, immediately she went with haste to greet her and to know what had been said about her by the Lord. And through divine love and the bond of kinship, she remained for three months, as the holy gospel says. But when the time of Elizabeth's giving birth drew near, and she understood her own conception, she went forth to the house of Joseph, and the holy Virgin did not let anyone know about the angel's Annunciation.

CHAPTER 3

THE NATIVITY

30 Nevertheless, when Joseph recognized her pregnancy, he could hardly bear it, because he was unaware of the great mystery. That is why he was filled with sadness, because he was a just man, and he thought that allowing her to remain in his own house would be a transgression of the Law and a cause of suspicion against himself. And he likewise thought that exposing her and handing her over to the high priests for punishment would be cruel, so on account of his great virtue and godly life, he spared her and had mercy on her. Therefore he decided to send her away from his house in secret (cf. Matt 1.19). *And as he was considering this, behold, an angel of the Lord appeared to him in a dream and said, "Joseph, son of David, do not fear* (Matt 1.20) because of her either from God or from punishment of the Law, nor of being brought into wrongful suspicion regarding Mary, who has been betrothed to you according to the custom of men and women." The angel called his betrothed *"wife,"* but she had not been given to him as wife in the manner of other women: by no means! Rather, she had been betrothed to his custody as divine treasure consecrated to the Lord. "Do not fear that she remain in your house, *for the one who will be born from her is of the Holy Spirit. And she will bear a son, and you will call his name Jesus, for he will save his people from their sins"* (Matt 1.20–21). With these words the angel dispelled the fear that was frightening Joseph, and he introduced another much greater fear, so that he would fear and respect the holy Virgin even more as one filled with the Holy Spirit and as the parent according to the flesh of the ineffable[1] and unapproachable Son, who was born before the ages and who will save his people from their sins, for that is why he descended from heaven to earth, the beneficent king, in order to save us, those glorifying and believing in him, from servitude to sin and from the tyranny of the evil demons.

31 Then was fulfilled the prophecy of the patriarch Jacob, who said, "In the decline of the rulers and leaders of Judah, hope will come to all the gentiles" (cf. Gen 49.10), that is, Christ the king who is truly the hope of the gentiles and also of the Jews who believe in his holy name. For not all who are from Israel are called Israel (cf. Rom 9.6), but those who have received the preaching of the gospel, as is written above. And so Simeon also informs us, for he named him *a light to enlighten the gentiles, and for the glory of the people of Israel* who have believed, and he called him the salvation of all peoples together: *My eyes have seen your salvation, which you have prepared in the presence of all peoples* (Luke 2.30–31). But why does Jacob say "in the decline of the rulers of Judah," since the Lord himself has come, who is the ruler[2] and leader of all and the true king, and he appeared from the tribe of Judah? It is thus clear that the patriarch's prophecy did not foretell a spiritual reign, but he spoke of mortal kings and worldly rulers. That is also why the Lord says, *"My kingdom is not of this world"* (John 18.36), even though in the end when the kings of Rome were ruling Judea completely (cf. §59), the Savior was nevertheless given reign over the Romans and all of the gentiles who believed in his holy name. I am not speaking only of the natural reign of his divinity, he who is king and Lord from age unto age, but of the voluntary submission to him by all the believers, as he has called all those who have submitted to his reign by a single new name, Christian. This indeed is the true and honorable name that has been appointed to us by him. So at that time when all the sovereignty and hegemony of the Jews had been diminished, and dominion over the entire world had been given to the Roman emperor, as the holy gospel says, *"In those days a decree went forth from Caesar Augustus that the entire world should be enrolled"* (Luke 2.1), then the true king and savior of the entire world was born. And so his Providence ordained that the sovereignty of the Jews was greatly diminished and absolute power of dominion had been given to the Romans. And they subdued[3] the Hebrews with a rod of iron (cf. Ps 2.9), which is the rule of the Romans (for it is called a rod of iron) by which the Jews were crushed[4] after the Passion and Resurrection of Christ, and they were devastated by a perpetual captivity. So then the Providence of Christ caused the Romans to rule over the Jews, but he himself reigned over the Romans and all the gentiles and over the Jews who believed, and he reigns over all creatures unto eternity.

32 Nevertheless, these visible events were symbolic of invisible mysteries. The census was a symbol of another census, for the rule of Caesar over all was a sign of the unique rule of the one true God and king of all. And the census represents the voluntary submission of all and the census in heaven of all those who desire it. And as the order then went forth to the whole world, so the preaching of Christ went forth in all the earth (cf. Ps 18.5), and each one who went up to his own city was a symbol of the return of everyone to their original home and citizenship, from which we were cast out and dispersed to various activities and lands. And the tax that all gave to the emperor was a symbol that we are all indebted to offer up to God spiritual fruits through good works and noble deeds and godly thoughts. So then by Providence from above, the census compelled Joseph to go to his homeland, from Galilee to Judea, from Nazareth to Bethlehem, so that the prophecies would be fulfilled: the one that *he will be called a Nazarene* (Matt 2.23), and the other that the Messiah comes from Bethlehem (cf. Matt 2.6), for the Annunciation took place in Nazareth, and the wondrous Nativity was accomplished in Bethlehem. We see, then, the twofold humility of the rich king who became poor for our sake, for Nazareth was an ordinary city, from which a prophet had never appeared: as Nathanael said, *"Can anything good come from Nazareth?"* (John 1.46). But Bethlehem, even though it had been honored by the saying of the prophet, was in all other things poor and humble, on account of which the prophet comforted it and said, *"And you, O Bethlehem, land of Judah, are not at all the least among the rulers of Judah, for from you will come forth a leader who will shepherd my people Israel"* (Matt 2.6; cf. Mic 5.2). Joseph was a citizen of this Bethlehem, and as it happened that many people from his homeland moved to another land or city, so Joseph wished to settle in Nazareth. And while he was there, the holy Virgin Mary was betrothed to him[5] by the priests on account of his righteousness and honesty, and there the archangel announced the inconceivable and glorious Annunciation.

33 Nevertheless, when the decree went forth from Caesar Augustus to enroll every land, and each person was enrolled in his homeland, *Joseph went up from Galilee from the city of Nazareth to Judea, to the city of David that is called Bethlehem, for he was from the house and family of David,* *in order to be enrolled with Mary, who was his betrothed* (Luke 2.4–5). And she had conceived by the Holy Spirit, and the time of her giving birth was near, but the emperor's decree also required Mary to go up to Bethlehem, for she too was from the house and family of David, and the Providence of God led her up to Bethlehem. Because the order that Joseph had recently received from the angel made him careful to serve Mary with reverence, for this reason his other sons and relatives were sent ahead, and he himself went forth slowly with holy Mary and his daughters. And when they reached Jerusalem and Bethlehem, the hour of the Nativity, wonderful and beyond comprehension, drew near. Nevertheless, because many people were gathered for the census, and the places and houses of Bethlehem were already occupied, they took their lodging[6] in a cave of Bethlehem (cf. *Protev* 18.1). Behold, the hardship and exile of the ruler of all creatures: no place nor dwelling was found for him. Therefore the incomprehensible and unbounded one was contained in a small cave and an unsuitable manger, and the beginningless and uncontainable Word of God, the creator of the entire world, was guiding his mother to the cave of Bethlehem, as the holy gospel says, *"And it happened that while they were there the days of her birth were fulfilled, and she gave birth to her firstborn son, and she wrapped him in swaddling clothes and laid him in a manger, because there was no place for them at the inn"* (Luke 2.6–7). Then the ruler of heaven and earth was wrapped in swaddling clothes. O glorious wonder! The one who nourishes all was nourished with milk, and the one who enrolls all was enrolled. Then was fulfilled the prophecy of David concerning Bethlehem and the birth of the Lord, as he says, *"I will not give sleep to my eyes nor slumber to my eyelids nor rest to my body until I find a place for the Lord and a dwelling place for the God of Jacob. Look, we have heard of it in Ephratha; we have found it in the field of the forest"* (Ps 131.4–6). He said this about Bethlehem, where the birth of the Lord took place. That is why he added, *"We will enter his dwelling place; we will venerate the place where his feet stood"* (Ps 131.7). Glory[7] to his immeasurable humility![8] Who will relate the powers of the Lord and make heard[9] all of his praises?

34 Nevertheless, at the time of the Lord's birth, the worthy Elizabeth, the mother of John the Forerunner and Baptist, was not absent, for her flight to the mountain with her child had not yet come to pass (*Protev* 22.5–9). But as she had been a prophet and witness of the conception by the holy Virgin, so also was she an attendant and an eyewitness of the glorious Nativity,[10] and after the Nativity she was a witness and proclaimer of her virginity. And she was full of joy, and she considered the ineffable Nativity a wonderful feast day. So then the dividing wall[11] of the fortified bulwark was torn down, and the irreconcilable animosity was destroyed (cf. Eph 2.14–16), and peace and joy spread to creation: God became a human being, and heaven and earth were joined. The angels drew near above the shepherds, and the shepherds were enlightened by the angels, and they rejoiced at the great announcement, and they saw the good and gracious shepherd as an immaculate lamb born in the cave. The earth learned the praise of heaven, and those in heaven rejoiced at the peace on earth and good will among human beings. Nevertheless, when the shepherds were afraid and terrified by the wondrous sight, the angel of light dispelled their fear and taught them joy. *"Fear not, for behold, I bring you good news of great joy that is for all people. For today is born for you in the city of David a savior, who is Christ the Lord. And this will be a sign for you: you will find a child wrapped in swaddling clothes and lying in a manger." And suddenly there was with the angel a multitude of the heavenly host, praising God and saying, "Glory to God in the highest, and on earth peace and good will among human beings"* (Luke 2.10–14). The shepherds, amazed by this awesome sight and sound, went by night to Bethlehem to look for the savior and light of all things. Then they gathered many others of their relatives and acquaintances, and they were amazed by the words of the shepherds (cf. Luke 2.15–18).

35 *But Mary kept these things and reflected on them in her heart* (Luke 2.19), not only those things regarding the shepherds, but those things that were seen and heard from the beginning in the Temple and after the Temple, the Annunciation by the angel, the seedless conception, the painless birth, and the virginity after the birth, that is, not only that she avoided the pains of motherhood and appeared as a mother and was preserved as a virgin, but also that she did not feel the birth. Behold the economy of divine activities and the transformation of natures, for the wondrous son did not make known to the immaculate mother the knowledge of his birth, and in an instant he was inexplicably found outside her womb and settled in her lap, so that just as her conception took place without seed and without awareness, so also the birth took place without corruption and without awareness. The dew on the fleece (cf. Judg 6.36–40) was a symbol of the glorious and wondrous Nativity,[12] but the reality was more exalted than the symbol, for although the dew came upon the fleece silently and of its own, it was not of its own squeezed out from the fleece but only by hand. But the divine dew, which gives life to all, just as he entered into the Virgin's holy womb silently and painlessly, so he did not make known his ineffable coming forth to the immaculate mother, but he put on human flesh from her, and so he went forth easily and supernaturally, the one who did not make his birth known, not only to others but even to his own mother. Such were the ineffable and unattainable wonders that the all-holy Mary kept and reflected on in her heart, and in all this she was content that the true God was born from her, the one who made his immaculate and most gracious mother blessed among all generations and glorified her in heaven and on earth and made her praised by all.

36 So then at the glorious birth of the Lord the great joy was announced to the shepherds, and they came to Bethlehem and reported to all what they had seen and heard concerning the glorious infant, *and those who heard it were amazed at what the shepherds told them* (Luke 2.18). Then suddenly, behold, the Magi came from the east guided by a star to show that the one born was Lord of heaven and earth. And this star was not one of the stars of the firmament, but it was a power sent from above that completely abolished the deception of astronomy and annihilated the darkness of such ignorance, for its path was not like that of the other stars, but it went slowly according to the pace of those whom it was leading. And sometimes it moved, and sometimes it stood still; and sometimes it appeared to them, and sometimes it was hidden. And its path was from north to south, for so is the route from Persia to Judea. And it did not appear in the heights, but it went close to the earth up to a small village, and it appeared at a small cave. And, what is greatest of all, it shone not only at night but even in the day to the extent that it covered the light and disc of the sun, not for a day or two, but until the Magi came from Persia to Jerusalem and Bethlehem.

Nevertheless, it appeared to them not at the birth of Christ but much earlier, so that by it those who were predicting the times of the Nativity were silenced. That is why it appeared a long time before. And it made their hearts faithful concerning the birth of the king and led them to follow a long route. And so it determined when they travelled and when they made camp so that they would find the King of Glory lying in a manger. All this is neither the nature nor character of a star, but it is clear that it was a rational power that understood every detail and was guiding them deliberately by the power and command of the creator and caretaker of all things.

37 And it was not in vain that it led them to Jerusalem,[13] and when they came to Jerusalem, it disappeared. And this event was ordained for two reasons. Firstly, so that the mystery would be revealed to all the inhabitants of Jerusalem, and it would be made known by the quest and the question of the Magi when they said, *"Where is he who has been born the king of the Jews? For we have seen his star in the east and have come to venerate him"* (Matt 2.2). That is also why the entire city was disturbed, and Herod was terrified at these words (cf. Matt 2.3). Secondly, so that the enemies themselves, the scribes and the Pharisees, would bear witness and reveal the place and time of the Lord's birth, and so that they would introduce the prophecy that says, *"And you, O Bethlehem, land of Judah, you are not at all the least among the rulers of Judah, for from you will come forth a ruler who will shepherd my people Israel"* (Matt 2.6; cf. Mic 5.2). For the other rulers were leaders according fleshly honor, but they were not shepherds, because they would not lay down their lives for the flock (cf. John 10.11). But this one is the true shepherd, because on the way of life he leads the flock that follows him to the pasture of Paradise, and he lays down his life for his sheep. See, then, how they bring together the words of the patriarch Jacob and the prophet Micah, for this one said that the Lord would come from Bethlehem, but that one foretold that in the weakening and decline of the rulers of Judah the hope of the nations would appear (cf. Gen 49.10; Mic 5.2). When the Magi heard these words, they confirmed them further by the appearance of the star, and they proclaimed Christ the true king.

38 That is why Herod was frightened, because he craved power, and he was frightened that this might occasion the downfall of his reign and dominion, for he was full of stupidity. That is also why *he assembled the high priests and scribes and asked them where the Christ is to be born* (Matt 2.4). Nevertheless, they wickedly revealed something and withheld something. They made known that the Christ is to be born in Bethlehem, as the prophet says, *"You, o Bethlehem, land of Judah, you are not at all the least among the rulers of Judah, for from you will come forth a ruler who will shepherd my people Israel"* (Mic 5.2). But they withheld the prophet's subsequent words, which say, *"His goings forth are from the beginning, from eternal days"* (Mic. 5.2), because even from that time they were seized with envy toward Christ and did not want his recognition as God. And they withheld the words foretelling[14] his glory, for their eyes were willfully closed and their ears shut to see and hear the truth (cf. Isa 6.10). Nevertheless, Herod, filled with wickedness, summoned the Magi secretly and questioned them about the child king, and he lied deceitfully and promised his veneration when they should find him and tell him where this King of Kings is (cf. Matt 2.7–8). So then the birth of the Lord was made known to the one by the other: to Jews[15] by the Magi and the appearance[16] of the star, to Herod by the both the Jews and the Magi, and the Magi were further persuaded when they heard the proclamation of the prophet, and when they saw Herod's jealousy and fear. But when they went forth from Jerusalem, suddenly their guiding star appeared again, nearby and brighter than the day. It shone even more in the gleam of the sun and led them to the sun of truth, the creator of the sun, the moon, the stars, and all creation. And it led them to Bethlehem as to heaven, to the small cave and the unsuitable tabernacle.

39 Nevertheless, when they arrived at this place, the star showed them what they desired with an intense brilliance like a finger, and when it had completed its service, it disappeared from them. Nevertheless, when they saw their guiding star, or rather, the angel appearing in this form, they were filled with great joy (cf. Matt 2.10), because they had obtained what they were searching for. And they saw a glorious wonder, for when they stood before the newborn infant, the first born before the ages, suddenly they were filled with grace, sweetness, and light, and indescribable joy suffused their hearts. Nevertheless, the sight and speech of the unwed and completely incorruptible mother was the height of grace and glory, and the character of her form was beyond all human understanding. Nothing of the customary pain and weakness of childbirth appeared in her, but she was brilliant and exceedingly beautiful after the birth, for she too was filled with the grace and light of the birth, and it was a wondrous thing for all those who saw it. The Magi, persuaded by all these miracles and splendors, rejoiced and gave thanks to the Lord. That is also why they worshiped him humbly as God and king, and they offered[17] precious gifts, gold, frankincense, and myrrh (cf. Matt 2.11), as to a king and God and to the one who became incarnate for our sake and who was headed for death so that we will receive from him immortality. Nevertheless, the grace of the Holy Spirit also made it known that they should offer such gifts so that they would become for us a model of offering such spiritual gifts, so that we will offer a good and holy character as gold, but comprehension and spiritual insight as frankincense, and mortification of the passions and bodily members as myrrh, from which arises impassibility and by which we receive the kingdom of heaven. Then the words of the holy and all-blessed Virgin were fulfilled: as she said before, *"the Mighty One has done great things for me, and holy is his name, and behold, from now on every generation will call me blessed"* (Luke 1.49, 48). For truly then her glories began to be manifest, and in the end her glory, praise, and blessedness will abound even more greatly.

40 So then the Magi met with what they desired. They saw the king of glory, and they worshiped him. They offered him visible gifts, and with them they offered themselves and their souls to the Lord, and they became the beginning of the conversion of the gentiles and precursors of their acceptance of service to Christ, the first believers and worshipers of Christ and preachers and witnesses of his reign by offering precious gifts and by their rejection of the lies of the Jews and by their contempt for Herod's dominance: for they were informed *in a dream not to return to Herod, and they departed to their own country by another way* (Matt 2.12). So then Christ the rich king chose poverty when he came into the world, and by his choice he made it honorable. And, O believer, when you hear of this humility and poverty,[18] do not leave your mind in such great poverty, but exchange the small cave and the unsuitable tabernacle for the heavens of heavens, the little manger for the brilliant star and the praise of the angels, the ordinary swaddling clothes and the tax demands for the gifts and veneration of the Magi and the faith of all the gentiles. And so do not let the lowliness of the Lord diminish the height of knowledge of God, but have even more faith in the exalted and glorious good things.

41 Nevertheless, when the blessed mother saw all of this, her heart was filled even more with faith, hope, and love for her son and king, and she expected even greater and more glorious things, as she truly saw and was satisfied. So again other signs of his humility were fulfilled, for after the birth of the Lord in an unsuitable cave and his lying in a little manger, *eight days were completed for his circumcision, and his name was called Jesus, which he had been named by the angel before he came to be in the womb* (Luke 2.21), which was the name of future blessedness, by which is proclaimed the removal of bodily passion and the gift of impassibility. And on the fortieth day *they brought the infant Jesus to Jerusalem to present him to the Lord, as it is written in the law of the Lord* (Luke 2.22–23). Nevertheless, it is not pointless to explain here the divergence of the accounts of the holy evangelists, insofar as Matthew relates the flight into Egypt, Herod's rage, and the slaughter of the infants immediately after the Nativity. Luke, however, relates the going up to Jerusalem on the fortieth day and the Presentation of Jesus in the Temple following the Nativity. Let it be made clear, then, that Matthew left out any mention of the Circumcision, the going up to Jerusalem, the Presentation in the Temple, Simeon's lifting him up, and other events that took place at that time. And what he relates took place after many days, just before the second year or a little earlier (cf. Matt 2.16):[19] Joseph's vision of the angel, the flight to Egypt, and the return again from Egypt. For this is the custom of the Scriptures: events that took place[20] much later are joined with things that took place earlier. The evangelist Matthew indicates as much below, for[21] he says that Joseph received a command in a vision, *and he came and dwelled in the city that is called Nazareth, so that the words of the prophet might be fulfilled, "He shall be called a Nazarene"* (Matt 2.23). And immediately he adds and says, *at that time John the Baptist came, preaching in the* *desert of Judea* (Matt 3.1). But the preaching of John was thirty years later, and he joins this account to the time of the Nativity. So it is when he describes the Nativity of the Lord, the arrival of the Magi, their veneration of the Lord, and their return to their country: he immediately adds Joseph's flight to Egypt with the Lord and the holy Virgin Theotokos. And then he relates the slaughter of the infants and what follows, as the Holy Spirit gave him to write. Nevertheless, by the grace of the Holy Spirit Luke described after the Nativity what Matthew left out concerning the Circumcision, the going up to Jerusalem, the Presentation in the Temple, Simeon's lifting him up, and the things that follow, for it was not given to a single evangelist to describe all of the divine economy, but one described certain deeds and miracles of the Lord, and the second or the third or the fourth described certain others. So then the explanation of this matter is as I have said.

42 But it must be asked, how then was Herod immediately greeted and defied by the Magi, and yet his wrath and fury did not appear at that time but only after so much time, because he was a very impious and wrathful man? And how did Matthew not say whether the infant was hidden from him at that time, or whether the Magi stole him away with his mother, for they understood his wrath, or whether he was moved from one place to another, as happened to many? There is a true[22] and ready explanation of this matter too, for so it has been made known to us that in those days when the Magi came to Jerusalem and asked about the infant's birth, and Herod wickedly lied and through the pretense of veneration had found a means of murder, a great tumult and conflict arose in his family. But this took place through Providence from above, which did not allow him the opportunity to search for the newborn king and Lord of all. This conflict and tumult had arisen for him from his wife and his sons. At that time he had achieved victory after a long struggle, and immediately he killed his wife, but he was not able to kill his sons without the emperor's consent: that is why he was raging with wrath against them. He mounted up and went forth to Rome, to the emperor, in order to obtain from him power over them. And so it came to be: from there he received the authority. He came and strangled his sons, and he sated his crazed, demonic, and

homicidal soul with their blood. And when the rage against them faded
from his heart, as if he had quieted a violent uprising against him, for
a second time he fell into an even worse and more wicked madness and
rage, and he remembered the greeting of the Magi and the birth of the
infant king. He feared that there would be a change of power, for he was
a slave of insatiability and a thirst for power. He was filled with envy
and wrath and with searching for the one infant king of all. He directed
his wrath against all the innocent children, and by the sword he merci-
lessly slaughtered all the children who were found in the environs of
Bethlehem *two years old and younger,*[23] *according to the time when he questioned the
Magi* (Matt 2.16).

43 Oh merciless mind, hostile to God! How was he not ashamed
of the slaughter of the innocents, when the human heart
would not undertake to kill even young animals like this, nor would it
wish to root out such a multitude of the seedlings of soulless plants, let
alone to slaughter human infants? But this godless man did not hesitate
to suffocate even his own grown children. Oh how wicked are love of
power and envy, the roots of all evils! One of the archangels, fallen away
from honor and service to God, went forth, and this power-hungry
enemy transformed into the devil and the opponent of God. And envy
also made this Belial, and by it he made the Jewish people[24]
God-murderers, and they forgot the Lord's innumerable mercies toward
the unfortunate. So also both these passions wickedly ruled the godless
Herod and made him a murderer first of his own children and then of
a multitude of innocent children, and even worse he intended the
murder of the king and Lord of all, and he attempted to kill the
one by whom he had been created. But, O Herod, enemy of God and
friend of the devil, if the words of the Magi were empty and false,[25]
why do you fear and tremble? If, alternatively, they are true and the
one proclaimed by the prophets has come, how do you not understand
that you are not able to kill him? O blind and ignorant man, who by
excessive envy brought upon yourself the wrath of God, and you were
removed[26] from power and from life, and you became the food of
maggots even before death, as you were fittingly and justly deserving.[27]
And even in this world your torment was horrible and frightful for

all those who saw the wrath that came upon you, and in eternity you have received an especially severe and wicked torment in the fire of Gehenna in accordance with your wicked deeds. But let us return to our original topic.

44 When the cruel judgment went forth from wretched Herod, and the multitude of innocents was gruesomely slaughtered by the sword, and there was no mercy whatsoever, it was not only as if a fire incinerated and demolished Bethlehem and its surroundings, but it shook and troubled all of Judea. And that is why a prophet had already spoken a lament of this event long ago: *"A voice was heard in Ramah, mourning, weeping, and great lamentation; Rachel was weeping for her children, and she would not be consoled, for they were no longer"* (Matt 2.18; cf. Jer 31.15). And thus are these words to be understood: Rachel was the mother of Benjamin, and when she *died she was buried on the road to Ephratha (this is Bethlehem)* (Gen 35.19), because Ramah is part of the tribe of Benjamin. And Benjamin was a son of Rachel, and the tomb of Rachel is near this place. That is why, on account of Benjamin and because of her tomb,[28] the slaughtered infants are called the children of Rachel. *She would not be consoled, for they were no longer.* This was not some small evil: it did not have any explanation, nor was there any expulsion or plunder. The destruction and elimination of the children of Rachel and Benjamin was complete. And so also was Bethlehem made glorious and revered not only on account of other glories but especially because of this. And Bethlehem fulfilled the Passover and was its fulfillment. It sacrificed not only one mute lamb but many, articulate and spotless, only just freed from the pain of birth and suddenly sent forth by the sword from the pains of this fleeting life to the other eternal world, these who had only just seen the visible light, and immediately for the sake of the intelligible light they lost the fleeting light and were transferred to the shadowless light. These heroes and martyrs, age-mates of Christ who unknowingly were knowers of the truth before reaching maturity and who were slaughtered for him before the other martyrs, they were sacrifices and offerings of Christ, offered for him and to him even before his Passion for our sake, for so it was fitting that with Christ's appearance among humanity great virtues were planted in the world.

45 Because of this, not only did incomprehensible and supernatural virginity shine forth from his immaculate mother, but the virtue of courage and service on behalf of[29] Christ was also shown by the young children, and the earth was purified[30] from the blood of impurity and the sacrifice to idols by the shedding of holy and innocent blood, which was a precursor[31] and foreshadowing of the glorious royal blood that was shed on the cross. Such is the story up to this point. But let us recall again for ourselves the Presentation of sweet Jesus in the Temple and the things that follow, for all of this is also praise and glorification of the incorruptible and supremely blessed mother. And when we say this about the Lord, she is also involved and joined to the story, for events that are joined by nature are not separated by words. So then the Circumcision took place on the eighth day after the Nativity, and his name was called Jesus as the archangel said before the conception. Nevertheless, this day was not only the eighth, but it also was the first, the Lord's Day. The angel gave the Annunciation to the Virgin on the Lord's Day. The Nativity from the Virgin also took place on this day. Also on this day he arose from the dead and raised with him our mortal and condemned nature. The resurrection of all and his second coming with heavenly glory to judge the living and the dead also will occur on the Lord's Day. That is why this one day of the week is honored and glorious, which is the holy Lord's Day because such mysteries were fulfilled on it.

CHAPTER 4
THE PRESENTATION IN THE TEMPLE

46 And on the fortieth day after the Nativity they *went up to Jerusalem to present him before the Lord, as is the ordinance of the Law, which says that every child that opens the womb shall be called holy to the Lord* (Luke 2.22–23). Now it is understood by all that he is purifying and also is purified.[1] But it is not known to all that this was seemingly spoken and fulfilled only with respect to every first-born child, who were also brought before the Lord according to the saying of the Law, and an offering of two turtledoves or two young doves was made on their behalf (cf. Lev 5.7), for purity and solitude are symbolized by the turtle-doves, and peace and innocence by the doves. So then the ordinance of the Law was fulfilled together by all, but it was not truly understood by all. And as other words and deeds of prophecy are hidden and unknown to many, so is this matter as well, for not every first-born child was holy to the Lord, as Cain and Reuben and Esau and many others both before and after bear witness. And moreover it is not the case that every first-born child opens the womb, but the woman's womb is opened by the man's bed, and the virginity is corrupted, and only later is the child born, and it comes forth from an already open womb. Nevertheless, if every first-born is holy from birth, how is this saying of prophecy ordained, "*Behold, I was conceived in lawlessness,*[2] *and in sin my mother brought me forth*" (Ps 50.7), for not only birth but also conception is accomplished according to the order and form of sin, even if since the Fall from Paradise the ordinance of the Law has made a pardon concerning this matter? Then again, even if we had observed the creator's commandment, and the propagation of our race had been ordained in another manner and not in corruption and pain, it is still clear that it is not the case that every first-born child would be called holy before the Lord.[3]

47 But there is only one child that is first-born and holy before the Lord, the one whose conception took place not through desire and the male seed—certainly not!—but through grace and the coming of the Holy Spirit, and his birth took place not in corruption and pain but through the power and wisdom of the most high God. That is why the child was born holy, and the Holy of Holies according to the words of Isaiah.[4] And not only was the holy womb opened by his birth, but it remained closed, as Ezekiel, the seer of invisible things, said, *"This gate will be closed, and it will not be opened, and no one will go forth through it, but the Lord God of Israel alone will enter in and come out through it, and the gate will be closed"* (Ezek 44.2). Truly, then, in both cases it remained closed and sealed, before the conception and at the conception, and after the conception and after the birth. But how was it both closed and open, inasmuch as it says, *"every child that opens the womb shall be called holy to the Lord"?* According to the nature of virginity it was closed and unopened,[5] but by the power of the one born, every closure of nature is open and obedient before him. Who else is there, then, who himself opened the mother's womb and kept it closed except the very one whose conception and birth is ineffable, supernatural, and incomprehensible? Behold, then, the truth of the prophecy, for it said that he will be called not just holy, but holy to the Lord. About whom else was it said that he was from birth called holy to the Lord except the one whose primogeniture was described by the angel of the Lord: "the one who is born will be called holy and the son of the Most High" (cf. Luke 1.32, 35)? What was likewise said about him, however, that *every child that opens the womb shall be called holy to the Lord*, this was so that the power of the words would be partly hidden in the words that were spoken, for this mystery is truly the most hidden of all mysteries.

48 But let us listen wisely to the words of Simeon, what he foretold about the sweet and desirable Jesus, for what is sweeter or so full of value as understanding the words spoken about him? So also with respect to his holy and completely immaculate mother, let us hear what prophecies and blessings the old man pronounced, this one *who was a righteous and holy man* and considerably advanced in age, for he had surpassed the limits of this fleeting human life, *and he was looking* *for the consolation of Israel, and the Holy Spirit was upon him. And it had been revealed to him by the Holy Spirit that he would not see death before he saw Christ, the anointed of the Lord. And by the Spirit he came to the Temple of the Lord* (Luke 2.25–27), that is, he was strengthened by the Holy Spirit to take up the desirable one on his lap, and he received from him freedom from this fleeting, difficult, and sorrowful life. Nevertheless, the blessed old man was weakened and immobile on account of his extreme age, and at just this moment he was strengthened and moving well and taking up the Lord onto his lap. And he was freed from this fleeting and difficult life, a symbol of our decrepit and weakened nature, which took on the Savior and liberator, who by his recognition of need and his mercy came to seek the lost, and our nature was freed from the ancient servitude of the passions, from the domination of demons, and from myriad temptations, and it was made worthy of the grace of the Holy Spirit.

49 What then does the evangelist say concerning this worthy old man? *"There was a man in Jerusalem whose name was Simeon, and this man was righteous and devout, and he was looking for the consolation of Israel, and the Holy Spirit was upon him. And it had been revealed to him by the Holy Spirit that he would not see death before he saw the anointed of the Lord. And by the Spirit he came to the Temple, and when the parents brought in the child Jesus, to do for him according to the custom of Law, he took him up in his arms and blessed God and said, 'Lord, let your servant now depart in peace, according to your word, for my eyes have seen your salvation which you prepared before the face of all peoples, a light to enlighten the Gentiles and the glory of your people Israel'"* (Luke 2.25–32). Truly he was full of the grace of the Holy Spirit, and his heart shone from the grace of the one that he took up in his arms. First he offered thanks on account of the goodness that he encountered, and then he spoke a fitting prophecy concerning his own going forth from the world. And he also gave thanks because his eyes saw the Savior Jesus, whom he had previously beheld in the mind, in the very circumstances and with the name that had been prepared before the ages. Nevertheless, he had been hidden as a great mystery, but now he was *prepared before the face of all peoples*, not only the Jews but also all peoples, *a light to enlighten the Gentiles and the glory of your people Israel*, for he was himself the one who shone light on those dwelling in darkness (cf. Isa 9.2). And he also was himself the light, and he was God and king and creator of all things and *the glory of your people Israel*, those who received him and were worthy to be called Israel. The glory and light of all, Christ, mercifully came from heaven to earth and put on flesh from the Holy Spirit and the Virgin Mary. All this had been revealed to the blessed old man by the Holy Spirit, *and Joseph and his mother were astonished by what was said about him* (Luke 2.33).

50 But you, O pious, see how just now the evangelist carefully separated Joseph from the Virgin after the Nativity and the resolution and satisfaction of doubts, for the Nativity was divine and the one born gloriously praised. That is why he said, *"and Joseph and his mother were astonished by what was said."*[6] He called his name Joseph because he was neither the infant's father nor the husband of the infant's mother. That is why he named him Joseph and nothing else, but he calls the blessed Virgin his mother. Simeon was also aware of this, because knowledge of the mysteries concerning this had been revealed to him by the Holy Spirit. He blessed them both because he knew of Joseph that he was a righteous man and he was serving well the mystery of the Lord: and *he blessed them* (Luke 2.34). And then he delivered his remarks to the glorious Mary, *and he said to Mary his mother*, because he knew that she was a treasure house of good things, receiving such a wonder and accomplishing this strange birth, *"Behold, this child is ordained for the fall and rise of many in Israel"* (Luke 2.34).

51 See now the truth of this statement, for the plan of salvation was before the face of all peoples, because the divine will was for the salvation and Deification of all, but the fall and rise was dependent on the will of many, those who believed and those who did not believe, especially in Israel. And it should be understood that the raising of the fallen, which is the conversion of the unbelievers, is clear and comprehensible. But the fall of those who are fallen, what is that unless it is an indication of their profound fall, for the punishment of all those who were unbelieving before the coming of the Lord and before the proclamation is not the same as that of those who remained in unbelief after the Incarnation of the Lord and the proclamation of his teachings. For this is indicated by the saying of the Lord that says, *"this gospel of the kingdom will be preached in all the world as a testimony to all nations"* (Matt 24.14), that is, for the exposure and judgment of unbelievers, because after the teaching and testimony they were deserving of greater punishment. And the guilt of the people of Israel was especially great: that is why it was not possible for their punishment to be merely of the same order. They happened to fall from all honor, and so their punishment will be worse than that of the gentiles if they remain in unbelief, because they did not accept the one whom all the prophets proclaimed, and these wretches considered the righteous and gracious one as a criminal, and in disbelief they became murderers of Christ. That is why he brought upon them the fall of disbelief, and the destruction of the city, and the annihilation and eviction of the people, and the downfall from all freedom and boldness. The faithful, however, met with the true rising, for they have been freed from the bondage and servitude of the old Law, and they have been buried with Christ in baptism (cf. Rom 6.4), and with him they have been raised and live in eternal life. With him they suffered persecution and torment, and with him they have been glorified in the kingdom of heaven.

52 And some of the Fathers also say that the Lord did not come for the fall of some and the rise of others, for he does not cause anyone to fall, but they fall themselves and rise themselves. They fall because of evil things and rise because of good things. If, then, the evils that oppress us do not fall and good things are destroyed, they do not rise among us; if unbelief does not fall, faith does not rise; if sin does not fall and righteousness is destroyed, it does not rise among us. As the apostle Paul says, *"when I am weak, then I am strong"* (2 Cor 12.10). He is himself weak and strong: weak in the flesh and strong in the spirit. So also the power of Christ proclaims[7] by the fall the rise of his believers: that they fall from the hardness and severity of sin and rise with the rise of righteousness. *Behold, this child is ordained for the fall and rise of many in Israel.* And the cross is called *a sign that is spoken against* (Luke 2.34), for it is the cause of glory and of reproach. It is for us who believe in Christ a glory, a sign of our salvation and the seal of our Lord, but it is spoken against because some[8] have understood this well and some wickedly, and some have mocked and despised it. But the believers long for it and honor it and venerate it. And Christ himself is called *a sign that is spoken against*, because he was a worker of supernatural wonders, and some accepted this well and have believed that he did these miracles by the Holy Spirit. Other evil and impure people have blasphemed and said that he did these miracles by the devil (cf. Matt 12.24), and they also said many other things about Christ. Some have said that his coming into the world took place without flesh; others have said that it took place unknowably; others have said that he put on flesh but did not receive a human mind. The senseless and ignorant have spoken thus, and slandering[9] and disputing the truth they have thrown in many other things.

53 And because of all this, he calls the things that were said before and the things just mentioned *a sign that is spoken against*. The old man revealed all this prophecy about this and about the Lord to the immaculate mother because he knew that the blessed one considered everything about her son for herself. That is also why he revealed not only the joyous things but also the sad things, so that when they occurred, the blessed mother would remember the prophecy and it would be a comfort to her. That is why he said, *"And a sword will pierce your own soul too"* (Luke 2.35), because at the time of the Passion, a sword of sorrow pierced the soul of the immaculate mother. When she saw the Passion of her son and king, how great was the sorrow of her heart! And the holy Fathers have also interpreted these words as referring to the Word that scrutinizes and discerns intentions as *a sword that pierces until it divides soul from spirit, joints from marrow, and it discerns the secret intentions and thoughts of the heart* (Heb 4.12), because at the time of Christ's Passion every soul underwent some sort of trial, according to the word of the Lord that says, *"you will all fall away because of me"* (Matt 26.31). Thus Simeon also says about the holy Virgin Mary, "When you stand before the cross and see the sufferings of your son and hear the cries, as it was, *'Eli, eli, lama sabachthani'* (Matt 27.46) and *'Father, into your hands I commit my spirit'* (Luke 23.46), and again when he said, *'I thirst,'* and they held forth vinegar, *and when he received the vinegar, Jesus said, 'Everything is* *finished,'* and he *bowed his head and gave up his spirit* (John 19.28–29), and when you hear and see other such dreadful events and words, after the Annunciation by Gabriel, after the ineffable Nativity of which you yourself are knowledgeable, after seeing the glorious miracles, a sadness will come upon your soul, for it is necessary that the gracious Lord should taste death on behalf of all and redeem all the world and justify all by his blood (cf. Rom 5.9). That is why I speak of your soul, you who are especially knowledgeable of all things: some[10] of the trials of the Lord will touch it, which are a sword that will reveal the thoughts of many." By this he indicates that after the grief and doubt that came upon the disciples at the Crucifixion of the Lord and struck the heart of the immaculate Mary like lightning, immediately, in an instant, healing and consolation were introduced by the Lord, who strengthened their hearts by her faith, so that her fortitude was made manifest. And so the words *"so that the thoughts of many would be revealed"* (Luke 2.35) also indicate this. For when he fulfilled the suffering on the cross, the mystery of our salvation was accomplished. And by this cause the thoughts of many have been revealed, the thoughts that each person has about Christ, either love and faith or envy and hate. For some were openly mocking and rejoicing at his Crucifixion, not only those who had openly been enemies from the beginning, but also some who hypocritically insisted on their friendship, whose thoughts and intentions time revealed. But others grieved and mourned and confessed him as God on the cross, as did the thief, *so that the thoughts of many would be revealed*, and many of those who erred were also strengthened by the Resurrection of the Lord, and they believed and shone with the grace of Christ.

54 Nevertheless, let us return again to our original topic. After the Presentation in the Temple and Simeon's taking him up and speaking these words of prophecy and the praise of Anna (cf. Luke 2.36–38), *when they had fulfilled everything according to the Law of the Lord, they returned to Galilee, to the city of Nazareth* (Luke 2.39), as the evangelist Luke says. Then *an angel of the Lord appeared to Joseph* and ordered him to *flee to Egypt* (Matt 2.13), according to the words of the evangelist Matthew. Then the child himself, an infant and God before the ages, arranged

THE LIFE OF THE VIRGIN

everything, and he himself undertook the flight into Egypt with his mother and Joseph. After that, as is written above (cf. §§42–43), the slaughter of the infants by the godless Herod took place. But then the great John, the Forerunner of the Lord, who while still in his mother's womb, before coming forth to the visible light, saw the true light and leapt for joy, a preacher before having a voice, a witness to the Word before coming to speak, at that time he was about to taste death and receive the martyr's crown with the other infants of his same age, because by family and by birth he was from Bethlehem and its surroundings. Although his birth had taken place six months earlier, the tyrant's iniquitous order ordained the slaughter of all children *two years old and less* or a little more *who were in Bethlehem and all of its surroundings* (Matt 2.16), so that those being sought could not flee anywhere. Nevertheless, God was the glorious Forerunner and Baptist's protector, the God and Lord that they were seeking to kill, and he was providentially fleeing to Egypt. He kept his predecessor safe so that he was not killed with the other children, but at the completion of his life he was his witness and predecessor among the dead in Hell to announce their deliverance. The benevolent one who came into the world for our sake saved Elizabeth and her son from the murderers' hands, she who fled with her son to the desert and said to the mountain, *"Mountain of God, receive a mother with her child"* (Protev 22.3), and the mountain received them and hid them by the order of the Lord. There Elizabeth left her son John, and she died herself. Nevertheless, from that time on, just as the conception and birth of the sun of righteousness and the bridegroom of the church are ineffable and inexpressible, so it is also true of the sun's friend who is called the candle of the light and *the voice of one crying* (Mark 1.3) and *the friend of the bridegroom* (John 3.29) and the knight of the king. His upbringing and dwelling and reception of nourishment and all of his existence in the desert until the day of his proclamation to Israel are indescribable (cf. Luke 1.80).[11] Nevertheless, when the wicked child-killers failed to seize Elizabeth and her son John, they returned and took out their rage on Zechariah, John's father, and by order of the impure Herod, they killed the blessed man while he was serving God in the Temple before the altar and offering the sacrifices of the Law, and so in this way he fulfilled his destiny (cf. Protev 23.2–3).

55 Nevertheless, when the young infant and king of all made the flight into Egypt, he put to flight and drove out the demons of Egypt and destroyed many debaucheries. For the Magi and the Egyptians were pagan, and more than the other pagans these two were enslaved to demons and had acquired[12] every evil. For the Egyptians more than all others were the servants and attendants of wicked idols and abominable reptiles and plants of the earth. And they sacrificed to a cow and believed[13] it to be a god, whom they called Apis, and they made a goat into a god, and they sacrificed to martens and mice. And they considered the crocodile, the beast of the river Nile, to be a god and worshipped garlic and onions and certain other worthless and abominable reptiles and plants. The Magi, however, served the demon guardians of the air and called upon them, and they were observing the stars and sacrificing to them and acquiring predictions and spells. By his coming into the world, Christ immediately released these two deeply misled nations from great debauchery, so that the enemy saw the plunder of his property, and the heart was no longer captured by other things. For at the time of his Nativity he called the Magi from Persia, and he destroyed every illusion of the demon guardians of the air and every debauchery of astrology and soothsaying. And a little while later he went down to Egypt himself as a human being with his immaculate mother, and he destroyed every impurity of the Egyptians and drove out the snakes and scorpions of Egypt and dispelled the fog of debauchery. Nevertheless, the mother of the Lord, the source of life, saw her family and friends in Judea as enemies and persecutors, and the Egyptian enemies and foreigners she found as friends. She had left Judea and was dwelling in Egypt. Then the Egyptians saw what had previously been said by the prophet Jeremiah, God incarnate and his immaculate virgin mother (cf. Jer 22.26?).[14] And so our Lord Jesus Christ and his all-holy mother dwelt in Egypt for two years, as the Fathers have taught us.[15] After this, the wicked Herod died a horrible death, and again *an angel of the Lord appeared to Joseph in Egypt and said, "Arise and lead the child and his mother forth and go forth to the land of Israel, for those who were seeking the child's life are dead." And he arose and led forth the child and his mother, and he came to the land of Israel* (Matt 2.19–21). And he received the command in a dream. *And he came and settled in a city that was called Nazareth so that the words of the prophets* *would be fulfilled*, one that *"He will be called a Nazarene"* (Matt 2.23), and the second *"Out of Egypt I have called my son"* (Matt 2.15). So then the going down to Egypt and the return from Egypt and the settling in Nazareth took place through the appearance and the words of the angel, as the evangelist Matthew teaches us.

56 If, however, anyone should say that the evangelist Luke does not mention the appearance of the angel and the settling in Nazareth but says that after the Presentation in the Temple, *when by it they had fulfilled everything according to the Law, they returned to the region of Galilee, to Nazareth* (Luke 2.39), there is nonetheless no mutual contradiction in the words of the blessed evangelists. Luke describes events prior to the going down to Egypt, because according to his account there was only their going up to Bethlehem and Judea. And when this was completed and the supernatural birth of the Lord took place, they remained there in Bethlehem until forty days had passed. Then they brought the child up to Jerusalem for the Presentation[16] before the Lord according to the ordinance of the Law, and the elderly Simeon took him up. When all of this took place by the Providence and command of the Lord, who was born from the Virgin for the mercy of humankind, they returned to their dwelling, to the city of Nazareth, where they had been before. There they spent two years, as we have learned from the Fathers, and then the angel of the Lord appeared to Joseph and ordered the Flight into Egypt when, after the upheavals of insurrection, Herod had the time and wanted to search out and kill the infant king. And then when they had remained in Egypt for two years, and the impure Herod died, the angel of the Lord again appeared to Joseph and ordered the return to the land of Israel. *And he arose and led forth the child and his mother, and he came to the land of Israel. And he heard that Archelaus reigned in Judea in the place of his father Herod. He was afraid to go there, and he received a command in a dream. And he came and settled in a city that was called Nazareth* (Matt 2.21–23).

57 Oh the glorious wonder of the immaculate and blessed mother! How great are the works and labors that befell her from beginning to end, although divine consolations were mixed in with the adversities. For after the Annunciation by Gabriel and the ineffable conception, there were Joseph's doubts: as the evangelist says, *"He decided to divorce her quietly"* (Matt 1.19). How great was the vain doubt that disturbed his pure soul, and the doubts were dispelled by the angel's appearance, which made him to understand that the conception was by the Holy Spirit and that his birth was for the salvation of the entire world. The time of the blessed Nativity drew near, and suddenly the emperor's order required them to go up to Bethlehem in Judea. They went forth from Nazareth in Galilee and went up to Judea with difficulty and hardship. When they drew near to Bethlehem, *the days of her birth were fulfilled, and she gave birth to a son, and she wrapped him in swaddling clothes and laid him in a manger, because there was no place for them at the inn* (Luke 2.6–7), and their life was one of poverty and hardship. But again, consolation was joined to the adversities: the annunciations and praise of the angels, the shepherds' running and searching for the newborn child, the proclamation to all when they heard about the child from the angels, and those who heard and marveled and glorified God. And then suddenly the arrival of the Magi guided by the star, and their adoration of the child, the king of all, with his all-holy mother, and their offering of precious gifts took place. After that, the going up to Jerusalem, the Presentation of the unfathomable infant in the Temple, and the taking up by Simeon and his blessing and prophecy took place.

58 When these consolations took place, time passed, and suddenly Herod's rage and hatred were stirred up. And the all-holy mother's flight into Egypt with her son, the blessed king of all, took place, and again there was adversity and poverty and hardship and fear, for Herod was seeking the life[17] of the child (cf. Matt 2.20) by whose hands every living soul exists, the one who had come to seek the lost sheep (cf. Luke 15.6) and the drachma that is the image of the king (cf. Luke 15.9, 20.24, and Gen 1.26). Then he fled to Egypt, the one who once delivered the people of Israel fleeing from Egypt and led them through the sea as if on dry land. These people, which he then saved from many misfortunes, were now pursuing him and seeking his life. The Lord and king of all things visible and invisible went forth and became a stranger in a foreign land, and he moved from place to place with his blessed mother. All these labors and adversities were of a maternal nature, of the one who bore in her bosom her infant son, God before the ages. And all this was a prefiguration and an image of the courage[18] and patience of the holy Virgin, just as her early life and character made known[19] the wisdom and the purity of the immaculate Virgin.

59 Nevertheless, when the mother of God returned from Egypt with Joseph and her gracious son, and they came again with difficulty to their land, the land of promise, the most-blessed mother found that the tyrant who was seeking her holy child had fittingly and justly fallen to a destruction of great evils. First, he eliminated his wife and children and all his family by himself, and then he died a horrible death, and his wicked soul went forth from him in a gruesome death. And his kingdom was divided into four provinces, and because Archelaus, one of his remaining sons, was in his place (since he was not able to eliminate everyone), Joseph then received the command from the angel. He went and settled in the city of Nazareth and did not go to Judea because the angel had told him this: he was in Egypt for the same reason. The angel did not tell Joseph to go up to Judea, but he said, *"Arise and lead the child and his mother forth and go forth to the land of Israel, for those who were seeking the child's life are dead"* (Matt 2.20). Nevertheless, it has been investigated by scholars how Archelaus reigned and Pilate ruled in Judea.[20] But so it should be understood that at the time of the Incarnation of Christ and even a little before, the kingship of the Jews and the high priesthood had been greatly diminished by the Romans, according to the words of the prophet that say, "In the decline of the rulers of Judah, hope will come to all the gentiles" (cf. Gen 49.10).[21] Therefore at that time Hyrcanus[22] was high priest and king, and he had a younger brother named Aristobulus, who rose up against his brother Hyrcanus as an enemy and an opponent and stirred up great disorder. Aristobulus was sent to Rome as a prisoner by the Roman general Pompey, and Pompey ordained that the high priests of Jerusalem would pay tribute to Rome.[23] After a little while, Herod, through great service to the emperor, a military alliance, and many gifts, was appointed by the emperor Augustus as king of Judea. He had the title of king but a condition of servitude, for he could not even enact his will against his own children without the emperor's order, and he had no authority over them. Nevertheless, after the death of Herod, the servitude of the Jews to the Romans became even greater, and even in Herod's own lifetime, when the decree went forth from the emperor Augustus to enroll the whole world, all Judea was enrolled like a slave. And also at that time a Roman governor was established over them, as the evangelist says, *"this was the first enrollment when Quirinius was governor of Syria"* (Luke 2.2), and from that time on the governors and judges, soldiers and guards of the land were all Roman, so that the Jews would not be able to make an uprising, because all the power and authority was Roman. And the kingship of Judea was given by the emperor to whomever the emperor saw fit from among them. And the one who was appointed king was not independent but submitted to the emperor in all things. That is why it is clear that in the reign of Archelaus[24] Pilate was the governor, and also when the son of the other Herod handed over our Lord Jesus Christ to Pilate to be crucified, Pilate was the governor, and Herod the tetrarch happened to be found in Jerusalem, having gone there as a guest (cf. Luke 23.5–12). And it was known by all that the power and authority of the emperor was in the Roman governors. But let us return to the original course of our discourse.

60 The holy gospel says, *"And the child grew and became strong in spirit, and he was filled with wisdom, and the grace of God was upon him"* (Luke 2.40).[25] These words are not attributed to his divinity, for what could be more perfect and more constant[26] than the one who is from the beginning perfect, more perfect than the perfect, more constant than the constant, and full of every good thing. But the evangelist speaks of growth and becoming strong with respect to human stature. And so the other words that follow should also be understood, which say, *"he increased in wisdom and grace"* (Luke 2.52), for increase in wisdom and grace are not attributed to his divinity, because it was from the beginning full and complete. And so also it should not be understood that he became stronger and became more full with respect to his humanity from the indwelling of the Holy Spirit in him, for he had the grace of indwelling completely from the beginning, because with the union of the two natures, immediately *"in him the entire fullness of the deity dwelt in the body"*

(Col 2.9), as the holy apostle Paul says. But the same words, *he was filled and increased in wisdom and grace*, indicate this: that the indwelling in him that from the beginning united divinity and humanity, full of grace and wisdom, appeared and shone forth more and more with the growth in stature of his body, not that he received more grace and wisdom anew, but he revealed and made known the completeness of his grace and wisdom by his glorious deeds, because, as the apostle says, *"he is himself before all things, and by him all things also are made firm, for in him the complete fullness was pleased to dwell and through him to reconcile all things to himself"* (Col 1.17, 19–20). Nevertheless, it did not seem fitting to make his wisdom manifest without respect to age, but as it is ordinary for our nature to reach the perfection of speech[27] in the twelfth year, so he also saw fit to do so in the twelfth year of his bodily age.

61 And at the time of the feast when the Jews much later enviously wanted to raise him up and hand him over to the Passion, at this feast and in the twelfth year of his human age, when his parents went up to Jerusalem, as was their custom, *when they had completed the days and they were returning, the boy Jesus remained behind in Jerusalem, and his parents did not know it* (Luke 2.42–43), neither his mother, who was truly his parent, nor Joseph, who was called his parent in name only, and they did not know anything about it. That is why he remained behind without them knowing, so that he would not be prevented by them from remaining behind there, and so that he would be prevented from being disobedient. But when he remained behind in Jerusalem, he went to the Temple and sat among the teachers. And without force or arrogance, he taught and instructed the teachers and priests, the one who was the unique source of all wisdom and knowledge and who gives speech and wisdom to all others. But in this he also knew the limits of his own age and honor, and he followed a different order. Therefore he allowed the teachers and priests to teach and instruct, but for his own part he asked questions eloquently and listened intelligently and responded thoughtfully. That is also why they were all amazed by his understanding and wisdom, for he was truly amazing. Nevertheless, when his all-holy mother with Joseph *sought him among their relatives and acquaintances and did not find him, they returned to Jerusalem, and they found him after three days sitting in the*

Temple among the teachers. He was listening to them and asking them questions, and all those who heard him were amazed by his understanding and his answers. His mother said to him, "Child, why have you done this to us? Behold, your father and I have been running[28] *around looking for you"* (Luke 2.44–48). Nevertheless, the gracious and sweet Lord made his blessed mother understand the truth, and he made known his true Father, and he explained to her so that she saw him not as an ordinary human being but as God incarnate, and that the house of the Father, which is the Temple, also is his, as everything else that is the Father's is also the Son's. It was as if he faulted those who were ignorant of all this and who were not able to come to a full understanding of the truth. That is why *he said to them, "Why were you looking for me? Did you not know that I must be in my Father's house?"* (Luke 2.49). In this place for the first time he spoke clearly about his true Father with divine eloquence, so that he made them to understand his divinity, and so that they would know that if God is his Father, then the Son also must be of the Father's same nature, for there is one nature of the Father and the Son, as he says in another place, *"He who has seen me has seen my Father"* (John 14.9). And again he said to his disciples, *"If you had known me, you would have known my Father also; from now on you know him and have seen him"* (John 14.7), as he said to them, "since you have seen me, you have seen the Father also" (cf. John 8.19).

62 This was the first teaching and divinely inspired doctrine of the wisdom and power of the infant Jesus. Thus he amazed his holy mother and Joseph and all those standing there, although they were not able to understand the meaning of his words completely (cf. Luke 2.50). *"And he went down with them and came to Nazareth, and he was obedient to them. And his mother kept all these sayings in her heart,"* as the holy evangelist says. *"And Jesus increased in wisdom and stature and grace before God and humankind"* (Luke 2.51–52). And all this time, from this moment until the baptism, transpired without the working of any public miracles. For the book that is called *The Infancy of Christ*[29] is not to be received, but it is alien to the order of the Church and contrary to what the holy evangelists have said and an adversary of truth that was composed by some foolish men and storytellers. But the evangelist Luke briefly relates the truth of the gospel's proclamation, and he says that *"Jesus increased in* *wisdom and stature and grace*[30] *before God and humankind,"* as we have made clear in the explanation of these words above. And he was truly full of all wisdom and grace, the source of wisdom and grace, and longed for by all wise and intelligent people, for he was handsome in bodily form, *"in beauty beyond the sons of men"* (Ps 44.3), as the prophet says, striking in proportion and ideal in the measure of his body, fittingly radiant, and captivating and eloquent in speech. And his entire life was joyous and full of the Holy Spirit, and to put it briefly, as in all other good things, so also in human behavior and speech he was the model and definition of every good virtue, but his peace and goodness were unattainable and inexpressible by all.

63 *A razor never came upon his head* (Judg 16.17; Num 6.5), nor did he make use of any human assistance except from his holy and all-blessed mother. And he did not give any other teaching until his baptism. But through his deeds and conduct, his entire life and behavior were a model and education in virtue, for what he ultimately taught with words to his disciples and the people after his baptism,[31] all this he accomplished perfectly himself from his childhood to his death, and then he taught others. Nevertheless, I say that he accomplished this with respect to human custom, nature, and stature, for one cannot speak of his accomplishment as God, and he is supremely exalted from age unto age, as the prophet David says, *"From age unto age, you are"* (Ps 89.2). But according to the human nature and body of the flesh that he put on from the Virgin Mary, he accomplished every virtuous deed and all the precepts of the Law that had been ordained by the words of Moses, which no one else could achieve completely and without compromise except only Jesus who became incarnate for our salvation: love of God and humanity, compassion, benevolence, and sweetness, peace, humility, and patience, honor and obedience to parents, fasting and prayer and every other good work, which the gracious one taught humanity first by deeds and then by words. From that time on the holy mother was a disciple of her sweet son, truly the mother of Wisdom and a daughter of Wisdom, for she no longer saw him as a human or as a mere human being, but[32] she served him reverently as God and received his words as the words of God. That is why she did not forget any of his words or deeds, as the evangelist says, *"And his mother kept all these sayings in her heart"* (Luke 2.51), and she awaited the time[33] of their clear manifestation. On the one hand she had his words and deeds as the rule and law of her life, and on the other hand as sign and prefiguration of the ineffable mysteries and miracles to come. Nevertheless, we remain silent about everything after this, about which the gospel also remained silent, because the Word of God himself, who became incarnate for our sake, revealed no sign or power of his divinity until he reached the perfection of human stature. And the time for the revelation of his divine economy and the manifestation of miracles and the life-giving Passion arrived, for each one received its cause from the other. For the miracles confirmed his teaching, and the teaching proclaimed the miracles, and both of these gave rise to the gathering of many people who gathered to see the miracles and hear his teachings. For this reason he gave rise to the envy of the high priests and Pharisees, on account of which they rose up against him as enemies and delivered him to the Passion, and thus were all the mysteries fulfilled.

CHAPTER 5

THE REVELATION (OR THE EPIPHANY)

64 And let us now hear the story of the revelation and the baptism of the Lord. Jesus was thirty years old, and John was a little older. At that time, *in the fifteenth year of emperor Tiberius, the word of God came to John the son of Zechariah in the desert, and he went to all the region surrounding the Jordan and proclaimed a baptism of repentance for forgiveness of sins* (Luke 3.1–3). *Then Jerusalem and Judea were going out to him, and all the country around the Jordan, and they were baptized by him in the Jordan and confessing their sins* (Matt 3.5–6), because his manner of living was beyond human nature. And everyone heard of his amazing asceticism, and they assembled around him and heard his teaching and were baptized by him. Nevertheless, all of this came upon him though Providence so that his fame spread and his teaching and witness to our Lord Jesus were credible, for he was preaching and saying, *"One greater than me is coming after me, for whom I am not worthy to loosen the thong of his sandals. I baptize you with water, but he will baptize you with the Holy Spirit." At that time Jesus came from Nazareth of Galilee and was baptized by John in the Jordan. And immediately as he was coming up from the water, he saw the heavens opened and the Holy Spirit descending upon him as a dove. And there was a voice from heaven: "You are my beloved son, in whom I am well pleased"* (Mark 1.7–11). These great mysteries required an equally great witness.[1] Consequently, the Lord exalted John and made him famous among all people so that his testimony also would be credible. Thus many also believed because of his message and became disciples of the Lord, as happened with Andrew, Peter, and John, who also wrote this: *"John was standing with two of the disciples"* (John 1.35). These were Andrew the brother of Peter (cf. John 1.40) and John the evangelist.

65 *And he watched Jesus as he was walking, and he said, "Behold, Christ, the Lamb of God!" The two disciples heard this* (John 1.36–37), and they went over to those of Jesus.[2] And many others believed as a result of John's witness, because, in light of his way of life, his strange diet and peculiar garb[3] (cf. Matt 3.4), and his audacious preaching, he was an astonishment to all, to the degree that they were wondering in their hearts, is this one the Christ? *And the Jews sent priests and Levites to him to ask, and he testified, "I am not the Christ. Nevertheless, among you stands one whom you do not know, the one who is coming after me, for whom I am not worthy to loosen the thong of his sandals"* (cf. John 1.19–20, 26–27). But what is the meaning of this statement, if he "is coming after me," and he "stands among you"? He is "coming after" with respect to preaching, because John began to preach first, and the Lord Jesus thereafter. And John appeared first and was honored by all, and then the Lord Jesus, who preceded him in honor and glory, for the knight comes first and then the king follows.[4] But he "stands among you" in the flesh because he came to be baptized similarly with all the others. Nevertheless, the Baptist bore witness not only with words, but he also indicated with a finger, for when he saw Jesus coming toward him, he said of him, *"Behold the Lamb of God, who takes away the sins of the world"* (John 1.29), because he did not need purification[5] but is the purifier of the entire world. And John continued and said, *"This is the one about whom I said, 'After me comes a man who is ahead of me because he is before me.' I did not know him myself, but in order that he would be revealed in Israel, for this reason I came baptizing with water." And John testified and said, "I saw the Spirit descending as a dove from heaven, and it remained on him. I did not know him myself,[6] but the one who sent me to baptize with water said to me: 'The one on whom you see the Spirit descend and remain, he is the one who baptizes with the Holy Spirit.' And I myself have seen and testify that this is the Son of God"* (John 1.30–34).

66 Nevertheless, the Holy Spirit remained on him not only at that moment, nor did it come upon him only then—for how could that be possible for the one in whom the whole fullness of the deity dwelled (cf. Col. 2.9) from the beginning—but this happened so that the one who is truly Son of God and truly God would be seen by all. And I think that just as he did many other magnificent deeds as signs for us, so too was this a sign for us of the coming of the Holy Spirit after baptism. Therefore the coming of the Holy Spirit took place in this way, and when it came, the voice of the Father was heard testifying about the Lord Jesus, *"This is my beloved son, with whom I am well pleased"* (Matt 3.17). And thus the Holy Trinity was revealed at the Jordan, united in one essence and separated in three hypostases:[7] three in hypostases because it is named individually in separate parts—the Son was seen in the body at the Jordan, the Holy Spirit descended on him as the dove, the Father bore witness to his beloved son from above—but one in essence because they are united and have appeared together. And not only this, but since we understand that Christ's hypostasis of divinity and humanity is one, because God became human and humanity became God unchangingly, for this reason the Father called the union of divinity and humanity in two natures and one hypostasis "beloved son." Therefore only John was worthy of the vision of the Holy Spirit, but the voice and testimony of the Father were heard by all the people as before on Mount Sinai, when God gave the Law to Moses (cf. Deut 4.33; 5.3–5; Exod 20). Moses alone saw the vision, but the voice was heard by all—not just by those who were present there but even among those present according to the worthiness of each one, excepting those who were unworthy of hearing and rebelled against the giving of the Law. Therefore both took place justly and fittingly at the baptism of Christ, for if the people and John had together been made worthy of seeing the Holy Spirit and hearing the voice from above, then no greater honor remained for the Forerunner and Baptist, but the vision of the awesome and glorious coming of the Holy Spirit would be understood as shared by all. And likewise, if the voice had not been heard by the people all together, the testimony given concerning Christ would have been unknown, and John's testimony would have been suspect, and they would have said that he testifies falsely or for profit.[8] But when the voice was heard by everyone, it made John's testimony believable and brought understanding of the Lord Jesus to all.

67 But after the baptism, Jesus went out to the desert at the direction of the Holy Spirit, in order to call forth the strength of that reclusive place to fight the enemy, so as to demonstrate for us the proper actions of the faithful following baptism: fasting and good works. He fasted for forty days and experienced hunger in the nature of his body. The tempter came and tempted him in various fashions, and in every instance the Lord Jesus Christ was victorious against this evil enemy,[9] and he was driven away. After the victory, *angels came and ministered to him* (Matt 4.11). This happened especially as a sign for us that after faith and baptism one must engage in good works, and following the good works, gifts and blessings are given to those who did the works. He went down again and came to the place where John was. And he saw him again and testified as before, this time not only once but twice. Then the disciples of John followed him, Andrew and John, the chiefs of virtue,[10] because Andrew was the model of courage and John the model of virginity. Andrew brought his brother Peter to be a disciple of the Lord: the younger became the leader of spiritual birth to the elder and first-born, so that Peter would not have seniority in everything. From that time on John entrusted his disciples and his proclamation to Christ the king. Nevertheless, he was himself cast into prison by Herod after a little while, because he was zealous to be the Forerunner of his Passion as he had been the Forerunner of his preaching and his baptism. What then does the holy gospel teach us? *"When Jesus heard that John had been cast into prison, he withdrew from there and went forth to Galilee. From that time Jesus began to preach and to say, 'Repent, for the kingdom of heaven has drawn near'"* (Matt 4.12, 17). The beginning of his preaching and teaching was in Galilee. There he received Philip and Nathanael as disciples (cf. John 1.44–49), for Peter, Andrew, James, and John had already been received.

68 After that *there was a wedding in Cana of Galilee* (John 2.1) and the beginning of the miracles, the changing of the water into wine. His immaculate and all-holy mother was there, a witness to the miracles and a hearer of the Lord's teachings. And the mediator of all good things was a mediator of this miracle also, for she desired as the immaculate mother to see the miracles of her son and Lord. Therefore she asked respectfully and cautiously and did not directly order that he do a miracle, but with modesty she merely made known the need of the situation and said, *"They have no wine"* (John 2.3). And the desire of her heart revealed that she wanted to see his working of miracles, because she knew that he was the creator of all things and the renewal and transformation of natures as he chooses, who supernaturally dwelt in her womb and preserved her virginity incorruptibly, and he went forth from her womb as he wished and preserved the womb as closed and unopened. She knew that he could accomplish whatever he wished, and she modestly made the situation known. Nevertheless, her son and gracious Lord, in order to teach his even greater humility and modesty, especially because he was beginning to reveal the power of his divinity, seemingly faulted her by saying, *"Woman, what have you to do with me? My hour has not yet come"* (John 2.4). But in fact he complied and fulfilled her request: he honored her as mother and yielded to the desire of her heart. Nevertheless, the blessed and all-holy one was aware of his goodness and power. *She said to the servants: "Whatever he tells you, do it"* (John 2.5). And thus the ineffable power of the Lord changed the water into excellent wine. But the water's change into wine also effected a change in the one who was the host. The bridegroom left the wedding and his home, and he followed and served the excellent guest,[11] the gracious Lord and king and the bridegroom of immaculate and holy souls. So also the bride served the all-holy mother of the Lord, so that the miracle done by the Lord not only turned water into wine, but it also changed marriage into virginity. So then the all-holy Virgin and mother of the Lord remained inseparable from the gracious Lord and her beloved son for as many days as it was possible. Wherever[12] he went, she went with him, and she was considered the life and the light of his eyes and soul, going with him and listening to his words.

69 And when the Lord entered Peter's house and healed his mother-in-law, who was weak from a fever (Matt 8.14–15), his all-blessed mother, the holy Virgin Mary, was with him, as well as the women who had become disciples of the Lord. Now Peter's healed mother-in-law along with her daughter, who was Peter's wife, heard the teachings of the Lord, and they went with the holy Theotokos, and they became her servants and her advisors. From there the Lord Jesus went forth again to Nazareth with his holy mother, because Joseph, the one to whom the holy Virgin had initially been betrothed, had completed one hundred and ten years full of excellent days, he who had been worthy to be the parent and servant of the Lord and king of all and God, Jesus Christ. And he became an eyewitness to the ineffable wonders of his birth and upbringing and, after his baptism, to his miracles. Thus he went forth to eternal life, and he received a blessing from the Lord Jesus Christ worthy of his virtue and faithful service. Nevertheless, his sons James and Jude followed Christ as disciples, and his daughters became disciples of the holy Theotokos (cf. *Protev* 9.2). And as the Lord in his wanderings preached the message of salvation and healed every illness and every mental affliction, they regularly accompanied him. And they served him and saw the miracles that were done by him, as it is written in the holy gospel, *"There were also many women there who followed Jesus from Galilee and provided for him"* (Matt 27.55), but the holy and glorious mother of the Lord was the leader of them all, their source of support and their mediator with the Lord her son. From there the one seeking the salvation of all went to the lake of Gennesaret (cf. Luke 5.1), which is great and famous, full of fish within and of various fruitful plants around it. There he ordered Simon Peter to fish,[13] after the teaching that he had taught the people from the boat (cf. Luke 5.3–4). They cast out the net, and they took in a great multitude of fish, and *astonishment seized Peter, and all those with him, at the great catch of fish that they had taken, and so also James and John, the sons of Zebedee, who were partners with Simon. And Jesus said to them, "Do not be afraid; henceforth you will be catching people." And they brought their ships to land, and they left everything and followed him* (Luke 5.9–11), as they had done before.

70 From Gennesaret the Lord went to Capernaum, where he healed the paralytic, who was a symbol of our old[14] and broken nature, for just as he restored him and ordered him to take his bed and return to his home (cf. Matt 9.1–8),[15] so also the gracious one has renewed our fallen and crippled nature, and he gathered together into one faith the scattered members, who were the dispersed gentiles, and made them one body, obedient to the head of all things, Christ our God. And he has ordered us to take on the yoke of his commandments and to go forth to the original homeland, which is Paradise, from which we have fallen away. After that there was a gathering of the people and innumerable miracles of the Lord that the evangelists were not able to describe in full, *which Jesus did, which, if each one of them were to be written, this world could not contain the books that would be written* (John 21.25), for the understanding of the people of this world cannot contain their abundance and most glorious power. Then Jesus was teaching the people and curing infirmities and diseases, not only those of the body but also those of the soul. The disciples, however, were teaching those who had been cured and brought to the faith, and they were baptizing them by the Lord's command. For just as in every other thing Christ fulfilled the old customs and was the beginning of the new Law, so also in baptism he received the baptism of John in the Jordan river, but thereafter he himself perfected baptism by the bestowal of the Holy Spirit, and he instructed the disciples to do the same. Then Zebedee, the father of James and John, died, and they asked the Lord to go and to bury their father, but the gracious one would not allow it (cf. Matt 8.21–22), so that they would think of nothing as more desirable than being with him. And then by his command they abandoned their own will. After that he ordered them to go and take care of their house and their mother. And they went forth and accomplished everything well, and they brought their mother and joined her to the servants of the holy Theotokos, in order to serve the Lord always with her. But at the Lord's instruction, they shared the considerable possessions that they had from their mother and father partly with the poor, and part they gave to their co-disciples. All the rest they sold, and they bought the house of Zion, which was to become the house of the immaculate mother of the Lord after the Crucifixion and Ascension of Christ, where the beloved disciple, when he received her from the Lord at the time of the Passion, brought her and served her at the instruction of the sweet king. After Galilee, Judea also was full of the miracles and wonders of Christ, and his holy mother was always with him, observing the great beauty of his miracles and listening to his teaching. There was there also a certain wealthy and honorable woman named Joanna (cf. Luke 8.3), and when she heard the teaching of Christ, that whoever wishes to be perfect should sell[16] her possessions and give them to the poor and *"take up her cross and follow me"* (Matt 16.24; cf. Matt 19.21), she renounced everything and abandoned her spouse and children, her house and land and all her possessions and followed the Lord, and she remained with his holy mother all the time thereafter.

71 Then there was the feast of Tabernacles (cf. John 7), when, among other miracles and healings, the Lord Jesus did this: he entered the Temple with a whip, and he found merchants selling cattle, sheep, and doves,[17] and moneychangers sitting there, and he drove them all out of the Temple (cf. Matt 21.12–13), the one who was a symbol of the old and new Law, because he both brought the old customs to an end and he initiated the new. When he had filled Judea with miracles, he again returned to Galilee and went around to the towns and villages. And he went to the town of Magdala, where he met Mary of Magdala, from whom the Lord had cast out seven demons (cf. Luke 8.2). She was distinguished by her wealth and noble birth, and she showed zeal in being a disciple of the Lord and served Christ and his pure mother faithfully. But she was also a symbol of human nature, because she had been beset by seven evil spirits, which are opposed to the seven divine graces, and so also human nature is afflicted by seven evils. The Magdalene found the healer and purifier of our nature, and the alleviator of every disease and mental affliction. And not only was she freed from all the demons by the grace of Christ, but she became filled with every grace, and she appeared very zealous in faith and good deeds and good thoughts. And she followed the Lord all the days of her time on earth. She was a disciple and a minister, a good and obedient companion of the queen, the holy Theotokos, and she served as a minister with her. And finally, she also became worthy of the grace of being an apostle, and she went about from city to city for Christ, and she came to Rome and received the crown of martyrdom, and she fought the good fight (cf. 2 Tim 4.7) until her blood was spilled. To put it briefly, as the blessed apostle Peter was zealous and outstanding among the [male] disciples, so was Mary Magdalene among the myrrhbearers and women, but her good works will also be well recalled when we come to the place of Christ's Crucifixion.

72 But now let us return to the original course of this discourse, and let us address the remainder of the life of the mother of the Lord and our queen, everything that she accomplished with her son and Lord, and also everything she did herself until her Assumption. Nevertheless, may readers and listeners forgive the length of this discourse, for our discourse concerns such great mysteries and grandeurs, for which every language and every art, all power and grace, all the time elapsed from now until eternity, both the present and the future, have been utilized, and are being utilized, and always and henceforth will be utilized, but they have been vanquished and have failed, and they will be vanquished and will fail, and no one will be able, not even the incorporeal and bodiless heavenly powers, to express these mysteries worthily and fittingly, but these divine and glorious events will always and in every instance be expressed and glorified only according to the limits of power and scope of each individual. But we have said this and we say it again, that after the recognitions of the exalted and ineffable birth of the Lord from the immaculate and blessed mother, the incorruptible mother was never separated from her gracious son and king. But already in the age of infancy he was Lord, and she raised him in the proper manner, and she served him as a servant, and she lived with him always inseparably. That is why when he was twelve years old in human age, and they went up to Jerusalem for the feast of Passover, and upon their return the child Jesus deliberately remained in Jerusalem, the immaculate mother went from place to place in distress and groaning and sought him. And when she found him, she said to him in distress, *"Child, why have you done this to us?"* (Luke 2.48) and what followed this. Then he returned with them, and they came to Nazareth, and the king and Lord of all things was obedient to them. But when he grew up[18] and was thirty years old, and was baptized in the Jordan by John, and the Holy Spirit came upon him in the form of a dove, and the Father bore witness to him from above as the beloved Son, and he began to preach and to work miracles, the holy mother went with him always, as much as was possible, seeing the miracles and hearing the teachings.

CHAPTER 6

ON THE PASSION

73 When the time of the life-giving Passion arrived, when the gracious and sweet Lord was judged by the high priests and princes and was tortured and crucified, not only was the immaculate mother inseparable from him, but she shared his pain. And I would say, even though it is a bold statement, that she suffered more than him and endured sorrows of the heart: for he was God and Lord of all things, and he willingly endured suffering in the flesh. But she possessed the frailty of a human being and a woman and was filled with such love toward her beloved and desirable son. And how could anyone express the magnitude of her sorrows and laments when she beheld the sufferings of the one who could not suffer, suffering so as a human being? For after the divinely adorned deeds of Christ's ministry on earth were complete, his innumerable miracles and divine teachings and doctrine, nothing was lacking except only the completion of the divine economy: the Crucifixion, burial, and Resurrection. Here were manifest the sufferings and pains of the holy Virgin, which are beyond thought and speech and the measure of her distinction from all others. For then the time of the Passion arrived like a fire: it made a consuming trial of all the other elements, for they left and took flight. But it separated out the immaculate and blessed mother as gold and revealed her only as even more holy and proven. For as her gracious son and God revealed her as both mother and virgin and took care of her at the time of his birth, so at the time of his Passion he revealed her as both invulnerable and compassionate: as compassionate in her very nature, and even more from the nature of the love that the blessed mother had for him, but invulnerable by the divine grace with which her soul was filled and by his assistance which he showed to his holy mother.

74 But let us return to the beginning of this topic. As we said, she was always inseparable from her Lord and king and son. And she held authority: as the Lord did over the twelve disciples and then the seventy, so did the holy mother over the other women who accompanied him. As the holy gospel says, *"There were many women who followed Jesus from Galilee and provided for him"* (Matt 27.55). The holy Theotokos was the leader and director of them all. For this reason, when the mysterious and glorious supper took place, and he sacrificed himself as a priest and was sacrificed, he offered and was offered,[1] at that time the Lord Jesus took care of the twelve disciples and whomever else he wished, and he gave them the exalted mysteries, the signs of the divine Passover. By the bread and the cup he gave his precious body and blood, and with great humility he revealed the glory beyond understanding, and he foreshadowed his Passion and Resurrection and consoled and affirmed his disciples, and he made a representation of the true Passover for us all and established for us giving with suffering and humility. Thus when he was reclining at table in the midst of the disciples, he nourished their souls and bodies with incorruptible nourishment and washed their feet with his own hands in order to teach them humility (cf. John 13.1–15), to strengthen them to run on the road of life, and to adorn them with the truth: as it is written, *"how beautiful are the feet of those who bring good news of peace"* (Isa 52.7). And at this same time the Lord entrusted his holy mother with the care and supervision of the women who accompanied him, in order to honor and glorify her, and she encouraged them and was his surrogate in their labor and ministry.

75 Then the evil dinner companion became a traitor, and the deceitful disciple became the robber of his gracious master, and the feet washed by incorruptible hands ran to the Jews to sell the one who is without price. Oh how could anyone express the savage thinking of this greed! *"What will you give me, if I deliver him to you,"* said the Iscariot to wicked high priests, *and they paid him thirty pieces of silver, and from that moment he was looking for the opportune moment to hand him over to them* (Matt 26.15–16). The false and deceitful disciple did this, but the gracious teacher and king of all things, according to the words of David, was handed over and did not go forth, that is, he did not flee, nor did he turn away,[2] but *as the sheep he was led to the slaughter* (Isa 53.7). And he did not resist, nor did he cry out, but he went willingly to the Passion. And he stood before the unworthy high priest, and from there he was handed over to Pilate. And they laid every kind of torment on him, but he *as a lamb stands silent before the shearer, so he does not open his mouth. In his humiliation his judgments were taken away. And who will be able to describe his generation?* (Isa 53.7–8). Then Pilate sent forth a decree for his crucifixion. The decree and judgment were made known to the immaculate mother. Consider here not only the unattainability of her sanctity and virginity, but also her love for her child and the full measure of her courage. For of all the other disciples and women, devoted companions,[3] friends, and acquaintances who abandoned him and fled at the time of his arrest, some went away, as it is written, "friends and loved ones *stood at a distance*" (Luke 23.49), while others followed him for a short time and soon denied him with an oath and then wept bitterly (cf. Matt 26.58, 69–75; John 18.15–18, 25–27). But the glorious and blessed one, truly his mother and imitator in valor,[4] who was faithful and confirmed her likeness not only in nature but also in similarities of virtue, showed the greatness of her courage and wisdom, and she safeguarded all the courage and wisdom not only of the men and women present then but of every sort of men and women, both those before and those to come. Just as in every other thing she was victorious over all things, so also was she at the time of these events.

76 This solitary virgin woman was unaccustomed to a throng of people, especially of such people as thieves and troops of armed soldiers, but she went everywhere fearlessly. And she was not separated from her beloved Lord and dear son, not even for a single moment, because she was bound to him in soul and body. Thus from the beginning of the arrest until the end of the Passion she remained near him. She saw everything and heard his words. Because of this, the majority of the words spoken at that time and the things that happened before the Crucifixion and after, these the beloved and most blessed one told to the Evangelists and the other disciples. But when our Lord Jesus Christ stood before Annas and Caiaphas and was judged, the immaculate Virgin also followed him and wanted to stand beside him, but the lawless tormentors did not allow her (cf. John 18.12–14, 19–24; Matt

26.57–68). Consequently, she stood outside and asked questions and carefully investigated what they had decided about him, and she asked those who were going in and coming out to tell her the truth. And she noted who was saddened[5] by the affair and who was glad, for there were some for whom the affair was difficult, who informed her secretly, and the blessed one understood those who were sympathetic, and there were also senseless others who shamelessly denied him, fools who said not only in their heart but also aloud that he is not God but an enemy of the Law. They have become truly corrupted and impure through their misdeeds. They said, "Come, let us kill the righteous man, Christ, because he is in opposition to us" (cf. Mark 12.7 and Wis 2.12).[6] And so they were agitated in this way and plotting in vain. But the blessed one, as an innocent dove among serpents and vipers or a peaceful sheep among evil beasts (cf. Matt 10.16), alone was full of wisdom because the right hand[7] of her son and Lord overshadowed her. With the eyes and ears of the flesh she saw and heard the judgments that were put forth against him, but mentally she was joined to her sweet son and what was happening to him. She was pierced in her heart because everyone had turned away all at once and had become useless. Those who were committing the transgression did not understand, and they condemned the life of all things to death.

77 O envy, the beginning, gathering, and end of all evils, who taught homicide[8] and defection from God in the first rebellion and proposed fratricide to Cain in the second, now you have persuaded the Jews to commit Deicide! The venom of your wickedness has been eradicated from the world! Then the king and ruler of all things was counted among prisoners, the untouchable one was bound by fetters, and the virgin mother again accompanied her son and Lord Jesus, and mentally she was tortured and crucified with him. Oh how many lamentations and sufferings came upon you then in your heart because of your son, mother of Christ! How many tears fell from your eyes when you saw the savior of all things with his hands bound behind him like a criminal, the liberator of those who are enslaved! The evil servant struck his cheek, the one who is praised and adored by myriads of angels. The useless and pitiful soldiers were mocking him and

insulting him. Infidels and impure men were spitting on the light-giving face and beating the life-giving body. Oh his forgiveness, forbearance, and infinite love of humanity, and your courage and patience, O blessed mother! They clothed him mockingly with a scarlet robe, he who clothed human nature with true divinity; they placed a crown of thorns on the king of all things, who gave human beings sovereignty over all visible things; they derisively led around the one who made the firmament of heaven to move around as he wished. They cast into prison the one who confined the sea from the sand and the earth from the depths. And in all this the heart of his immaculate mother was bitterly disturbed; for as his birth was supernatural, so also was her ineffable and inexpressible love and compassion for him.

78 The time of the greatest deed arrived, and a cross was set up so that they could crucify the king of angels, and they crucified the creator of human beings and all creatures, the master and ruler of all things visible and invisible. Behold, how did the earth sustain it and not melt away! How did heaven behold it and not collapse (cf. 2 Pet 3.12) when the one seated on thrones of cherubim (cf. Ps 79.2 and 98.1) and glorified by seraphim, whose dominion[9] is the heavens of heavens, was hung upon a tree by evildoers! The one seated with the Father and the Holy Spirit was scornfully crucified, the one who was clothed with light (cf. Ps 103.2) was nailed naked to the cross, and the murderers removed[10] and divided the garment woven by the hands of the holy and immaculate mother. With nails they fixed the hands that created all things, that uphold heaven and earth. Oh the goodness of the king! Oh the boundless forbearance! Who will describe the powers of the Lord and make all of his praises understood? Then, O mother of Christ, a sword pierced through your soul, as Simeon told you. Then the nails that pierced the Lord's hands pierced your heart. These sufferings overcame you more than your all-powerful son, for he suffered voluntarily and knew everything that would come upon him, and so he suffered[11] as much as his authority wished. He had to lay down his soul and his authority, and he had to take them up again, as he says in the gospel (cf. John 10.17), but you suffered unimaginably, and you were still[12] ignorant of the mystery of the Passion. And the abundance of the sufferings and the wounds pierced your heart: streams of blood came down from his[13] incorruptible wounds, but fountains of tears came down from your eyes. How could you bear to behold such a dreadful sight, unless the grace and power of your son and Lord strengthened you and confirmed for you the glory of his mercy.

79 Then the gracious one prayed to the Father for the evildoers and sought forgiveness for them (cf. Luke 23.34). Oh the sweetness of the king! But the godless were gnashing their teeth at him like dogs, taking vengeance and scorning him, and reproaching and mocking him. David expressed their thoughts and deeds well and spoke in place of the Lord: *"they opened their mouths at me, like a raging and roaring lion; like many dogs they surrounded me, and an evil crowd encircled me; they have pierced my hands and my feet, and they have counted[14] my bones"* (Ps 21.14, 17–18). So the holy gospel also bears witness: *"Those passing by maligned him, and they were shaking their heads and saying, 'You there, who would destroy the Temple and build it in three days, save yourself and come down from the cross'"* (Mark 15.29–30). So also the great David foretold, *"The insults of your insulters have fallen on me"* (Ps 68.10). And he also says, *"My soul has borne reproach and poverty; I waited for a sympathizer, and there was no one for a comforter,[15] and I did not find one"* (Ps 68.21). But tell us, O prophet, what they substituted in place of comfort. *"They gave me gall as my food, and for my thirst they gave me vinegar to drink"* (Ps 68.22). Such were their comforts and sympathies; such were their substitutes for good deeds. But when the immaculate and blessed mother saw and heard all this, the words of those reproaching him pierced her as arrows. And her son's nails wounded her heart as spears. Then the earth shook, and Hell below was crushed, and the heaven was darkened, because the light of lights was slain, and all creatures mourned, and the powers of the heaven of heavens trembled above. Some looked on from heaven and beheld the wonder; others came to the place of the skull, and they were astonished by the audacity of the Jews, and they glorified the forbearance of the king. And they were incensed by the apostate and evil servants, and they started to submerge the God-murderers into the netherworlds, so that Hell would be the grave of them all. But the power and mercy of Christ put a stop to their vengeance, and in an instant he reined in all the visible and invisible creatures so that[16] they did not destroy the world. For before them, he called Moses as a witness to the treachery of the Jews, as he said: *"Behold, O heaven, and I will speak, and let the earth hear the words of my mouth,"* and what follows this (Deut 32.1ff.). And he forcefully reproached them through Jeremiah and said: *"Heaven was astonished by this, and the earth trembled, says the Lord"* (Jer 2.12),[17] because they forgot his innumerable[18] mercies and returned evil for good things.

80 So then, all of the amazed creatures were trembling, but the all-holy mother was lamenting greatly about all of this, and she had no consolation, but as in an eternal night, she was surrounded by sadness and grief, and she wanted to draw near and speak to the gracious and sweet Lord. Yet because of the great multitude of people surrounding the area, she could not draw near, but she stood and lamented from afar. She stretched forth her hands, beat her breast, and groaned from the depths of her heart, and she endured her torments and drenched the earth with her tears. But when the crucifiers had shown every wickedness at the Crucifixion and the adversaries of God were dispersed—some went to have dinner, some dispersed for another reason—they were celebrating and rejoicing as if there had been some kind of victory, and the soldiers were neglecting to keep a frequent watch.[19] Then the grieving mother approached the beloved son, and what she said and how she acted, what language can express it? Her words were mixed with tears and wisdom, for she was the mother of Wisdom. And even though it was not possible for her to say or evince anything improper, she nevertheless kept everything orderly, and her mourning was in many respects decorous and calm. And she bitterly lamented the sufferings and wounds of her sweet Lord and son, and she glorified the forbearance and endurance of the one who suffered and was crucified for us, and she was amazed. And she condemned the ingratitude and audacity of the God-murderers, and I say that she wept because of their corruption and said to the Lord:

81 "What is this, O my king and Lord and God? How is your forbearance so vast? How is that you, the sinless one, are counted among the evildoers, and even more, you, the one bearing the sins of the world, are among the condemned, you the judge of the living and the dead? What is the boundless depth of your immense humility and forgiveness and love of humanity? Was it not enough that you, who are God, became a human being for us? Such great troubles and miseries, trials and persecutions, envies and hostilities, slanders and accusations that you have endured from the Jews from birth until now for the salvation of humanity, were they not enough? But behold, now they have hung you nailed to a tree. Oh their malice, ingratitude, and audacity, and your beneficent endurance and forgiveness! Such is the recompense for your old and new mercies! The malevolent Jews tortured you in many different ways, you who tortured the Egyptians in various ways on their behalf.[20] First they dressed you in the robe of mockery, you who one time covered them with a cloud of light and led them as a father leads children and kept them as the pupil of the eye (cf. Matt 27.28–31; John 19.2–5; Exod 40.34–38; Num 9.15–16; Deut 32.10). They placed on you a crown of thorns, the one who crowned them with glory and honor (cf. Matt 27.29; Ps 8.6). They struck you with a reed, they on whose behalf you ordered Moses to strike the sea with a rod, and you divided it and led them across, although the sea covered their enemies (cf. Matt 27.30; Exod 14.16). The evil ones dared to strike you on the cheek, you who have shown the light of your face and given us life, who one time glorified the face of Moses (cf. Matt 26.67; John 19.3; Prov 16.15; Exod 34.30). They were not ashamed to spit on you,—oh the astonishment! oh their malevolence!—you who with spittle opened the eyes of the man blind from birth (cf. Matt 27.30; John 9.6).[21] They nailed your hands and feet with nails, you who led them out from the bonds of servitude in Egypt and now have released the bonds of the original curse (cf. Ps 21.17; Exod 13.14). In return for the cleansing of lepers, they placed wounds upon you; in return for the resurrection of the dead, they condemned you to death; in return for the illumination of the blind, O my light, they hastened to darken your eyes. In your place, O my life, they asked for Barabbas, and they gave you over to death. Oh dreadful sight: how did the earth merely tremble and not collapse into the underworld? How were the luminaries merely darkened and did not fall down completely? How was heaven disturbed and did not completely disintegrate? How did the angels tremble and endure and not overturn the world? But it is clear that this happened through your mercy and forbearance, O my son and my God, and you rule over everything, and you do not allow to come upon the world what did in the time of Noah. O my son, would that I were tormented instead of you! Oh would that your wounds were upon me! Oh would that I might take death upon me instead of you! But now it is[22] more bitter to me than death that I cannot substitute myself for you. I die neither instead of you nor before you, but I entreat you, give me a word of mercy, a word of consolation; ordain my life for the remainder of my days as it seems best to you. Let me hear the voice of greeting and rejoicing when I see you again, O my light, when I embrace you, O my life, when I hear your sweet voice, my life-giver. Although you kept me untouched from all affliction and pain at your birth, now the sword of sorrow has pierced through my soul at seeing your Passion. Show me then also, I beg you, your Resurrection and glory, as you promised me many times."

82 When the immaculate and blessed mother was mourning with such lamentations, the gracious and all-merciful Lord looked upon her with sweetness. And when he saw standing by her the beloved disciple, full of love for his Lord and master, Wisdom herself opened her sweet mouth, and mercy itself spoke a few words, as was fitting for the moment. And he entrusted her to the beloved disciple, who more than all the disciples showed fidelity and love for his Lord and master, as well as courage and bravery of heart, for all the others fled, and he alone stood inseparably before his cross. For this reason he said to his blessed mother, *"Woman, behold your son!" Then he said to the disciple, "Behold your mother!"* (John 19.26–27). And he gave his virgin mother once again a virgin son, and he gave him in place of himself, not that he would refuse to care for his immaculate mother himself—by no means!—but he consoled his mother's grief with a visible consolation. But invisibly he was himself the caretaker of both the mother and the disciple and of all their hopes. And he gave her over to the disciple as a result of his love and faithfulness and his standing there at the time of the Passion, and he honored him with a great honor, for he established him in his own place. And he also gave us a command to care for and look after our parents until death, even if through Providence he did not show complete obedience in other instances.

For as the evangelist says before the baptism, *"he was obedient to them"* (Luke 2.51), but after the baptism, when they were in Cana of Galilee, he says, *"He said to her, 'Woman, what have you to do with me?'"* (John 2.4). And again when they said, *"Your mother and your brothers are seeking you." He said, "Who is my mother? My mother and my brothers are these"* (Mark 3.32–33). And even if he spoke in this way then according to the divine economy, nevertheless now he has clearly shown complete care and proper devotion. And in his place he established the beloved disciple to take care of her, *"and he said to him, 'Behold, your mother!'"* And he comforted his orphanhood, and he established his holy mother as a caregiver and queen for him. When the disciple heard this he led her to his house on Zion, which is written about above, and he served her properly by the grace of Christ.

83 After that the Godless crucifiers then accomplished every outrage and torment against the gracious king, and *Jesus saw that everything was finished, and he said, in order to fulfill scripture, "I thirst"* (John 19.28). And as soon as he was thirsty, in order to pile even more torment upon him, they gave him, alas, the sweetness of life and source of immortality, vinegar and gall. They showed this example of their wickedness mixed with bitterness and cruelty so that nothing spoken about him by the prophets would be left out (cf. Ps 68.22). Nevertheless, this took place not only for the sake of prophecy, but the prophecy foreshadowed what was to take place, for the prophecy was not the cause of their audacity, but the audacity of their malice was the cause of the prophecy. These wicked and ungrateful men dared to do such things, and they did not remember the bitter waters of Marah. He made them sweet for them (cf. Exod 15.25), and many times he satisfied their thirst and made them want for nothing in the waterless desert by the thirst-quenching word: *He fed them honey from the rock and oil from the solid rock* (Deut 32.13). Nor did they remember the more recently done miracle,[23] the changing of water into wine at Cana of Galilee. In truth, *their vineyard is from the vineyard of Sodom, and their vines from Gomorrah; their grapes are grapes of gall, and their grapes are of bitterness* (Deut 32.32), and as follows. But let us understand that the immaculate and all-holy one saw all of this, and the greatest bitterness assailed her heart, for when she heard *"I thirst"* from the sweet and beloved mouth, what flame of the furnace did not pass through her heart? Then her heart was full of desire and was thirsty and was burning like a fire to finally[24] cool the flame of her son's thirst, but the murderers did not allow her give him a good drink. But she begged each of them to allow her to go to him and give him water to drink. But the wild beasts did not allow her to go and did not allow her to comfort him, but *they opened their evil mouths against her as ravenous and raging lions* (Ps 21.14). And instead of cool water they gave him gall and vinegar to drink. And before the Crucifixion *they offered him wine mixed with myrrh, but he did not want it* (Mark 15.23), so that they would not be able attribute his sudden and quick death to the poison instead of to his own will and consent. But now he took the vinegar mixed with gall and said, *"Everything is finished"; and he bowed his head and gave up his spirit* (John 19.30) of his own will and authority.

84 Nevertheless, it is neither in our power nor anyone else's power to describe the holy Virgin's sufferings and tears and the groanings of her heart at each moment, for they are beyond nature, and as her birthing was beyond nature, so also her sorrow, which was occasioned by the Crucifixion of the Lord, is inexpressible by human beings. But she who suffered alone knows, and she alone completely understands the Lord who was born from her. Nonetheless, when *Jesus cried out with a loud voice and yielded up his spirit* (Matt 27.50)—for even the head of all things bowed his head—and the moment of death transpired, she stood by him as a servant, and the king fulfilled the mystery through his divine economy. Oh blessed soul of the immaculate mother, which is stronger than a diamond and made of precious stones that no sword could cut completely! How did the immaculate mother endure the pain? How did she not give up her spirit as well? But it is clear that the grace and power of the crucified Lord sustained her. He gave up his spirit himself as he saw it was necessary, but his power sustained the soul of his mother so that she was invested in every action as he was himself. Fear and trembling have seized my tongue, and it is not possible to describe the events that followed; yet the arrows of the pains of her suffering have stricken me, O king, and do not allow me to remain silent concerning the desired account.

85 What more did these enemies and opponents dare to do even after his death? Indeed, the lees of their bitterness still were not spent by the offer of gall and vinegar, but even after his death the evil beasts and faithless God-murderers showed their excessive envy and wrath. And the laments of the immaculate mother, on whom even the wild beasts would show mercy,[25] did not stop them, and she suffered with him. But even after his death, these ruthless men, harder than stone, pierced his life-giving side with a spear, so that not a single one of his parts would remain without suffering. His head endured the blows of the reed, his cheeks the slaps to the face, his mouth the drink of bitterness, and before that they spat in his face, his shoulders endured a beating, his hands and feet the nails, and now his side the blow of the spear, in order to bring forth life for us, the good fountain of water and blood (John 19.34), by which the Holy Spirit is given to us. You, however, consider the sword's piercing into the heart of the blessed mother at that moment, and how she suffered with him in everything and suffered even more, for now, when she saw her son dead, it was as if she herself were dead, and she was worried about his burial. And suddenly the spear in his side pierced her heart as well, and it renewed fresh pains, and made streams of tears flow from her eyes and made blood drip[26] into her heart, so that she said, *"My heart was hot within me, and my troubles were renewed"* (Ps 38.3–4). And suddenly she rushed forth, and not only was she an eyewitness, but she also became a recipient and an heir of double riches: with reverence and care she received the blood and water flowing forth from the side of the giver of life, and the good and most blessed mother received the new and perpetual immortality.

86 And again she mourned only a little, as was fitting, and spoke words of lamentation. And immediately her concern focused on the burial of the life-giving body, for she could not bear for it to be hanging thus, above the beating, the reproach, and the torment of the enemies. She wanted to find a suitable grave, but nothing at all was found that was worthy or suitable for the life-giving body, as her completely immaculate womb had been found worthy to receive the complete fullness of the divinity. No other such place was found, but she was searching for a place suited to her desires and wishes. For this reason she went around the entire place of the skull, strengthened by the grace of the life-giving corpse. Her feet went here and there, but her eyes and her mind were not dislodged from her beloved son and king.[27] Then by the guidance of his grace she found very near to the cross a beautiful tomb, with a verdant garden around it. The tomb was empty and new, and recently hewn from the rock: as the holy gospel informs us, it had not received any other corpse but was expecting a new corpse, the Lord God of all things. According to Providence it was completely empty, for the sake of the Resurrection, so that no one could say that the body of someone else had been resurrected and not that of Christ. For this reason no one had been laid in it, as the evangelist says: *"There was in the place where he was crucified a garden, and in the garden a new tomb where no one had been laid"* (John 19.41; cf. Luke 23.53). It was new for the new Adam, and because it had not received anyone and was untouched by every human fault and sin, it was protected so that no one could bear false witness or commit larceny. Thus it was impregnable from every side: it was unhewn rock for the cornerstone, it was solid[28] for the indivisible one, and it was deep for the unwavering foundation. The garden was a symbol of Eden, and it was the place of the skull because Adam is buried there. The Passion was the destruction of our sufferings, and the death was the destruction of death.

87 Thus when the holy mother of the Lord saw this place that was nearby and suitable, a beautiful and new tomb where it was fitting to bury the incorruptible body, she inquired and learned that it belonged to Joseph, *who was a disciple of Jesus secretly, for fear of the Jews* (John 19.38). Immediately, she sent word to him, as was fitting for the mother of the Word, the mother of Wisdom. She not only asked for the tomb, because she knew that this was easy for him and that it was highly desirable for him to bestow upon his tomb the good companion and gracious master and to store up treasure as in a treasury, but she told him to go himself and take him down and bury him, because this was difficult. Then great boldness was required of him. Joseph was a rich and honest man, and an acquaintance of Pilate. The holy Theotokos called upon him and said to him, "Behold, O my friend, these enemies and murderers fulfilled the envy and rage that they had against my God and king, Christ my son. And they brought a bitter and reproachful death upon him, and they showed many blows and offenses both before the Crucifixion and after the Crucifixion. And the dead body hangs naked on a tree—awful to behold for me and for all creatures—which even after death they pierced in the side with a spear, and blood and water came forth, a glorious miracle, and even so the God-murderers were not ashamed. The sun darkened and the earth shook, the rocks were split, the curtain was torn in two, and they remain merciless in their atrocity, and they rebuke him and mock him and shake their heads. Now, then, show an act of your devotion and love and fidelity to your master and king and a consolation of my mourning and[29] lament for him. Go to Pilate and ask for his body, which is hanging on the cross, and bury him yourself in your tomb, and with a little courage store up as treasure for yourself the treasure of the world, and with little cost[30] purchase and acquire the life of all living things. Give this final service and grace to your master. Now be braver and better than the other disciples, because some of them have completely fallen away, and others have fled and fallen far away. But I alone, both weak and a stranger, have remained with one disciple amongst so many savage beasts. I am utterly poor and powerless, and rich and powerful only in tears and pain, and I have no consolation from anyone else. My king and son himself will be a traveler with you, this dead one who resurrects the dead, who shook the earth and darkened the sun and terrified all creatures."

88 Thus the one who is wise and blessed among women strengthened Joseph and sent him to Pilate. And he went in to Pilate and was given courage and the ability to speak by the Lord, and he asked for the body of Jesus. He feared neither the power nor the wrath of the Jews, and for this reason he obtained his heart's desire. He asked and received, and God the Word was the exchange for his words; in exchange for the garden, he bought heaven, and in exchange for the tomb, life; in exchange for his request to the governor, courage before the king of all things. Truly, Joseph was not only rich but also wise, and wiser than the merchant about whom it is written in the holy gospel that *"he found a pearl of great price, and he went and sold everything that he had and bought* *it alone"* (Matt 13.46). Now, he did not give everything that he had, but a little readiness and courage and a single tomb and a large stone, and he bought the pearl without price and placed it in an impenetrable grave. This Joseph was the disciple who was completely the opposite of Judas: that one blasphemed and plotted to deliver the gracious master to the enemies of the Lord, but this one quickly took care to go to the enemies and to ask for the body of the Lord and master. That one handed him over to the murderers for a little silver, but this one, by his words of supplication and his expense of wealth, requested him from the murderers and buried him honorably. That one kissed him with treachery and gave him over to crucifixion; this one took him down from the cross and kissed him devoutly, embraced him with love and took care of him honorably. That one brought the evil assembly of the Jews against him with swords and clubs (cf. Mark 14.43),[31] and the treacherous disciple handed the gracious leader[32] over to them; this one took him down from the cross and pulled out the nails and gave to the sweet mother the sweet and life-giving gift who is without equal among creatures.

89 Then the blessed mother was helping Joseph remove her son and king from the cross. She dampened the earth with her tears, and with her hands she helped in the removal. She clutched the nails to her bosom and kissed the wounded members devoutly. She washed away the blood with her tears and was weeping bitterly for the sweetness desired by men and angels. Nevertheless, when he was taken down from the cross and this body more exalted than the heavens was brought down to the earth, then she collapsed completely and embraced him and washed him with the most ardent tears. And with divine words she uttered a hymn of praise for the burial. "Oh completion of the tremendous mystery! Oh revelation of counsels hidden for centuries (cf. Rom 16.25)! Oh death more wonderful than the wonderful Incarnation! The creator of all souls lies inanimate, the one who gives life to all lies dead. The Word of the Father is speechless, the creator of all articulate nature. The one by whose word and wink all moving things move, at whose glance mountains melt (cf. Ps 96.5), *who looks on the earth and makes it tremble, touches mountains and they smoke* (Ps 103.32), who sees the thoughts of human beings, *who scrutinizes hearts and reins* (Ps 7.10), whose gestures the sons of men scrutinized, who illuminates and instructs the blind, is motionless and with closed eyes. Alas, where is your beauty, O my son and my God? Where is your face, more beautiful to behold than all the other sons of men, which established all the beauties of the earth, you who are sweetness itself and desirable in every way? You received blows and wounds, you who healed the unhealable wounds of our nature, scars and wounds both old and new: so you, O king, were merciful, and you were beaten for our sake, and by your wounds we have all been healed (cf. Isa 53.5; 1 Pet 2.24). And behold, the mystery of the divine economy and your gracious forbearance and love of humanity has been fulfilled. Now, then, reveal your power; hasten and come to our aid. I know truly that you will arise and have mercy on your mother first of all, and then on Zion and Jerusalem, which have sinned bitterly, where you will summon all the gentiles and establish the church, the temple of life, from the gentiles. But blessed will be the day when you will make me to hear your sweet voice again, when I will see your divinely beautiful face and be filled with your desirable grace. Blessed will it be when I see you clearly, true God and Lord of the living and the dead."

90 But how could I, unworthy and unlearned, appropriately express and describe the words spoken by the Theotokos then? Even all the tongues of the sages and scholars put together are not capable of expressing it, but I have expressed a meager representation of the words spoken then, in order to satisfy the understanding of the pious. With such words and rites and painful tears and incorruptible hands she took care of the immaculate and life-giving body of the Lord Jesus with Joseph and Nicodemus, and they embalmed it and wrapped[33] it *in linen cloths with spices* (John 19.40). They laid him in a *new tomb, where no one had been laid* (John 19.41; cf. Luke 23.53), and they *rolled a stone against the door of the tomb* (Mark 15.46). And when Joseph and Nicodemus had completed their service well, they went away from the tomb, they and the others who were with them. Nevertheless, the holy and entirely immaculate mother of the Lord remained there alone, and she watched with the unsleeping eyes of the soul and the body. She bent her knees ceaselessly and prayed without interruption: she was crying out and waiting for the moment when the sweet light of the Resurrection would shine forth.

91 *But standing by the cross of Jesus were his mother, and his mother's sister, Mary the wife of Clopas, and Mary of Magdala* (John 19.25): we have said more about the last person above, in order to clarify a topic of interest to many. As the three other evangelists relate, *"The women who had followed Jesus from Galilee were looking on from a distance"* (Matt 27.55). But only the great theologian and evangelist John says that his mother and the other Marys, Mary the wife of Clopas and Mary of Magdala, were standing by the cross of Jesus. Let it be known that both of these statements are true, and that both things took place as described. For *there were many women who followed Jesus from Galilee and provided for him* (Matt 27.55; cf. Luke 8.2-3), among whom were these two Marys. But the men were not equal to them in boldness and fearlessness, nor in excellence to the others. That is why some evangelists mentioned the names, and some evangelists did not mention the names, and some did not recall the names. But he acknowledged them for their renown and made them known according to their family relations: his mother's sister, Mary the wife of Clopas, and Mary of Magdala. Now Mary the wife of Clopas was the sister-in-law of Joseph, to whom the holy Virgin Mary was betrothed, for Clopas was the brother of Joseph. And he also makes holy Mary the Theotokos related according to the cousinage of her mother, and therefore he calls her her sister and says "the sister of his mother." Nevertheless, Matthew says it in this way: *"There were also many women there who were looking on from a distance, among whom were Mary of Magdala and Mary the mother of James and Joses, and the mother of the sons of Zebedee"* (Matt 27.55–56; cf. Mark 15.40). Thus Mark also names them, and Luke does not recall the names, but he says, *"All his acquaintances and the women who had followed him from Galilee stood at a distance and saw this"* (Luke 23.49). For when the betrayal of the Lord took place and they led him away to be crucified, some other women stood far off, and when they crucified him, again they stood at a distance and watched. But the two Marys were more zealous than the others in their love of the Lord, and they were assisting his immaculate mother and struggling alongside of her when they saw the fearlessness and courage of her mind and how she stood inseparably before the cross of her son. And they put on courage of the mind and withdrew from the others, and they drew near to her, and they comforted her and shared her sorrow. Therefore the evangelist said, *"But standing by the cross of Jesus were his mother, and his mother's sister, Mary the wife of Clopas, and Mary of Magdala"* (John 19.25). Nevertheless, although they were more courageous than the other women, they were not able to match the courage of the holy Theotokos. Therefore at that time when the tumult of the Jews subsided a little, they had the courage to approach the place where the immaculate and supremely blessed one stood before the cross of the Lord. Nevertheless, when the Lord Jesus cried out, *"I thirst,"* and the God-murderers began to rise up and mix[34] the vinegar with gall, they were afraid, and they left. The most blessed one, however, stood without fear in that place,[35] inseparable from her son, and she saw everything that took place.[36] And likewise at the time of the removal from the cross and the burial they did not dare to come near, but they *were sitting opposite the tomb* (Matt 27.61), that is, far from the tomb, and they looked on, as the evangelist says (cf. Matt 27.55). And especially when the high priests and scribes went with an army to the tomb, and they led soldiers there to guard it, and they secured the tomb and sealed the stone (cf. Matt 27.66), fear seized the women, and they fled. Fear of the Jews and the desire for Christ came upon them. They went forth and bought perfumes, and *after the Sabbath* they went again *to see the tomb*, in order to anoint the holy body of the Lord (cf. Matt 28.1; Mark 16.1). If they had not gone away, how did they come? But it is clear that they went away and came back again with perfumes in order to show their devotion and faith.

CHAPTER 7

ON THE RESURRECTION

92 Nevertheless, the immaculate mother was inseparable from the tomb, and she was watching and listening to everything that was happening and being said. She saw the great earthquake that woke the *first fruits*[1] *of those who have fallen asleep* (cf. 1 Cor 15.20) and put the guards to sleep and rolled away the stone (cf. Matt 28.2, 4), and then the waking of the guards again and their entry into the city (cf. Matt 28.11). All this the women who had gone and come back again were not able to see, but the blessed mother of the Lord, seized by love of her son and standing inseparably at the tomb, was a witness to everything until she saw even his glorious Resurrection. For the other women saw the stone rolled away and the angel sitting on it; but when and how this took place, they did not know this at all. Only the immaculate mother of the Lord standing there knew everything. And because of this, she received the good news of the Resurrection before everyone else, and before everyone else she became worthy of the longed for height of every good thing and divinely beautiful vision of her Lord and son. And she heard the sweet voice and believed in all the mysteries of his divine economy: as previously in those of the Incarnation, so now in those of the Resurrection. Not only because she was the immaculate and holy mother, but also because she thus remained with him willingly at the time of the Passion and ardently cared for him, when she was enabled by him through desire[2] as if to die with him, that is why she is living and glorified with him. So then the all-holy mother of the Lord saw the Resurrection of her son before anyone else. And she informed his disciples and announced it before the myrrh-bearing women.[3] Even though the evangelists mentioned none of this in the account of the Resurrection, it is for this reason that they left out the mother's witness:

to preclude any doubt and so that no one would take it as reason for disbelief that the vision of the Resurrection was reported by the mother. And furthermore, some would also have said that the evangelists wrote this in order to bestow favor and respect on the holy queen.[4] On account of all this, they mentioned nothing about this but wrote the things said by the other myrrh-bearing women.

93 So then the holy Theotokos saw with her eyes the Resurrection of her son and king, and she was filled with joy, and she went from there to the house of the beloved disciple and was awaiting the time of Christ's Ascension. Nevertheless, this house was Zion, as was written above: for after the death of his father Zebedee, John the Evangelist sold the hereditary property and possessions that he had in Galilee, and he purchased the house of Zion in Jerusalem where he received the holy Theotokos according to the command of his Lord and master, and he served her. Because of this house, he became known to the High Priest, as he says in the gospel, *"this disciple became known to the High Priest"* (John 18.15), and the disciples were in the house *because of fear of the Jews* (John 20.19). And the Lord appeared there and entered through closed doors after the Resurrection (cf. John 20.26). And *he breathed on them and said to them, "Receive the Holy Spirit"* (John 20.22). There also after eight days he satisfied Thomas and showed him the mark of the nails (cf. John 20.27). There after the Ascension, the apostles celebrated the first mystery of the holy liturgy, and the holy Theotokos had this house as her dwelling place after the Ascension of the Lord. And there, before the Ascension, after he arose from the dead, his holy and all-glorious mother was in the same house, and she was awaiting his Ascension, for this was the completion of his divine economy and life on earth. Nevertheless, between the Resurrection and the Ascension, the Lord appeared to his holy mother many times, whenever it seemed good to him, and he comforted her, as was appropriate for her. Nevertheless, he did not appear often to the disciples, but only when it was necessary, and he also received food in front of them so that they would believe that he was not appearing as an illusion but was truly the Lord Jesus Christ, their king and master. Then, when he had made them understand many mysteries, he promised them the coming of the Holy Spirit and ordered them to *remain in Jerusalem until you are clothed with power from above. Then he led them out from the city as far as Bethany, and he blessed them* (Luke 24.49–50). The holy Theotokos was also there, for so it was necessary, so that, as at the time of the Passion her heart had been wounded more than any other, and she had stood inseparably by him, so also she saw his glorious Ascension and was filled with joy.

94 The Lord promised his disciples the coming of the Holy Spirit, and he blessed them. Nevertheless, his all-holy and immaculate mother was blessed from the beginning, from when she heard *rejoice, favored one, the Lord is with you; blessed are you among women* (Luke 1.28) and received the true blessing in the womb and gave birth to the destruction of every curse. Thus from the very beginning she was full of the Holy Spirit and clothed with the power from above. From this day the Holy Spirit came upon her, and the power of the Most High overshadowed her, as the archangel Gabriel said to her, *"the Holy Spirit will come upon you, and the power of the Most High will overshadow you"* (Luke 1.35). Thus, every promise was fulfilled in her, and she received the crown of the kingdom of heaven and earth, just as her son received all power in heaven and on earth when he arose from the dead not only as God but as a human being. Then, when the Lord ascended to heaven and the apostles looked to heaven with the holy Virgin, immediately he sent angels to them to console them and to announce his second coming (cf. Acts 1.10–11). And so they worshipped and returned to Jerusalem with great joy. And *they were devoted to prayer with the women[5] and Mary the mother of Jesus and his brothers* (Acts 1.14), for the holy Theotokos was always a participant and a leader in every good thing. After the Ascension of Christ, she, the treasure house of all good things, being thus in her own country, took charge of every good thing, and while she was dwelling in the land, she was herself the model and leader of all good things. Thus, after his Ascension, the holy mother of Christ was the model and leader of every good activity for men and for women through the grace and support of her glorious king and son. And that is why she then instructed the holy apostles in fasting and prayer, and they were devoted to fasting and prayer and supplication until the fiftieth day was completed, and they were filled with the grace of the comforting Holy

Spirit. And from there the worthy apostles went forth to preach the gospel, and they spread the word of life in Jerusalem and all Judea, and after a little while they went forth to the ends of the earth, wherever the Holy Spirit ordered them. And they made disciples of all nations and baptized in the name of the Father, the Son, and the Holy Spirit, according to the command of the Lord.

95 Nevertheless, the mother of the Lord was dwelling in the house of the beloved disciple on Zion, and in accordance with her glory and praise, she completed the holy and immaculate days of her divinely graced life, for how extremely wonderful and beyond the limits of nature was her life after that time! And I will say that it was more exalted and more wonderful than her earlier life, excepting only her awesome and ineffable conception and giving birth, for this mystery is exalted beyond every order and concept of nature. But I will speak about her ministry and godly life, for her final actions were not at all inferior to her earlier ones. Therefore consider not the supernatural birth and wonderful rearing, which conceived and gave birth to the Son and Word of God, king and God of all, an inconceivable, unattainable,[6] and inexpressible act. But from that time she has shown activity exceeding the limits of nature all the days of her life, and through many actions she showed unvanquished triumphs over nature and routed the enemy of humanity entirely. And then she struggled in[7] the fulfillment of his contendings and endured many afflictions, tribulations, sorrows, and lamentations at the Crucifixion of the Lord, and in every instance she was arrayed with victory and assumed myriad crowns of victory and was ordained queen of all creatures. And then, what is the greatest of all, she saw her son resurrected from the tomb and ascending into heaven with the nature that he had received from her, the Son and Word of the Father, true God and king of all things. After all this glory, she did not then win an easy and effortless life and was not made carefree from all labor and ministry—far from it! Rather, as if she began her godly life and ministry only now, she *gave neither sleep to her eyes nor slumber to her eyelids nor rest to her body* (Ps 131.4). But when the apostles were dispersed to the entire world, the holy mother of Christ, as the queen of all, was dwelling at the center of the whole world, in Jerusalem, at

Zion with the beloved disciple, who had been given to her as a son by the Lord Jesus Christ.

96 She sent forth the other disciples to preach to those far and near. Nevertheless, while she herself remained in the royal city of Zion, she once again endured alone more afflictions and attacks on account of her son. For his sake she opposed and fought against the adversaries, the wicked Jews, and once again she was an intercessor and mediator with him on behalf of all, not only on behalf of the believers, but also on behalf of the enemies, that he might have mercy on them and they would be brought to knowledge and repentance, for this she had also learned from her gracious son, when he said on the cross, *"Father, forgive them; for they know not what they do"* (Luke 23.34). And she herself was also gracious and merciful, and she desired that all humanity would be saved and arrive at knowledge of the truth. And she was not satisfied only with this, but she added the work of fasting and prayer. She would not depart from the tomb of the Lord, but it was her dwelling: this place was her bedroom, the stone her pillow, prayers to her son and visions her daily course,[8] discourses of praise her table, accounts and teachings of the doctrine and Passion of the Lord her nourishment, tears were her drink and bath, kneeling her rest and delight, for it is said by truthful teachers and has come to us that her holy hands were very calloused from frequent prostration, the hands with which she previously embraced in her bosom the Lord born from her without seed. And now again she was beseeching and supplicating. And who could describe completely her divinely graced[9] labors and deeds, which, if someone were perhaps to relate or describe them individually, would result in an enormous amount of writing. But it is well known and recognized that, as she remained after her son and king as steward[10] on his behalf and teacher and queen of all the believers and those who hope in his name, men and women, his friends and disciples, so she had care and concern for them all. And the eyes of all hoped in her, and they saw living among humanity in the place of the bodily Lord Jesus Christ his immaculate and most blessed mother who gave birth to him according to the flesh. She was a comfort to them and an inspiration in struggles and labors and every act of charity.

97 But she was not only an inspiration and a teacher of endurance and ministry to the blessed apostles and the other believers, she was also a co-minister with the disciples of the Lord. She helped with the preaching, and she shared mentally in their struggles and torments and imprisonments. And she suffered with them as she previously had shared the Passion of her Lord and son through sufferings of the heart. So now also she comforted his worthy disciples with actions as much as she could. She strengthened them with words and presented as an example for them the Passion of her king and son. She reminded them of the rewards and crowns of the kingdom of heaven and the unending blessedness and delight unto the ages of ages. Then, when Herod seized Peter, the head of the apostles, and threw him into prison bound in chains (cf. Acts 12.6–7), she was mentally captive with him, and the most blessed mother of Christ shared in his fetters, and she prayed for him and ordered the church to pray for him. And before this, when the wicked Jews stoned Stephen (cf. Acts 7.59), and when Herod murdered James the brother of John (cf. Acts 12.2), the sufferings and afflictions and torments of both pierced the heart of the holy queen. She was tormented with them[11] through the pains of her heart and the lamentations of her tears. Nevertheless, this tradition has also come down to us from the Fathers, that when the holy apostles went forth to preach, each one in the countries and lands that had fallen to them individually, and Saint John the Evangelist and Theologian remained to serve and take care of the holy Theotokos, whose son he had become by the order of the Lord, at that time the holy queen, his mother by the grace of Christ, said to him, "It does not seem right to me, O my son, that your friends and brothers will go forth and preach the name of Christ, my son and God, and make disciples of the nations, and you will stand idle only for the sake of my care. And likewise I am hesitant to separate you from me, in case it might not please the Lord, who ordered us to remain together. So then go: go forth to the land that has been appointed to you, and I will come with you so that both things will be accomplished, your preaching and your remaining inseparable from me." Thus she commanded the beloved, and she went forth to go and preach, and Mary of Magdala and the other myrrh-bearing women went with them.

98 Then her benevolent Lord and son appeared in a vision and ordered her to turn back from the road. As for the beloved disciple, however, he ordered him to go forth and the myrrh-bearing women with him to help him and care for him. He initially allowed her to go forth so that the zeal and enthusiasm of the holy queen would be known and also so that the Evangelist would be willing, because he did not want to abandon the holy Theotokos. Afterwards, he ordered her to turn back so that her honor would be unique and not joined with that of the apostles, but so that she would send them[12] forth and not be sent forth, and so that she would lead the believing people and direct the church in Jerusalem with James the brother of the Lord who was appointed as bishop there. Thus, wherever[13] she went she consecrated the earth with her footsteps. And she returned to Jerusalem again and dwelled in the house of John. The Theologian and Evangelist, however, following the command of the Lord went forth to Ephesus, city of the land of Asia, and the myrrh-bearing women with him and Prochorus, one of the seven deacons (cf. Acts 6.5). There he preached the name of Christ God and illuminated those who were in darkness. There the worthy myrrh-bearing women ministered with him and became co-apostles.[14] And there some died in their ministry, and some in martyrdom and bloodshed, and they went to their king and master Christ wearing crowns. Nevertheless, after the departure of Saint John the Evangelist, the blessed James the son of Joseph, who was called the brother of the Lord on account of his great virtue, served and took care of the holy mother of Christ. And he became the first bishop of Jerusalem. He took care of and served the holy Theotokos in the place of John the Evangelist. Thus, the return of the holy Theotokos to Jerusalem was excellent, for she was the strength, the haven, and the rampart for the believers who were there. And every need and ministry of the Christians was entrusted to the all-immaculate one, for they were living among a malicious and apostate people, the Jews. And the believers in Christ were beset from all sides by struggles and death, and she consoled and strengthened them all.

99 And she was the blessed hope of the Christians of that time and those to follow, and until the end of the world she is the mediator and the helper of the faithful. Nevertheless, her care and ministry were especially abundant at that time, in order to strengthen and guide the new Law of Christianity and to glorify the name of Christ. And the trials that fell upon the churches, the seizure of the homes of believers, the execution of many Christians, the arrests and various torments, the deeds and travails of the apostles who were dispersed here and there, all this affected her. And she suffered for them all, and by word and deed she ministered to them. And she was the model of goodness and the teacher of excellence in the place of her Lord and son, and she was a mediator and intercessor with him[15] for all the believers, and she asked that her mercy and assistance be spread forth over all. And she was a leader and a teacher to the holy apostles, and when anything was needed, they would tell her. And they received direction and good counsel from her, to the extent that those who were near the environs of Jerusalem would return. One after the other they went before her and reported everything that they were doing and how they were preaching, and they accomplished everything according to her direction. But once they went forth to distant lands, they were sure from year to year to go to Jerusalem for Easter and to celebrate the feast of Christ's Resurrection with the holy Theotokos. And each one of them reported the success of their preaching[16] and the sufferings that befell them from the Jews and gentiles. And again they went forth to the work of their preaching, armed with her prayers and teachings. Thus they did from year to year, so long as nothing significant happened to anyone that would pose a hindrance, except for Thomas: he could not come because of the great distance and the difficult journey from India. But all the others came from year to year to greet the holy queen, and armed with her prayers they went forth again to preach the gospel.

100 Yet who will count the attacks and animosities of the godless Jews, the rages and revolts of the murderers of God? Who will describe the blasphemies and mockeries, the denials of the Savior's miracles, the slanders and scorn against the Resurrection of Christ? For they were saying that the disciples stole his body: as it is written in the holy gospel, *"this story persists among the Jews until the present day"* (Matt 28.15). They frequently assembled and wanted to stone the house where the holy mother of the Lord was living, but the power of

Christ thwarted their intentions. Nevertheless, one time the children of wrath, the offspring of impurity, *a deceitful and crooked generation, a foolish and unwise people, a nation counseling destruction in which there is no understanding* (Deut 32.5–6, 32.28), whose *wrath is like a venomous and deaf snake whose ears are closed* (cf. Ps 57.4), conspired a gathering of vanity. These lawless and God-murdering people plotted to set fire to the house where the treasure house of life, the mother of the Lord Jesus Christ, was dwelling and to destroy it to its foundation.[17] They had in their hands fire, stones, and iron[18] bars for destroying the walls. They filled the city of God with insurrection and shouting, but they were not able to touch her, because the Holy City became even more steadfast and stronger,[19] concerning which the prophet said, *"Glorious things of you are spoken, O city of God"* (Ps 86.3).[20] For the fire turned back against them and burned many of the godless, the stones that they rained down on the roof of the holy house came back at them and smote the godless, their hammers and bars shattered and became dust, and their evil plan failed. Their *torment was turned back onto* themselves, *and their* perfidy *fell upon* their *head* (Ps 7.17); their sword pierced their heart, and their bows were shattered (cf. Jer 51.56), as Hell out of wrath devoured many of them alive.

101 The believers saw all this and gave thanks to Christ: *"the righteous will rejoice when he sees the vengeance,"* says the prophet (Ps 57.11). Such are the deeds of the wicked Jews, who did not cease from evil deeds from the beginning until they accomplished all their transgressions[21] and sentenced the gracious Lord and creator of all to death by the death of the cross. And now again they have shown audacious animosity to his immaculate and all-holy mother, but their torment was turned back onto themselves. And in the face of such great and numerous miracles they were not ashamed, but at the time of her death and translation from the world, yet again they showed their wickedness and God-defying[22] wrath, as we will relate when we reach this place. But now we will keep to the path of our discourse, because when such wonders took place then and these enemies and opponents of Christ and his holy mother were justly punished, the malefactors no longer dared to pursue such lawlessness. And the holy Virgin and mother of the Lord no longer was defamed by them, but they viewed her with respect and caution. They revered her with fear, and they forgot the innate canine rage of their habit, not only because of the wonders that were worked at that time and their just punishment, but because of the miracles that were worked from day to day by her grace and intercession, for demons were cast out, incurable diseases were cured, and myriad wonders and miracles were accomplished by her. With all these miracles, great light and glory shone from her face, and she dispensed grace on the believers but terror and fear on the enemies, because Christ the king of all things, her son, glorified his immaculate and holy mother, and he made her house unapproachable to all enemies and attackers, and by the grace and intercession of the all blessed Theotokos the people of the believers prospered and multiplied, and the faith of the Christians was confirmed.

102 For because of this our Lord Jesus Christ thought it fitting that his all-holy mother should remain in this world many years, so that the believers would be greatly strengthened by her grace and the church of Christians would exceed in praising the Father and the Son and the Holy Spirit. Nevertheless, the blessed and all-praised mother of God, honored by her son with such great honor, reached old age, for the queen of all creatures was approaching the eightieth year of this fleeting life, and she did not cease from labor, prayer, and supplication to her son, but from day to day she increased them, exceeding in every good work. She always appeared humble, and she increased her current activities and charitable work. As we have been well informed, after many years the bendings[23] of her holy knees were still to be found in the marble of Zion, and whenever the bodily nature required a little sleep, her bed was a stone. In all this she had great poverty, and her generosity overcame the poverty. This golden and precious pair, with the one aided by the other: amazing abundance in great destitution, riches and generosity of heart in need. Nevertheless, her mercy was not only toward loved ones and acquaintances but toward strangers and enemies, for she truly was the mother of the merciful one; she was the mother of the benevolent one and the lover of humankind *who makes the sun to shine on the good and the evil and sends rain on the righteous and sinners* (Matt 5.45). She was the mother of the one who became flesh and was crucified for us, enemies and apostates, in order to spread his mercy upon us. She was the mother of the poor and needy and of the enrichment of all, because for our sake the rich one was made poor in order to enrich us, the downcast and the poor. Now, then, may the discourse up to this point be about her deeds, her benefactions, and her glories. In all this I will say a lot very briefly: she gave birth supernaturally to a son, the Word of God incarnate, and her life and conduct also came to an end supernaturally, and in everything before this and everything after, she was made victorious by the abundance and wealth of her benevolence and good works. So greatly was she magnified: she became greater than all, as the sun is brighter than the stars.

CHAPTER 8

THE DORMITION[1]

103 Now by her grace let us speak about her Dormition and removal from the world to the eternal kingdom, for it is the joy and the light of pious souls to hear such a story. When Christ our God wanted to bring his all-holy and immaculate mother forth from the world and lead her into the kingdom of heaven so that she would receive the eternal crown of virtues and supernatural labors, and so that he could place her at his right hand beautifully adorned with golden tassels in many colors (cf. Ps 44.10, 14) and proclaim her queen of all creatures, and so that she would pass behind the veil and dwell in the Holy of Holies, he revealed her glorious Dormition to her in advance. And he sent the archangel Gabriel to her again to announce her glorious Dormition, as he had before the wondrous conception. Thus the archangel came and brought her a branch from a date palm, which is a sign of victory: as once they went with branches of date palms to meet her son (cf. John 12.13), the victor over death and vanquisher of Hell, so the archangel also brought the branch to the holy queen, a sign of victory over suffering and fearlessness before death. And he said to her, "Your son and Lord bids you: 'It is time for my mother to come to me.' Therefore he has sent me again to bring good news to you, O blessed among women. Just as you have filled the inhabitants of the earth with joy, O blessed one, so now you will cause the host of heaven to rejoice by your ascension and make the souls of the saints to shine even more. Rejoice, as you cried out before, for you have the title 'favored one' as an honor forever: *Rejoice, favored one, the Lord is with you* (Luke 1.28). Your prayers and supplications have gone up before your son in heaven, and according to your request, he bids you to relinquish this world and ascend to the dwelling places of heaven and to be with him in the true and unending life." When the holy Theotokos Mary heard this, she was filled with joy, and she responded to the angel with her original reply:

"Behold, the handmaid of the Lord; let it be to me now again *according to your word"* (Luke 1.38). And the angel departed from her.

104 Then the ever-blessed and glorious Theotokos Mary arose, and full of joy she went forth to the Mount of Olives to offer thanks and prayers to the Lord in peace, both for herself and for the entire world. When she had ascended the mountain, she extended her hands and offered prayers and thanks to Christ her son. Then a glorious miracle took place, as is known to those who have been made worthy of such knowledge, and from them it has come down to us. For while she was praying and offering her supplications to the Lord, in veneration all the trees standing there bent to the ground and venerated her. Thus, when she finished her prayer and thanksgiving and had been consoled by the Lord, she returned again to Zion, and immediately the Lord sent John the Evangelist and Theologian on a cloud, because the holy Virgin wanted to see him, since he had been decreed her son by the Lord.[2] She who is blessed among women saw him and rejoiced greatly and enjoined prayer. And the holy queen prayed, and after her prayer she informed John and the other virgins who were there about the annunciation of her Dormition by the angel, and she showed them the date palm branch that the angel had brought her. And she told them to prepare the house and to light the candles and to cense with incense, for she adorned the house as bridal chamber worthy to receive her immortal bridegroom and all-gracious son, because she was waiting with steadfast hope. When this was done, she informed her friends and acquaintances about the mystery of her Dormition, and they gathered around her. And they wept and lamented her separation from them, for after God they had her as their hope and intercessor.

105 But the holy[3] queen and mother of the Lord consoled each one of them individually and all of them together, and she gave them an impassioned greeting and said, "Rejoice, O blessed children, and do not make my Dormition a cause for grief, but be full of the greatest joy, for I am going into eternal joy, and may the grace and mercy of the Lord be with you always." Then she looked at John the Evangelist and told him to give her two garments to the two widows who were serving her. And she revealed to them the mysteries and true signs of her poverty and graciousness. After this she explained how they should anoint her holy and completely immaculate body with myrrh and specified where they should bury it. And so the glorious mother of Christ lay down on her bed, the bed that until that time had been bathed from night to night[4] with the tears of her eyes in longing for her son Christ and enlightened by her prayers and supplications. And again she told them to light the candles, and the believers gathered there again wept even more when they were informed about the Dormition of their queen, the holy Virgin. They fell down before her and begged her not to leave them as orphans, but if she were to go forth from the world, to be with them through grace and intercession.

106 Then the holy Theotokos opened her incorruptible and completely immaculate mouth and said to them, "May the will of my son and God be upon me. He is my God, and I will glorify and exalt him, the God of my father. He is my son, born from me according to the flesh, but the father is also God the creator of his mother. Therefore I desire to go to the one who gives life and being to all things. And when I stand before him, I will not cease to pray and intercede on behalf of you and all Christians and the entire world, so that the one who sees mercy as necessary will have mercy on all believers and make them steadfast and guide them on the way of life, and he will convert the unbelievers and make all into one flock of the good shepherd, who laid down his life[5] for the sake of his sheep, and he knows his own, and his own know him (cf. John 10.11, 14–16)." When the all-blessed mother of Christ spoke thus and blessed them, suddenly there was the sound of great thunder and a cloud on a gentle breeze. And behold, like fragrant drops of dew the holy disciples and apostles of Christ descended from the beautiful cloud, and in front of the house of the holy Virgin, the Theotokos, they came together from the ends of the earth. But John the Evangelist and Theologian met them and greeted them, and he brought them in before the holy and blessed Virgin. Not only were the Twelve there, but also many others of their distinguished disciples and those who were worthy of the honor of apostleship, as the great Dionysius the Areopagite informs us in his letter written to Timothy that, according to him, Dionysius, Timothy, Hierotheus, and others of their friends came there with the apostles for the Dormition of the queen.[6] They went in before her and greeted her with fear and respect.

107 And the blessed and all-holy one blessed them and informed them about her departure from the world. She told them about the Dormition that had been related to her by the archangel, and she showed them the symbol of her Dormition, the date palm branch given[7] to her by the chief of the angels, and she consoled them and blessed them. She strengthened them and encouraged them to carry out their excellent preaching. She greeted Peter and Paul and all the others and said, "Rejoice, O children, friends, and disciples of my son and God. Blessed are you who have thus been found worthy to be disciples of the gracious and glorious Lord and master, and he entrusted you with the ministry of such mysteries, and you have been called[8] to share in his persecution and suffering, so that the Lord of glory will make you worthy to partake of his kingdom and glory, as he himself promised and commanded you." Such a blessing and teaching she spoke to them according to her glory, and she explained to them the rites of anointing her with myrrh and her burial. And she extended her hands and began to give thanks to the Lord and said:

"I bless you, O king and only-begotten Son of the beginningless Father, true God of true God, who consented to become incarnate from me, your handmaid, through the incalculable, philanthropic good will of the Father and the assistance of the Holy Spirit.

I bless you, the giver of every blessing, who spread forth light.

I bless you, the source of every life of goodness and peace, who bestow on us knowledge of yourself and of your beginningless Father and of the co-beginningless and life-giving Holy Spirit.

I bless you, who were ineffably pleased to dwell in my womb.

I bless you, who so loved human nature that you endured crucifixion and death for our sake, and by your Resurrection you
resurrected our nature from the depths of Hell, and led it up
to heaven and glorified it with an incomprehensible glory.

I bless you and glorify your words, which you have given us in truth,
and I believe that all the things that you have said to me will
be fulfilled."

108 When the holy and all-blessed Theotokos was silent after
her thanksgiving and prayer, the holy apostles began to
speak at the command of the Holy Spirit, and they were singing and
glorifying, each one as he was able and as the Holy Spirit gave it to him.
They praised and exalted the inestimable beneficence of God's power,
and with their wondrous theology they brought great joy to the heart
of the glorious mother of Christ, as the above-mentioned St. Dionysius
says in the chapter where he shows "What is the power of prayer, and
concerning the blessed Hierotheus, and concerning the writing of
theology with reverence."[9] And his writing is to Timothy,[10] and in this
chapter he recalls[11] the gathering of the holy apostles for the Dormition
of the holy Theotokos, and how by the command and grace of the
Holy Spirit each one of them spoke praises and sang of the incalculable
power and beneficence of Christ our God, who deemed it worthy to
come into the world inseparably from the bosom of the Father and to
become incarnate from the holy Virgin, the one who *bowed the heavens and
descended* (Ps 17.10) and found the holy and altogether praised Mary, who
was chosen and exalted above all the human race, and he consented to
dwell within her, and from her he put on human nature, and he had
mercy and saved the human race through his glorious and ineffable[12]
economy. Blessing and praise to his inestimable goodness and mercy![13]
And so it is written in the discourse of the blessed Dionysius,[14] "I will
relate to you the complete theological discourse that the holy apostles
and our bishops pronounced at that time, for it was exalted beyond
words, as you yourself know, O brother Timothy, and how after the
great apostles, the blessed Hierotheus, the philosopher and disciple of
the great apostle Paul, also spoke praises of Christ God and praise and
glorification[15] of his immaculate and blessed mother by the grace of the

Holy Spirit, as the theologians and apostles themselves recognized: 'The Holy Spirit opened his mouth to speak such words of glorification.'" After this the Holy Theotokos blessed them again, and her heart was filled with divine consolation.

109 And behold, the glorious and wonderful arrival of Christ her God and son took place, and there were with him innumerable hosts of angels and archangels and other hosts of seraphim and cherubim and thrones: they all stood with awe before the Lord, for wherever the king is, the hosts also accompany him. The Holy Theotokos knew about all of this from the beginning, and she was waiting with steadfast hope. Therefore she said, "I believe that all the things that you have said to me will be fulfilled," and at that time she clearly saw the apostles as well,[16] and they beheld the glory, each one according to his ability. And this present coming of the Lord was more glorious and tremendous than the first, for he appeared more radiant than the brilliance and Transfiguration that occurred on Tabor, although it was less than his natural glory, for that is unfathomable and invisible. Then the apostles were terrified, and they fell to the ground as if dead (cf. Matt 17.6). But the Lord said to them, "Peace be with you," as he had said before when he entered in through closed doors (cf. John 20.19, 26), for at that time they were also gathered together in the house of John: then because of fear of the Jews, and now for the Dormition of the mother of the Lord. When the apostles heard the sweet and pleasant voice of the Lord, they were revived and strengthened in soul and body, and with reverence they began to look upon the brilliance of his glory and his divinely beautiful face. Nevertheless, the all-holy, immaculate, and blessed mother of Christ was filled with joy, and her glorious face shone with brilliance and divine glory. But she also beheld with fear and reverence the glory and brilliance that shone forth from her king and son Jesus Christ. She glorified his divinity even more and prayed for the apostles and for all those who were standing there. And she sought intercession for all the faithful, wherever[17] they were. She made an offering for the entire world and for every soul that calls upon the Lord and calls to mind the name of his mother, and wherever they observe a commemoration of her, she asked that a blessing would spread throughout that place. Then again the holy Virgin Mary looked and beheld the glory of her son, which human language is not capable of expressing.

I I O And she said, "Bless me, O Lord, with your right hand, and bless all those who glorify you and invoke your name, and receive[18] all their prayers and supplications." Then the Lord held forth his right hand, blessed his mother and said to her, "Let your heart rejoice and be glad, O Mary blessed among women, for every grace and gift has been given to you by my heavenly Father, and every soul that calls on your name with holiness will not be put to shame but will find mercy and comfort both in this life and in the age to come. You, however, come forth to the eternal dwelling places, to unending peace and joy, to the treasure houses of my Father, so that you will see my glory and rejoice by the grace of the Holy Spirit." And immediately at the Lord's command the angels began to sing hymns with a sweet voice, a clear and pleasant voice, and through the Holy Spirit the holy apostles stood shoulder to shoulder[19] and sang with the angelic hymns. And thus the all-holy mother of the Lord entrusted her blessed and immaculate soul to her Lord, king, and son, and slept a sweet and pleasant sleep. As she escaped the pains of childbirth in the ineffable Nativity, so the pains of death did not come upon her at the time of her Dormition, for both then and now the king and Lord of natures altered the course of nature. Then the host of angels invisibly applauded the sendoff of her holy soul. The house and the surrounding area were filled by a waft of indescribable perfume, and unapproachable light (cf. 1 Tim 6.16) spread forth over the holy body. And in this way the master and the disciples, and heaven and earth led forth[20] the holy Virgin: the gracious and glorious Lord and master led away the holy soul of his immaculate mother to heaven; the disciples took care of her immaculate body on earth, anointing it with myrrh and tending to the things that she had planned. And after a little while, her son and God wished to translate the body to Paradise or somewhere.[21] The holy apostles encircled[22] the bed on which lay the holy Theotokos' body, wider than heaven. They honored it with hymns and praise; they embraced it with fear and trembling. They not only showed faith and devotion but were also gratified to receive grace and great benefit, and the work of faith had only just begun.[23]

III Nevertheless, as soon as news of the holy queen's Dormition had spread, all the sick and infirm assembled there. Then the eyes of the blind were opened, the ears of the deaf were unblocked, the lame stood up to walk (cf. Isa 35.5–6), demons were expelled, and every suffering and sickness was cured. The sky and the heavens of heavens were sanctified by the ascension of the holy soul, and the earth likewise was made worthy of the honor of sanctity by the immaculate body. Then the apostles called on blessed Peter to deliver a funeral prayer. Peter pressed Paul and John to pray. They refused and honored him as the head of the apostles. The blessed Peter complied with their words, as was fitting for this occasion and this mystery. He prayed, and immediately they wrapped in a holy shroud and anointed with myrrh the body that contained the uncontainable, the king and creator of all things visible and invisible, and they laid it on a bed. And again Peter began to sing a hymn, and all the assembly of the apostles joined in, and the powers of heaven sang with them invisibly, and the air shone and was made fragrant with lamps and incense. Then the holy apostles took up the honorable bed on their shoulders, and through the guidance of the Holy Spirit they went forth to the area of Gethsemane, as the Theotokos had previously directed. The angels went ahead and were surrounding them[24] and followed behind, covering them with their wings.[25] The apostles were singing hymns, and all the believers accompanied them with faith. The procession of the glorious and praised one was itself glorious and praised. All the infirm and the sick were cured, and there were not only sixty strong men around the bed of the king, as Scripture says (cf. Cant 3.7), but visibly the numerous apostles and their innumerable followers and all the faithful, and invisibly the innumerable host of angels.

II2 And at that time the adversary and enemy of truth did not refrain from showing his treachery, but again he stirred up the evil Jews to envy and violence. For when they saw the glorious procession of the immaculate and all-praised mother of Christ, and the multitude of the faithful that was accompanying the apostles, and the innumerable miracles that they were working by the grace of the holy queen, and they heard the voices of the divinely beautiful singing, wicked envy seized *the deranged and unwise people, the nation deliberating on destruction, in whom there is no understanding* (Deut 32.6 and 32.28).[26] As before when the crowds of innocent children went forth to meet Christ the king of all things with branches from date palms and said, "Hosanna! Blessed is he who comes in the name of the Lord, the king of Israel!" (cf. Matt 21.9 and 21.16), and the godless high priests and the scribes were enraged and fought with wicked envy against the one who is gracious and compassionate to all, to the point that they condemned him to death by death on a cross, so now also they gathered to attack the procession of his gloriously immaculate mother and to obstruct the orderly and adorned company of the apostles and the faithful, and with perverse cries they came to destroy the divine assembly.[27]

113 Then one of the reprobates, who was more brazenly insidious and shameless than the others, insolently tore through the crowd of the faithful that was following the ark of holiness. He reached the holy apostles, who were bearing the treasure house of heaven that contained the uncontainable and unbounded nature. He stretched forth his impure hands and seized the bed on which lay the immaculate body of the most blessed queen, before which even angels tremble, which even the cherubim look upon with awe. This bed the arrogant and foolish man tried to throw down to the ground. Oh savage soul! Oh deranged mind! But immediately he saw just retribution for his deeds, for in the very touching of the holy bed with his hands, both hands were instantly severed from the shoulders when he dared to approach the one whom he was not even worthy to look upon.[28] The wrath of God came upon him as he cried out and screamed. Wailing and moaning overcame him and the other Jews with him. The wrath of fury came by the hand of the angel of wrath. They were turned back and were put to shame, and the angel of the Lord pursued them. This miracle took place to bring shame and fear[29] to the Jews, but it was a source of great courage and glory to the faithful. And then the one who was initially seized by great folly and was counted among the enemies and slanderers of God, when he was punished in accordance with his deeds, he was ashamed. And he understood and converted his former rebuke into faith, and his wicked envy into fear and repentance, and his calumnies and reproaches into contrition and prayer. He was no longer able to raise his hands in prayer, but with ardent tears and a penitent voice he called on the holy Theotokos and asked for mercy.

114 Nevertheless, the one who is the cause of all things and the source of all joy does not wish to inflict suffering and misery and mourning and unending sorrow[30] on the sinner, but with a small wound of the flesh, he cured the incurable wounds of the soul and made him worthy to become a Christian and by the grace of baptism to be called a child of God. Then he mercifully healed the wound of his hands, for when the justly punished Jew understood his error, he began to repent and to pray with ardent tears, and he invoked the name of Christ and of his holy mother Mary. The holy apostle Peter ordered that the holy bed be set down, and they all cried out to the holy Theotokos with prayers and supplications, and they brought before her the wounded sinner, shattered and repenting with the blood of his wound and drenched with the tears of his eyes. Then he touched the holy bed, no longer as before, but he prayed with fear and trembling. And the blessed Peter placed the severed hands in their place, and immediately by the grace of Christ and his all-holy mother, the hands severed from the shoulders were fitted and attached to his body. And not only did the pains and anguish disappear, but there was no trace of the wound at all. From that point, this man believed in Christ, and he was baptized and joined to the number of the believers, and he glorified Christ and his all-immaculate and glorious mother. This miracle, the sudden wound and the swift cure, strengthened the faith of many who had doubts and converted many of the Jews to the faith, and they confessed that the one crucified by them, Jesus Christ the Lord, was God, and they proclaimed his holy mother the Theotokos.

115 And so with utmost glory and radiant honor the apostles again took upon their worthy shoulders the bed, vested and glorious with the light of the holy queen, surrounded by the ranks of heaven and earth, invisibly adorned by armies of angels and archangels with visible praises and comprehensible songs. And they brought it to Gethsemane, and they laid in the tomb the immaculate body, the all-holy bodily throne of God, the Holy of Holies, the ransom of our nature, the awesome mystery, the mediator of the union between divinity and humanity, the city of God, on account of which she is called glorious from generation to generation (cf. Ps 86.3, Luke 1.48), *the mountain on which it pleased God to dwell*, through which *the processions of our God and king, who is in the holy place* have appeared (cf. Ps 67.16–17, 25), the closed door that no one has passed through except God alone, and it remained closed (cf. Ezek 44.2–3), the unique virgin among mothers, the unique immaculate Theotokos. Nevertheless, it is not astonishing that the mother of life was placed in the tomb, for her son also, who is himself life and immortality, endured death in the flesh and deposition in the tomb, and by his death he destroyed death and gave life to the world. And it is not fitting to keep silent as to how the body of the holy queen was laid in the tomb, for when they brought her to the tomb and set down the bed bearing the treasure without price, it was necessary to lift the blessed body from the bed and lay it in the tomb, but all the holy apostles and those who were with them were afraid, and they did not dare to lay their hands upon the holy and utterly blessed body, for they saw the light that enveloped it and the grace of God that was upon it.

116 Thus all of the apostles again called on Peter and Paul to lay the holy body in the tomb, for John the evangelist was carrying a censer, and he censed the holy body of the queen with fragrant incense and drenched it with tears. Then Peter and Paul did not touch the holy body with their hands, but with fear and reverence they took hold of the shroud that was hanging from here and from there, and thus they lifted the blessed body from the bed, and using the shroud they laid it in the tomb. As the glorious and most revered apostles had properly and worthily served her son, so they also served his mother, and they honored the one honored by men and angels, whom all generations call blessed and glorify, as the blessed one said with her own holy mouth (cf. Luke 1.48). Thus, when the holy one and the Holy of Holies, the body of the most blessed Theotokos and ever-virgin Mary, was sealed in the tomb, the holy apostles remained there for three days, and they heard the beautiful singing of the holy angels, sweet and pleasant singing that it is not possible for human language to describe: as the prophet David said, *"I will go forth to the marvelous dwelling place*[31] *in the house of God with the sound of singing and acknowledgement, with the sound of a festival"* (Ps 41.5), for here is truly the dwelling place of the Lord, the marvelous house of God in which the Lord of glory, God, the king of peace was pleased to dwell.

117

Nevertheless, we have learned something else from truthful and reliable informants, and it has been written about before us and is trustworthy and reliable: that in the assembly of the holy apostles for the Dormition of the queen, one of the apostles was providentially not able to arrive with the others. And the holy apostles were expecting him, so that he perchance would also receive a blessing from the blessed and beloved body. Nevertheless, on the third day that apostle also arrived, and he found his other comrades singing in front of the holy tomb, and he also heard the clear and sweet sound of the angels singing. And he besought the holy apostles to open the venerable tomb so that he could embrace the all-holy body of the glorious Theotokos. Through the guidance of the Holy Spirit, the blessed apostles heard their brother's plea and opened the holy tomb with fear. But when they opened it, they did not find the glorious body of the holy mother of Christ, for it had been translated wherever[32] her son and God wished. For as he himself was placed in a tomb when he endured death in the flesh for the sake of our salvation and gloriously arose on the third day, so it also seemed fitting to place the immaculate body of his mother in a tomb and likewise to translate it into eternal incorruptibility as he wished, either so that both elements were again united with each other, for so the creator of all things was pleased to honor the one who gave him birth, or in some other way that the king of glory and the lord of life and death alone knows.[33] So then the tomb was found empty. They found only the burial wrappings and the shroud in which they had laid her to rest, and the body of the immaculate Virgin was not there, but it had been raised up to her son and God so that she will live and reign with him completely, and thus our nature was raised up to heaven in the eternal kingdom not only by her son but also by the immaculate mother.

118 Then the blessed apostles were filled with astonishment and joy, and they understood that the late arrival of one of the apostles had taken place providentially for the revelation of this mystery, so that for his sake the tomb would be opened and the holy body's translation would be made known. And they glorified Christ, who had fully glorified his all-holy and immaculate mother, for they were suffused with light and fragrance from the holy tomb in which the body of the holy Virgin, wider than heaven, had been placed, and the brilliance and fragrance spread throughout the whole area of Gethsemane. So again they closed[34] the holy tomb, and the Dormition of the holy Theotokos was proclaimed to the entire world. Nevertheless, a report has been circulated and has come to our ears that the apostle who arrived on the third day was Thomas, coming from India, so that, as the Resurrection of Christ had previously been made more credible by Thomas, when on the eighth day the Lord entered through closed doors and showed him his hands[35] and his holy side (cf. also John 20.26–27), in this way now the translation of the incorruptibly immaculate body of the holy and all-glorious Theotokos and ever-virgin Mary also would be made known by Thomas. Then with prayers and mutual greetings, the holy apostles again dispersed, each one to the land of his preaching, and they taught the true faith to all peoples through the direction and assistance of the Lord and works of miracles. So then the heavens and the hosts of angels were perfected by the ascent of the soul and then the body of the holy and blessed Virgin. And the earth was made holy by her walking on the earth and by her placement in the tomb, and from the holy burial wrappings of her immaculate body. And the skies[36] and all creatures receive grace from her invisible and eternal regard and generosity, and every land and every city and all faithful people are full and overflowing with the ceaseless working of miracles and healing of illnesses and innumerable benefactions that the holy mother of Christ God shows to all individually. And who can relate her acts of care and assistance for us all, or what tongue will sufficiently express the abundance of her benefactions?[37]

119 But let us make known through our discourse on the glory of Christ God and in praise of his holy and immaculate mother, our hope and intercessor in all things, how the holy

Theotokos conferred her incorruptible garment as a precious relic to the great city of Constantinople, and how she brought this gift as a sign[38] to the faithful people and established[39] the sacrosanct treasure in a church. At the time of Leo the Great, the faithful emperor of the Greeks who reigned after Marcian, there were two noblemen, one named Galbius and the other Candidus. They were brothers in nature and brothers in charity. They were adorned with every good deed except only the one that is the pinnacle of every good thing, the true faith. In this they were deficient, for they had been seized by the seductive heresy of Arius. And they were from the family of Aspar and Ardaburius, who at that time exercised great authority in the imperial city. And God destroyed[40] them, for they were openly supporting the Arian heresy. Nevertheless, because of their good deeds, the grace of God did not leave Galbius and Candidus in heresy, but it turned them away from seduction to the truth, to the point that they not only established themselves firmly in the orthodox faith, but they were also teaching the truth[41] to many others who had been taught to be in error and leading them to salvation. Thus, when they were living virtuously in accordance with the orthodox faith, they undertook great benevolence and charity for the poor, in order to find complete favor with the Lord. For this reason also the holy and completely immaculate mother of Christ thought it appropriate to bestow some item of her incorruptible clothing on her city. It pleased her to carry out this act of Providence through these pious men, and it took place in the following way.

120 A yearning and desire to go to Jerusalem and venerate the holy places came upon the princes. They notified the emperor Leo and empress Verina, and with their consent they went forth, and with them many of their family and friends and a great multitude of soldiers. They reached Palestine, and they started on the road going to Galilee, in order to see both Nazareth and Capernaum. When they arrived there, it was night, and they needed lodging, and this took place through the Providence of God. Therefore they lodged in a small town where among many others lived a virgin woman advanced in age, a Jew legally, to tell the truth, but decent and zealous in every other affair, for at the time her soul was a land of darkness but useful to receiving the light of knowledge of God.⁴² In the possession of this elderly woman was the holy garment of the glorious mother of Christ. Nevertheless, by the Providence of the Lord, Galbius and Candidus made a stop at her house. And when they sat down to dinner, they noticed the interior of the house, and they saw another room,⁴³ in which many large candles were burning. It was filled with the perfume of incense, and many sick people were lying there. From this they understood that there was some sort of divine activity within, and they wanted to know what it was. Thus they sent and invited the old woman to dine with them, in order to question her about this activity. But she did not want to come and made a pretext of the Law's prescription that Jews may not eat Christian food. Nevertheless, they again insisted⁴⁴ that she come, and then they also explained⁴⁵ that this was no obstacle: "Take food that you have prepared yourself and use it, and sit with us only to speak and converse." The woman obeyed the distinguished men, and she drew near to them and sat down, and they began to speak with her. After much conversation and the removal of the table, they asked her in detail what was within the room, for they were thinking it was something of the Old Covenant.

121 Nevertheless, the woman discussed these things but did not want to reveal the cause of these things. So she said to them, "Do you see, my lords, the multitude of the infirm? By the will of God demons are driven away in that place: sight is given to the blind, movement is given to the lame, the deaf hear, and every other disease is cured." But the perceptive and distinguished men said again, "And what is the cause of such miracles: tell us." And she said, "A family tradition has come down to us that in this place God appeared to one of the patriarchs, and since then there is grace in this place." When she said this the wise men⁴⁶ were suspicious that she had not told the truth. And again they pleaded with her to tell the truth, "because for this reason we have undertaken⁴⁷ this labor and journey, in order that we would be worthy to venerate the holy places." And again she said, "I do not know anything more than this." And again they recognized that she was reluctant to tell them, for the holy queen, who wanted to bestow this great treasure on the Byzantines, spoke in their hearts so that they would seek out the truth. Therefore they besought her with more supplications that she reveal the truth to them, and they swore a great oath, and thus with much effort they pressed her to tell them the truth. Then she spoke from the soul, and her tears flowed, and she looked at them and spoke ashamedly: "O men, this mystery has been revealed to no one until this very day, for my parents entrusted me, their only daughter, with an oath. They commended this to a virgin so that she also would entrust it to another at the time of her death. But since I, the one whom you have seen, O honorable and distinguished men, and the ones who came before me in our family are virgin women,[48] and there is no one after me that I could tell it to her, therefore I will reveal this matter to you— but guard the information carefully. The garment of Mary the Theotokos lies there in safe keeping, for thus we have been informed by our ancestors: at the time of her death Mary the Theotokos left her two garments to the two women who had served her, one of whom was from my family. The first one received the garment, and she placed it in a coffer, and then she left it to her relatives, generation after generation. And she ordered that the keeper[49] of the treasure should be a virgin, and now the coffer is within this house, and within it is the garment of Mary the Theotokos, by which these miracles are worked. This, O honorable men, is the truth of the matter, and this has been made known to no one from Israel."[50]

122 The distinguished men were overwhelmed when they heard this, and their hearts were divided between fear and joy. And they fell down before the woman and said, "Be assured that no one in Jerusalem will hear this information from us: we bear witness to you[51] by the holy Theotokos herself. Nevertheless, we beseech you that we may spend the night in the place where the holy treasure lies." The woman allowed it, and when they entered the room,[52] they *gave neither sleep to their eyes nor slumber to their eyelids* (Ps 131.4), but they spent the entire night in prayer and supplication, and they offered thanks that such an excellent thing had been revealed to them. When they saw that all the sick had fallen asleep, they took complete measures of the coffer containing this abundant wealth, and they studied carefully the nature of the coffer's wood. And early in the morning they went forth and bid the woman farewell, and they said, "If you need anything from Jerusalem, let us know, because we will come here on our return trip." But she replied, "I need nothing else except your prayers that I will see you again in peace." Galbius and Candidus went forth to Jerusalem, and they fulfilled their promise to the Lord. They prayed in the holy places and distributed large sums to the poor, to the monasteries, and to the churches. Nevertheless, while they were there, they called for a skilled carpenter and instructed him secretly to make for them a coffer of this measure and form from old boards, and they told him exactly what they needed. The carpenter made it as they instructed, and they tied a beautiful cover embroidered with gold to the coffer. And when they had made pilgrimage to the holy places and monasteries and had received prayers from everyone and a blessing from the Patriarch, they took provisions for their journey and set out again on their way, and they had with them[53] the coffer that they had fashioned. And they arrived again in the village with joy, and they stayed in the old woman's house. They brought her beautiful candles and much incense and rich perfume. The woman received the distinguished men enthusiastically, as friends and acquaintances.

123 And they asked to stay again in the room with the treasure of grace, and she allowed them. They entered therein with authority, and they offered a prayer to God. And they prayed to his holy mother with ardent tears and said, "We your servants are not ignorant, O glorious queen, of what happened to Uzzah when he touched the Ark of the Covenant with his hand (cf. 2 Sam 6.6–7). How then can we, who are guilty of many sins, dare to touch this ark in which is such a treasure is kept? How can we place our hands on it if you do not command us? Therefore we beseech you and pray to you that it may please you to realize the desire of our hearts, for we desire to take away this treasure to the city that glorifies your name, so that it will have an eternal palladium and an intercessory rampart." They offered such prayer the whole night and drenched the earth[54] with their tears, and they were satisfied that the mother of Christ God had heard their prayer. They drew near to the holy ark with fear and trembling, for everyone who was there had fallen asleep. They took it and placed it among their possessions by the good pleasure of divine grace, and in its stead they placed what they had fashioned in its likeness in Jerusalem, and they covered it with the garment embroidered with gold that they had tied to it. And early in the morning they greeted the woman and bid her farewell. And they showed her the beautiful cover that they had draped over the coffer, which pleased the woman, and she promised that it would always be there. Then they distributed wealth to all the sick and disabled, and with joy they went forth on their way. And when they reached Constantinople, that is, the city of Byzantium, they did not wish to make their glorious deed known to either the Emperor or the Patriarch, for they feared that the Emperor would seize their great treasure and they would lose this splendid object. Thus they decided to keep this precious pearl unbeknownst to others with the assistance of the holy Theotokos. And they had a place where their houses were, near the wall by the seashore: the place was called Blachernai. There they built a church, and they were utterly diligent not to reveal their secret. That is why they called the church that they had built by the name of Saint Peter the Apostle and Mark the Evangelist. Then they placed the great treasure in it, and they took care to adorn the shrine with constant singing and endless incense of fragrant perfumes and the inextinguishable light of lamps and candles. And thus for a long time the secret remained a secret.

124 Nevertheless, it did not please the holy queen, the hope and intercessor of Christians, that such a wonderful thing was confined among these two men alone and hidden in silence, and that this wealth common to all was kept for their enjoyment[55] alone. She moved the hearts of these worthy noblemen to reveal the hidden mystery. Thus they went before Leo, the pious and faithful emperor, and disclosed the secret and explained how this great wealth had actually come to the imperial city. The faithful emperor heard this, and he was filled with great joy. And he immediately divulged this hidden mystery,[56] and Galbius and Candidus, who had performed this divine service, were blessed by everyone[57] and honored by all. Then Emperor Leo, the servant of God, and Verina, the faithful empress, built in this place with imperial subvention a beautiful shrine to glorify the holy Theotokos,[58] and they prepared a coffer of silver covered with gold, and they placed the holy treasure in it, and they adorned the shrine with numerous gifts and ornaments to their eternal memory. Thus Leo and Verina completed the time of their reign well and with virtue, and they passed into life eternal. Likewise Galbius and Candidus, the faithful and devoted servants of the holy Theotokos, died faithful and pious. Nevertheless, the ark of the mystery remained an eternal wealth[59] for the faithful people and the believing city, wherein sit not the tablets carved by Moses, but there lies the holy and venerable garment of the glorious and all-blessed Theotokos, which she not only wore on her incorruptible and immaculate body, but when Christ God became incarnate and was born from her for our salvation and when he was an infant, he, the life and nurturer of all flesh, was wrapped in it many times and nursed in the manner of infants. And that is why the holy garment of the immaculate and all-praised Theotokos remains incorrupt from then until now.[60] In the same way the immaculate mother of Christ also bestowed on this same city her holy girdle, which encircled the body that contained the uncontainable king of all things. And for this a beautiful shrine was also built by the faithful emperors to the glory of the holy Theotokos, which is called Chalkoprateia. And there is kept her incorruptible girdle as a crown of grace and a steadfast wall for the faithful city and as a source of victory to the pious emperors.

CHAPTER 9

CONCLUSION

125 Behold, what mind will fathom, or what tongue will express, or what master scribe's hand will write the innumerable multitude of the graces and benevolences of the holy and ever-virgin Theotokos, which she manifested and manifests from day to day among the human race?

She is the ardent intercessor with her son, Christ God, for all those who entreat her.

She is the calm harbor of all those buffeted by waves, who rescues them from spiritual[1] and fleshly waves.

She is the guide on the way of life for all who have gone astray.

She is the one who seeks and converts those who are lost.

She is the help and support of those who are afflicted.

She is the intercessor and mediator of those who are penitent.

And I will say even more than the above:[2]

She is the resurrection of the fallen Adam.

She is the destruction of Eve's tears.

She is the comforter of those who mourn.

She is the throne of the king, who bears the one who bears all.

She is the one who renews the old world.

She is the ladder that reaches to heaven, by which God descended to the earth.

She is the bridge that leads from earth to Paradise.

She is the wonder of angels, and she is the wound of demons and their destruction.

She is the root of the incorruptible shoot.

She is the tree of immortal fruit.

She worked on the worker, the lover of humanity.

She sprouted forth the planter of life.

She is the furrow sprouting forth the wheat that strengthens hearts.

She is the table bearing eternal delight.

She is the incense offered to God for intercession on our behalf.

She is the ransom of the world.

She is the cause of boldness before God for mortal humans.

She is the mother of the good shepherd.

She is the dwelling place of the rational sheep.

She is the chasing away of the invisible enemies.

She is the opening of the gates of Paradise.

She is the unsilenced mouth of the apostles.

She is the invincible courage of the martyrs.

She is the power and strength of Christians.

She is the dawn of the undarkening day.

She is the bearer of the sun of truth.

Through her the raging tyrant was banished from his dominion.

Through her the Lord Christ, the lover of humanity, has appeared to us as savior.

Through her we have been saved from the mire of many sins, and we have been freed from the rule of various passions.

She is the raising of human beings and the downfall of demons.

She is the rock of life from which the thirsty drink the water of immortality.

She is the pillar of light leading and illuminating those in darkness.

She is the urn receiving the manna coming from heaven.

She is the land of promise producing sweetness.

She is the flower of incorruptibility, the crown of virtue, the model of the life of angels.

She is the thickly leaved tree in whose shade the weary rest, the bearer of the redeemer of captives, the guide of those who have gone astray.

She is our intercessor before the just judge.

She is the destroyer of the records of our sins.

She is the garment of those who are bare of any good.

She is the door of great mystery.

She is the unquestioned pride of the faithful.

She is the one who received the uncontainable[3] God.

She is the holy throne of the one seated on the cherubim.

She is the virtuous inheritance of the one glorified by the seraphim.

She leads forth the angels and humans together.

She united virginity and childbearing, for she was both the immaculate Virgin and the mother of Emmanuel.

Through her was the curse removed.

On her account was Paradise opened.

She is the key of the kingdom of heaven.

She is the cause of eternal good things.

She is the one receiving the Wisdom of God.

She is the treasure house of his Providence.

She is the pillar of virginity.

She is the gate of salvation.

She is the beginning of our renewal.

She is the cause of divine mercy toward humanity.

She is the crown of the invisible sun.

She is the brilliance of the undarkening light.

She is the lightning that illuminates souls.

She is the thunder that shatters[4] the enemies and the deceptive demons.

She is the one who engendered the source of life.

She is the font that purifies thoughts.

She is the cup brimming with joy.

She is the tent of the Word of God.

She is the saint of saints, the height of all sanctity.

She is the ark covered by the Holy Spirit.

She is the precious crown of faithful kings.

She is the pride and ornament of worthy and holy bishops.

She is the unshakable tower of the catholic church.

She is the impregnable wall of the city of the faithful, about which David said,[5] *"Who will lead me to the fortified city?"* (Ps 59.11), which is the assembly of the faithful, gathered from the nations.

She is the healer of our infirmities.

She is hope and helper of our souls.

126 And what more will I say, for the time is too short for me to relate the glories and praises of our supremely blessed and all-glorious queen, the Theotokos and ever-virgin Mary, and if even the tongues of angels and humans joined together are not capable of praising and glorifying her appropriately and worthily, then I, weak and unworthy, ignorant and stuttering, am not able to say anything properly or worthily, but the gracious mother of the gracious and benevolent Lord will receive[6] even this our inept discourse, prepared by her grace and gifts and not by our ability and knowledge. That is also why I entreat you,[7] all the pious believers in Christ who glorify the holy Theotokos with zeal and desire, that you will always assemble adorned with spiritual virtues to celebrate the brilliant and glorious feast of her Dormition with divine praise and hymns, for she is truly great and glorious and adorned[8] in every way, and great wonders and divine mysteries were accomplished in her. The archangel Gabriel was sent again by God to announce the Dormition, and he brought the sign of victory, the branch of the date palm, in order to show that she had been victorious over every order of nature. Then the gathering of the holy apostles, caught up by clouds from the ends of the earth, assembled. The glorious Twelve and many others who followed them came in an instant to glorify the holy and glorious mother of the Lord. And the mystery of the second coming was made manifest here, as the blessed apostle Paul says, *"we will be caught up by clouds to meet the Lord in the air, and so we will always be with the Lord"* (1 Thess 4.17). This, then, is the mystery of the lifting up by clouds at that time. Now at the Dormition of the queen a great[9] and glorious wonder was fulfilled: the arrival of such a multitude from the ends of the earth and from distant lands and their appearance at Zion before the ever-virgin Mary in the blink of an eye. Then came Christ himself, the king of glory, her Lord and son, who saw fit by the good pleasure of his Father[10] and by the assistance[11] of the Holy Spirit to dwell in her womb and to take on flesh from her. And he fulfilled the plan of our salvation: he was crucified and buried and arose on the third day; then he ascended into Heaven and was seated at the right hand of the Father. This gracious king also came now with an assembly of angels and archangels. And he received the holy and glorious soul of his blessed and desirable mother and took it up to the glorious dwelling place of his Father, to the good things that *no eye has seen, nor ear heard, nor have entered into the human heart, which God has prepared for those who love him* (1 Cor 2.9), and above all for his immaculate mother.

127 Nevertheless, by the grace of the apostles and by the command of their Lord, God, and master, they brought the holy and immaculate body of their queen from Zion to Gethsemane and placed it in a tomb, as Joseph and Nicodemus once did with the body of the Lord Jesus. And as the Lord of glory arose on the third day, so also now on the third day the body of his holy mother was not found in the tomb, but it had been translated to where[12] her son wished. She was buried as one of the dead according to the order of nature, and she was translated as the mother of God, in order to confirm[13] and make credible the Resurrection of the Lord born from her and the assumption of the nature that he had put on from her, and to confirm our ascension and incorruptibility that truly will come later. As her giving birth was without corruption, so her death also took place without corruption. As her giving birth was beyond words and nature, so her Dormition took place in a manner beyond the temporal and natural order. And she was wondrous, because as her soul ascended to heaven without her body, so her body also without her soul, so that[14] she showed to her son and his servants both communion and separation. She ascended to Heaven by the grace and assistance of her son before the general resurrection to draw our attention to the coming resurrection. She was assumed completely, but first her holy soul separately, when she gave it over to the Lord, and then the immaculate body, as the Lord willed. Thus we confess the human beauty that the desirable one possessed, and the glorious grace with which her son glorified her. So this feast is revered and wonderful in every way, revered by angels and human beings and adorned by the grace of the holy Theotokos. And the time of this glorious feast also is good and blessed, full of all fruit: the harvest is complete, the vintage is matured, the fruits of the trees and every sort of produce are spread forth. And this honor is also a glorification of our nature by the creator and a remembrance of the delights of Paradise, and all this is given for the honor of the holy feast and for the delight of those who glorify her. And this time of the year is good and beneficial for humankind and full of benefits and delights.

128 Now our nature had been raised to Heaven by the ascension and translation of the holy Virgin, as before by the Ascension of her son. She has become more exalted than the thrones, cherubim, and seraphim,[15] for truly she has become far more exalted and glorious than all the other bodiless and immaterial creatures, the blessed mother of our savior Christ God, clothed in royal splendor, praised and venerated by the powers and dominions and every name that has been named, not only those in this world but those in the one to come, which are invisible and unknown to us. I have said what is more brilliant and useful for us[16] than all the rest. Now a second mediator has gone forth to the first[17] mediator, a devout human being to the incarnate God, a second offering of our nature to the Father after the first one who was himself sacrificed one time on behalf of all (cf. Heb 10.12), and she is ever living to intercede on behalf of those who approach God through her. But now such things are beyond our words and ability, and we are not able to grasp them with the mind, nor express them with language. That is why we have left out the hidden mysteries, because everything that the Lord wished, he did in the heavens and on earth. But let us, according to our own ability, offer thanks to the Lord and fulfill the debt of our discourse of praise and prayer to our Lord Jesus Christ and his supremely blessed and all-holy mother.

129 We thank you, O king and custodian of all mysteries, on account of all your good things and that you have chosen such a one to be a servant of your mysteries. We give thanks for your ineffable wisdom and the power of your love of humanity, you who not only joined and deified our nature but also saw fit to choose your mother from among us and established her as queen of all things. We thank you who took upon yourself the Passion of Crucifixion and death for our sake, and you saw fit for the sake of your name to take upon yourself your holy mother in this world of so much labor and hardship, in order to make her a partaker of your glory and by her prayers and intercessions to grant us eternal life. We thank you who gave yourself as a ransom for our sake and also in your benevolence gave us your all-holy mother as a helper and intercessor for our sake, O lover of humanity and sweet king. We thank you also, O blessed and glorious queen, who always take pity on us and suffer on account of our miseries, and you entreat your son to forgive our sins and temptations. We do not mourn your death and burial, but we celebrate your translation with glory, because even though you have been transferred to heaven, you have not abandoned those of us dwelling on earth. Although you have been removed from the struggles[18] and labors of this fleeting life and have entered into the ineffable and infinite bliss, you have not forgotten our poverty, but now you remember us even more and deliver us from various and diverse miseries and temptations. You do not abandon us from your assistance and desirable grace as orphans, but you care for us and cover us in the shade of your glory and offer constant intercession and prayer to your son and our God on behalf of those who hymn and glorify you, for now you truly stand as the queen of all at the right hand of the king, *adorned with a gold-woven robe* by the grace of the Holy Spirit *and dressed with diverse adornment* by the adornment of virtues (Ps 44.10), and *the rich of the people will seek your favor* (Ps 44.13b), the souls of the holy and righteous, who are rich in good deeds, which is the true wealth.

130 Now you have from the hands of your son and God the crown of beauty and the scepter of rule and adornment in every dominion. But we entreat you: do not forget the people who glorify your son and praise your name, for you have all power before your gracious son who loves humanity, and he generously fulfills all your prayers and petitions, and you also are merciful to all those who serve you and trust in you. And this is manifest by your perpetual and daily wonders, your spiritual and bodily ministrations and cures, which you show to each one of those who entreat you, which are indescribable and more innumerable than the sand of the sea, and, what is greater and more sublime than all else, your intercessions[19] and petitions for clemency[20] with your son on behalf of those who have sinned, and the prosperity and protection[21] of the righteous by your grace, your rescues and mercies in all the world and for each person individually. Because of this *the king desired your beauty* (Ps 44.12), your great love of humanity and mercy and goodness, imitating the greatness of his mercy. And although your other virtues are innumerable, purity, wisdom, courage, and all the rest, in goodness and mercy you are above all the imitator of your son and God, and so through your intercessions with him, the gracious and benevolent one spreads forth his mercies and delights even more upon us, because *"we have him* alone *as an advocate with the Father, Jesus Christ the righteous,"* as John the Evangelist and Theologian says, *"and he is the expiation for our sins"* (1 John 2.1–2). And you are also our advocate and intercessor with him: you turn away his wrath and anger, which comes justly on account of our sins and transgressions, but you spread forth his mercy and sweetness upon us. How great are your supernatural benefactions and mercies, O holy Virgin!

131 Truly you have surpassed the limits of nature, not only in the unfathomable Nativity but also in preternatural benevolence. Through you the curse of the first mother has been undone. Through you the dividing[22] wall of hostility has been torn down (cf. Eph 2.14). Through you the dominion of death has been destroyed. Through you we have become victorious over sin. Through you virginity has been planted among humanity. Through you we have learned courage in good deeds. Through you we have been given wisdom, humility, love, and every other virtue. We did not appear so victorious as long as we were conquered. But even more, we have been expelled from Eden, and through you we have received both heaven and Eden. We were removed through the Tree of Knowledge and were lacking the Tree of Life, but through you we have gained the creator of the Tree. Through disobedience we were stripped of the divine raiment, and through you we have put on God and been united to him, and he has given us the power to become children of God. So many, O virgin Theotokos, are your gifts and graces for us, which you granted us when you were in this life. And now after the Dormition, even more now you are living and glorious, and you dwell with life and the giver of life, your son, and you see that the one born from you is one of the Trinity, the one who was contained within you and is uncontainable by heaven and earth, the one who generously fulfills your prayers and[23] richly grants mercy in regard to what you ask. And even if some should sin again and entreat you again, then you still have mercy and ask forgiveness on their behalf, which is even more wondrous and glorious. Truly you are the gate of life, always open to those entering in, even though the prophet has called you the closed gate that no one will pass through except only[24] God, and still it remained closed (cf. Ezek 44.2). But now that you have been transferred from this world, through your intercession with your son and your assistance and embrace of those who entreat you, the gate of your grace and mercy is open to all, and you receive everyone and fulfill their requests.

132

O treasure house of all virtues! O facilitator of supernatural benefactions! O flower of every perfume! O pride of human nature, our joy and life, glory and peace, victory and wisdom and sovereignty, gathering of every good thing, which no tongue can express, no mind can grasp, and no span of time can age![25] O divine gift to humanity and offering from humanity[26] to God! O one full of grace and of the glory of the holy Trinity, domain of every good thing! O unwedded bride, the mother of God Emmanuel! O dwelling place of the Holy Spirit, queen of all things, urn of gold receiving the manna, rod that sprouted from the root of Jesse, about which Isaiah says, "Blessed is the root of Jesse, *and a rod will come forth from the root of Jesse, a flower will sprout from his roots*" (Isa 11.1; cf. Heb 9.4), the lampstand of light (cf. Heb 9.2; Exod 25.31–35), couch of the king (cf. Cant 1.12), table of life, temple of light, ark of holiness, source of immortality, intellectual Paradise, cloud of light, unwavering pillar of brilliance (cf. Exod 13.21–22), paten of the bread of life, gate of God, which he alone passed through and it remained closed (cf. Ezek 44.2), all-holy mountain, Eden of the second Adam, exalted heaven and elevated throne, uninflammable bush (cf. Exod 3.2), resting place of the Lord,[27] as David said of you, *"Rise up, O Lord, to your resting place"* (Ps 131.8), and everything else that the prophets called you with symbols and metaphors. Who will hear your many names and not be amazed? But your short and true name is mother of God, immaculate Virgin, most blessed Theotokos and ever-virgin Mary. This is your new and revealed true name. Those, your old names, spoken metaphorically, foreshadow[28] the new ones, and these new ones confirm the old ones. You are truly the living book in which the Word of the Father was ineffably written by the pen of the life-giving Holy Spirit. You are truly the divinely penned scroll of the New Testament, the life-giving testament, which God has laid down for humanity. You are the mediator and intercessor and bearer of our salvation, as you always are watching over and helping the faithful people.

133 Now watch over us even more and have mercy on us your flock and your people, whom your son has purchased with his precious blood, and pray for us and establish us in your inheritance. And from day to day you are merciful and sustain all people in general and each person individually, so that they all will become one body in the spiritual[29] stature of perfection, and they will have one head, Jesus Christ your son. Embrace your people and accept your inheritance, O all-holy queen, and keep them safe in the cloak of your mercy and intercession and chase away from them the invisible predators that murder souls. Keep them safe from visible struggles and temptations, even if because of our many sins and transgressions we are silent and deserving of torment. But do not remember our transgressions, and aid us quickly with your grace, for we are greatly impoverished. Deliver us and relieve us from our sins by your intercession with your son. Sustain us in this life and protect us from the snares and traps of the devil, and relieve us from all our visible and invisible temptations and sins. And in the age to come lead us into the eternal dwelling places, the resting places where the light of the face of Christ your son is spread forth, so that the people who glorify you will reign before you. And we rejoice in your name because you are blessed among women and blessed by all peoples and generations and glorified in heaven and on earth, because every tongue glorifies you and proclaims you the mother of life. All creation is full of your glory, and through you all things glorify the holy Trinity, three in hypostases and one in being, our glorious God.

134 Such are, O all-holy queen Theotokos, the mysteries of your glorious life. These are the story of your going forth, the hymn of your Dormition, the glory before your Dormition, the praise of your burial, and the wonders of your glorious translation. And now, O all-praised and glorified queen Theotokos, receive these humble words of your praise and glory given to you by your incapable and unworthy servant, which I have spoken according to my ability with faith and desire for your grace, for my mind is not able to accomplish more. Even if all the minds and tongues of the visible and invisible were joined together, they would not succeed in praising and glorifying you worthily. But in exchange for this humble and inept offering, pour forth your grace and mercy and intercession abundantly upon me, your unworthy servant, and upon all those who glorify your name. O all-praised Mother of God, who gave birth to the Holy of Holies, the Word of God, receive the prayer of your servants and keep us safe from every affliction and temptation and deliver us from eternal torment, and in the unending life of the righteous make us worthy of a share in the goodness of eternal life through Jesus Christ your son and God, to whom is due all honor, glory, and worship with the beginningless Father and the all-holy, benevolent, and life-giving Spirit, now and forever and unto the ages of ages. Amen.

O Christ, king of glory, through the intercession of the one who gave you birth, the holy Virgin Mary, have mercy and save the soul of humble Euthymius, who translated this holy book, the *Life of the Holy Theotokos* from Greek into Georgian on the Holy Mountain of Athos.

APPENDIX

A Guide to Liturgical Reading of the *Life of the Virgin*
from an Eleventh-Century Manuscript from the
Monastery of Mar Saba near Bethlehem

December 25, Reading IV: "Nevertheless, at the time when the archangel made the Annunciation" (§24) until "There is a true and ready explanation of this matter too" (§42).

December 26,[1] Reading XVI: "Nevertheless, this tradition also has also come down to us" (§97) until "in the place of John the Evangelist" (§98).

December 29,[2] Reading V: "for so it has been made known to us" (§42) until "because such mysteries were fulfilled on it" (§45).

January 6, Reading IX: "And let us now hear the story of the revelation and the baptism" (§64) until "he had been the Forerunner of his preaching and his baptism" (§67).

January 16,[3] Reading XVI: "Nevertheless, the mother of the Lord was dwelling in the house of the beloved disciple" (§95) until "And they went to their king and master Christ wearing crowns" (§98).

February 2, Reading VI: "And on the fortieth day after the Nativity" (§46) until "shone with the grace of Christ" (§53).

March 25, Reading III: "One day, in the middle of the night, she was standing" (§14) until "Afterwards, the blessed Virgin revealed the archangel's Annunciation" (§24).

Holy Wednesday, Reading XI: "But now let us return to the original course of this discourse" (§72) until "The holy Theotokos was the leader and director of them all" (§74).

Holy Thursday, Reading XII: "For this reason, when the mysterious and glorious supper" (§74) until "her ineffable and inexpressible love and compassion for him" (§77).

Holy Friday, Reading XIII: "The time of the greatest deed arrived" (§78) until "and the death was the destruction of death" (§86).

Holy Saturday, Reading XIV: "Thus when the holy mother of the Lord saw" (§87) until "in order to show their devotion and faith" (§91).

3rd Sunday after Easter,[4] Reading X: "What then does the holy gospel teach us?" (§67) until "when we come to the place of Christ's Crucifixion" (§71).

Ascension, Reading XV: "Nevertheless the immaculate mother was inseparable from the tomb" (§92) until "and the Holy Spirit, according to the command of the Lord" (§94).

April 30,[5] Reading XVI: "Nevertheless, the mother of the Lord was dwelling in the house of the beloved disciple" (§95) until "And they went to their king and master Christ wearing crowns" (§98).

May 15,[6] Reading VIII: "Nevertheless, when the young infant and king of all" (§55) until "and thus were all the mysteries fulfilled" (§63).

June 24,[7] Reading VII: "Nevertheless, let us return again to our original topic" (§54) until "and so in this way he fulfilled his destiny" (§54).

July 2,[8] Reading XX: "But let us make known through our discourse" (§119) until "remains incorrupt from then until now" (§124).

July 13,[9] Reading III: "One day, in the middle of the night, she was standing" (§14) until "Afterwards, the blessed Virgin revealed the archangel's Annunciation" (§24).

July 22,[10] Reading X: "Then there was the feast of Tabernacles" (§71) until "when we come to the place of Christ's Crucifixion" (§71).

July 25,[11] Reading I: "The praise and glory, laud and honor" (§1) until "are led there subsequently by her intercession" (§5).

August 14,[12] Reading XVII: "Thus, the return of the holy Theotokos to Jerusalem was excellent" (§98) until "praising the Father and the Son and the Holy Spirit" (§102).

August 15, Reading XVIII: "Nevertheless, the blessed and all-praised mother of God" (§102) until "and gave life to the world" (§115).

August 16,[13] Reading XIX: "And it is not fitting to keep silent" (§115) until "the abundance of benefactions" (§118).

August 31,[14] Reading XXI: "In the same way the immaculate mother of Christ" (§124) until the end.

September 5,[15] Reading VII: "Nevertheless, let us return again to our original topic" (§54) until "and so in this way he fulfilled his destiny" (§54).

September 8,[16] Reading I: "The praise and glory, laud and honor" (§1) until "are led there subsequently by her intercession" (§5).

October 23,[17] Reading XVI: "Nevertheless, this tradition has also come down to us from the Fathers" (§97) until "in the place of John the Evangelist" (§98).

November 21,[18] Reading II: "When she had passed the age of nursing" (§5) until "with humility and tranquility, with fear and love of God" (§14).

Sunday before the Nativity, For the Commemoration of David and Joseph the Servant of the Holy Theotokos and James the Brother of the Lord, Reading X: "What then does the holy gospel teach us?" (§67) until "and she remained with his holy mother all the time thereafter" (§70). One also reads the same on 30 April, Reading X: "What then does the holy gospel teach us?" (§67).

A Reading for the Holy Theotokos Whenever You Like: "Behold, what mind will fathom" (§125) until the end.

NOTES

INTRODUCTION

1   Although Korneli Kekelidze had previously characterized Euthymius as a somewhat careless translator, Michel van Esbroeck has exploded this myth and demonstrated convincingly the reliability of Euthymius' translations. See Michel van Esbroeck, "Euthyme l'Hagiorite: le traducteur et ses traductions," *Revue des études géorgiennes et caucasiennes* 4 (1988): 73–107. See also Stephen J. Shoemaker, "The Georgian *Life of the Virgin* attributed to Maximus the Confessor: Its Authenticity(?) and Importance," in *Mémorial R.P. Michel van Esbroeck, S.J.*, ed. Alexey Muraviev and Basil Lourié, Scrinium 2 (St. Petersburg: Vizantinorossika, 2006), 307–28, 312–13.

2   Euthymius' considerable output can best be surveyed in Michael Tarchnišvili, *Geschichte der kirchlichen georgischen Literatur, auf Grund des ersten Bandes der georgischen Literaturgeschichte von K. Kekelidze*, Studi e testi 185 (Città del Vaticano: Biblioteca apostolica vaticana, 1955), 126–54, where the *Life of the Virgin* is discussed on pp. 133–4. On the *Balavariani* and the *Life of Barlaam and Iosaph*, see David Marshall Lang, *The Balavariani (Barlaam and Josaphat)* (Berkeley: University of California Press, 1966); and George Ratcliffe Woodward and Harold Mattingly, *St. John Damascene: Barlaam and Ioasaph*, The Loeb Classical Library 34 (London: W. Heinemann, 1914). Regarding the importance of Maximus the Confessor in the Georgian tradition, and the significance of these translations in particular, see now Tamila Mgaloblishvili and Lela Khoperia, eds., *Maximus the Confessor and Georgia*, Iberica Caucasica 3 (London: Bennett & Bloom, 2009).

3   The various manuscripts are described in Michel van Esbroeck, ed., *Maxime le Confesseur: Vie de la Vierge*, 2 vols., Corpus Scriptorum Christianorum Orientalium 478–479, Scriptores Iberici, 21–22 (Lovanii: E. Peeters, 1986), v–xvii (Geor).

4   In his initial remarks on the *Life of the Virgin*, Kekelidze seems to allow for the possibility that the life is authentic: see Korneli Kekeliże, **Сведения грузинских источников о преподобном Максиме Исповедкине** (Svedenija gruzinskikh istochnikov o prepodobnom Maksime Ispovedkine [Information from Georgian Sources Concerning the Venerable Maximus the Confessor])," *Труды Киевской духовной академий (Trudy Kievskoj dukhovnoj akademii)* sentjabr-nojabr (1912): 1–41, 451–86; I have consulted the reprint of this article in Korneli Kekeliże, ექეთუდები

ძველი ქართული ლიტერატურის ისტორიიდან *(Etiudebi żveli
k'art'uli literaturis istoriidan [Studies in the History of Old Georgian Literature])*, vol. 7
(Tiblisi: Sak'art'velos SSR mec'nierebat'a akademiis gamomc'emloba, 1967),
14–54, here at pp. 35–6. Nevertheless, in the first edition of his history
of Old Georgian literature, Kekelidze rejects the attribution, offering the
explanation above in a footnote added only in subsequent editions: Korneli
Kekeliże, ქართული ლიტერატურის ისტორია *(K'art'uli literaturis
istoria [History of Georgian Literature])*, 1st ed., 2 vols., vol. 1, Żveli mcerloba
(Tbilisi: Gamomc'emeli T'oma Č'ik'vanaia, 1923), 192–4. In the most
recent edition, Korneli Kekeliże, ძველი ქართული ლიტერატურულის
ისტორია *(Żveli k'art'uli literaturis istoria [History of Old Georgian Literature])*,
5th ed., 2 vols. (Tbilisi: Mec'niereba, 1980), vol. 1, 195–7, esp. 197, n. 1 (this
note is not in the first edition). Note that Tarchnišvili, *Geschichte der kirchlichen
georgischen Literatur*, 133–4, which is based on the 2nd ed. of Kekelidze's history,
fails to translate the final section of Kekelidze's entry, and thus does not
reproduce his remarks concerning the *Life*'s attribution to Maximus.

5 Concerning these events from Maximus' trial, see *Dispute at Bizya* 14 (Pauline
Allen and Bronwen Neil, eds., *Scripta saeculi VII Vitam Maximi Confessoris
illustrantia*, Corpus Christianorum, Series Graeca 39 (Turnhout: Brepols,
1999), 143–5; Pauline Allen and Bronwen Neil, eds., *Maximus the Confessor and
his Companions: Documents from Exile*, Oxford Early Christian Texts (Oxford:
Oxford University Press, 2002), 114–17). In this account Maximus publicly
and unambiguously identifies Mary as Theotokos and condemns all those
who do not. On the composition of this text shortly after the events
described, in 656 or 657, see ibid., 36.

6 There is an Italian translation of the *Life of the Virgin*, but it is a translation
of van Esbroeck's French rather than a translation of the Georgian: Georges
Gharib, *Testi mariani del primo Millennio*, 4 vols. (Rome: Città Nuova Editrice,
1988–91), vol. 2, 185–289.

7 Zurab Sarjvelaże et al., *Altgeorgisch–deutsches Wörterbuch*, Handbook of Oriental
Studies. Section Eight, Central Asia 12 (Leiden: Brill, 2005). Also important
in this regard is Donald Rayfield, *A Comprehensive Georgian–English Dictionary*, 2
vols. (London: Garnett Press, 2006).

8 *Thesaurus Indogermanischer Text- und Sprachmaterialien (TITUS)* ([cited 5 Feb 2011]);
available from http://titus.uni–frankfurt.de/.

9 On the as yet incomplete status of Old Georgian lexicography, see, e.g.,
Rayfield, *A Comprehensive Georgian–English Dictionary*, vol. 1, xiii.

10 Bruce M. Metzger, *The Early Versions of the New Testament: Their Origin, Transmission,
and Limitations* (Oxford: Clarendon Press, 1977), 182–200.

11 Patrick H. Alexander, *The SBL Handbook of Style for Ancient Near Eastern, Biblical,
and Early Christian Studies* (Peabody, Mass.: Hendrickson Publishers, 1999),
73–89.

12   The original text of the letter is published in Michel van Esbroeck, "Some Earlier Features in the Life of the Virgin," *Marianum* 63 (2001): 297–308, 297–8, n. 2.

13   E.g., Aidan Nichols, *Byzantine Gospel: Maximus the Confessor in Modern Scholarship* (Edinburgh: T & T Clark, 1993), 111–19; Jean-Claude Larchet, *La divinisation de l'homme selon saint Maxime le Confesseur*, Cogitatio fidei 194 (Paris: Éditions du Cerf, 1996); Jean-Claude Larchet, *Maxime le Confesseur, médiateur entre l'Orient et l'Occident*, Cogitatio fidei, 208 (Paris: Les Éditions du Cerf, 1998). Note that Larchet remarks in the former work that the authenticity is "still poorly established" (13). Simon Mimouni also accepts van Esbroeck's arguments for Maximus' authorship: Simon C. Mimouni, "Les Vies de la Vierge: État de la question," *Apocrypha* 5 (1994): 211–48, esp. 216–20.

14   See especially Andrew Louth, *Maximus the Confessor*, Early Church Fathers (London: Routledge, 1996); Andrew Louth, "Recent Research on St Maximus the Confessor: A Survey," *St. Vladimir's Theological Quarterly* 42 (1998): 67–84; Lars Thunberg, *Microcosm and Mediator: The Theological Anthropology of Maximus the Confessor*, 2nd ed. (Chicago: Open Court, 1995). See also Paul M. Blowers, *Exegesis and Spiritual Pedagogy in Maximus the Confessor: An Investigation of the Quaestiones ad Thalassium*, Christianity and Judaism in Antiquity 7 (Notre Dame, Ind.: University of Notre Dame Press, 1991); Paul M. Blowers and Robert Louis Wilken, *On the Cosmic Mystery of Jesus Christ: Selected Writings from St. Maximus the Confessor* (Crestwood, N.Y.: St. Vladimir's Seminary Press, 2003); Demetrios Bathrellos, *The Byzantine Christ: Person, Nature, and Will in the Christology of St Maximus the Confessor*, Oxford Early Christian Studies (Oxford: Oxford University Press, 2004); Adam G. Cooper, *The Body in St. Maximus the Confessor: Holy Flesh, Wholly Deified*, Oxford Early Christian Studies (Oxford: Oxford University Press, 2005); Pascal Mueller-Jourdan, *Typologie spatio-temporelle de l'ecclesia byzantine: la Mystagogie de Maxime le Confesseur dans la culture philosophique de l'antiquité tardive*, Supplements to Vigiliae Christianae 74 (Leiden: Brill, 2005); Melchisedec Törönen, *Union and Distinction in the Thought of St. Maximus the Confessor*, Oxford Early Christian Studies (Oxford: Oxford University Press, 2007); Torstein Tollefsen, *The Christocentric Cosmology of St. Maximus the Confessor*, Oxford Early Christian Studies (Oxford: Oxford University Press, 2008); Nikolaos Loudovikos, *A Eucharistic Ontology: Maximus the Confessor's Eschatological Ontology of Being as Dialogical Reciprocity* (Brookline, Mass.: Holy Cross Orthodox Press, 2010); Maximus the Confessor, *Questions and Doubts*, trans. Despina D. Prassas (DeKalb, Ill.: Northern Illinois University Press, 2010).

15   Maurice Geerard et al., *Clavis Patrum Graecorum: Supplementum*, Corpus Christianorum (Turnhout: Brepols, 1998), 440, #7712; Angelo Di Berardino, ed., *Patrology: The Eastern Fathers from the Council of Chalcedon (451) to John of Damascus (750)* (Cambridge: James Clarke & Co., 2006), 148.

16 Ermanno M. Toniolo, "L'Akathistos nella Vita di Maria di Massimo il
Confessore," in *Virgo Liber Dei: Miscellanea di studi in onore di P. Giuseppe M. Besutti,
O.S.M.*, ed. Ignazio M. Calabuig (Roma: Edizioni Marianum, 1991), 209–28.

17 Shoemaker, "Georgian *Life of the Virgin*," esp. 316–20.

18 As van Esbroeck rightly notes, if Maximus is the *Life*'s author, then it most likely
was composed sometime before he fled Constantinople: van Esbroeck, ed.,
Maxime le Confesseur: Vie de la Vierge, xxx–xxxii (Fr). Regarding the complications
of Maximus' biography, see below, as well as Louth, *Maximus the Confessor*, 4–7.

19 E.g., Larchet, *La divinisation de l'homme*, 83, 264, 355; Larchet, *Maxime le Confesseur*, 81.

20 See, e.g., Di Berardino, ed., *Patrology: The Eastern Fathers*, 301–7, 402.

21 Hippolyte Delehaye, *L'Ancienne hagiographie byzantine: les sources, les premiers
modèles, la formation des genres*, Subsidia hagiographica 73 (Bruxelles: Société
des Bollandistes, 1991), 51; Alexander Kazhdan, *A History of Byzantine Literature
(650–850)* (Athens: National Hellenic Research Foundation, Institute for
Byzantine Research, 1999), 22.

22 Claudia Rapp, "Byzantine Hagiographers as Antiquarians, Seventh to Tenth
Centuries," *Byzantinische Forschungen* 21 (1995): 31–44, 35.

23 John Moschus, *Spiritual Meadow* prol. (Patrologia Graeca [hereafter PG], ed.
J. P. Migne, 162 vols., Paris, 1857–66, 87.2851); trans. John Moschus, *The
Spiritual Meadow*, trans. John Wortley, Cistercian Studies Series (Kalamazoo,
Mich.: Cistercian Publications, 1992), 3.

24 E.g., *Letter* 13, PG 91.533A.

25 For the Greek *Life*, see PG 90.68–109. The Syriac *Life* has been published
with translation in Sebastian P. Brock, "An Early Syriac Life of Maximus
the Confessor," *Analecta Bollandiana* 91 (1973): 299–346. See also the helpful
discussion of these two rival biographies in Louth, *Maximus the Confessor*, 4–7.

26 Louth, *Maximus the Confessor*, 4; Wolfgang Lackner, "Zu Quellen und
Datierung der Maximosvita (BHG3 1234)," *Analecta Bollandiana* 85 (1967):
285–316.

27 This despite the fact that many scholars of Maximus, such as Larchet,
La divinisation de l'homme, 7–20 and Nichols, *Byzantine Gospel*, 15, have simply
rejected the Syriac *Life* more or less out of hand. Louth, however, raises
some legitimate concerns regarding Maximus' imperial service and
the sophistication of his learning in light of the Syriac *Life*'s account:
Louth, *Maximus the Confessor*, 6. Nevertheless, these issues have now been
persuasively addressed by Christian Boudignon, "Maxime le Confesseur
était-il constantinopolitain?, " in *Philomathestatos. Studies in Greek and Byzantine
Texts Presented to Jacques Noret for his Sixty-Fifth Birthday*, ed. B. Janssens, B.
Roosen, and P. van Deun (Leuven: Peeters, 2004), 11–43. See also Christian
Boudignon, "Le pouvoir de l'anathème ou Maxime le Confesseur et les
moines palestiniens du VIIe siècle, " in *Foundations of Power and Conflicts of
Authority in Late-Antique Monasticism. Proceedings of the International Seminar, Turin,*

December 2–4, 2004, ed. A. Camplani and G. Filoramo, Orientalia Lovaniensia Analecta 157 (Leuven: Peeters, 2007), 245–74; and I.-H. Dalmais, "La Vie de Saint Maxime le Confesseur reconsidérée, " *Studia Patristica* 17 (1982): 26–30.

28 R. Devreesse, "La fin inédite d'une lettre de saint Maxime: un baptême forcé de Juifs et de Samaritains à Carthage, en 632, " *Revue des sciences religieuses* 17 (1937): 25–35, 32–3

29 François Halkin, ed., *Bibliotheca hagiographica graeca*, 3rd ed., 3 vols. (Bruxelles: Société des Bollandistes, 1957), vol. 2, 80 (#1042). Kazhdan simply notes that the authorship is "disputed": Kazhdan, *History of Byzantine Literature (650–850)*, 65. Di Berardino identifies it as one of many works "falsely or doubtfully" ascribed to Sophronius without further explanation: Di Berardino, ed., *Patrology: The Eastern Fathers*, 305.

30 Hans Georg Beck, *Kirche und theologische Literatur im Byzantinischen Reich*, Handbuch der Altertumswissenschaft (München: C. H. Beck, 1959), 435, maintains that a predominantly anonymous transmission and stylistic differences "forbid" the attribution to Sophronius. Nevertheless, according to a more recent publication, the work is "generally attributed" to Sophronius in the manuscript tradition: Alice-Mary Talbot, ed., *Holy Women of Byzantium: Ten Saints' Lives in English Translation*, Byzantine Saints' Lives in Translation (Washington, D.C.: Dumbarton Oaks Research Library and Collection, 1996), 66.

31 Karl Krumbacher, *Geschichte der byzantinischen Litteratur von Justinian bis zum Ende des oströmischen Reiches, 527–1453*, 2nd ed., Handbuch der Klassischen Altertumswissenschaft (München: C. H. Beck, 1897), 189; Delehaye, *L'Ancienne hagiographie byzantine*, 53; Derwas J. Chitty, *The Desert a City: An Introduction to the Study of Egyptian and Palestinian Monasticism under the Christian Empire* (Oxford: Blackwell, 1966), 155. See also F. Delmas, "Remarques sur la Vie de Sainte Marie l'Égyptienne, " *Échos d'Orient* 4 (1900–1): 35–42.

32 Stephen J. Shoemaker, "A Mother's Passion: Mary's Role in the Crucifixion and Resurrection in the Earliest Life of the Virgin and its Influence on George of Nicomedia's Passion Homilies," in *The Cult of the Mother of God in Byzantium*, ed. Leslie Brubaker and Mary Cunningham (Aldershot: Ashgate, 2011), 53–67; Stephen J. Shoemaker, "The Virgin Mary in the Ministry of Jesus and the Early Church according to the Earliest *Life of the Virgin*," *Harvard Theological Review* 98 (2005): 441–67, 458–60.

33 Epiphanius the Monk, *Life of the Virgin* (PG 120.185–216). Mimouni, "Les Vies de la Vierge, " 223; Kazhdan, *History of Byzantine Literature (650–850)*, 307, 396–7.

34 Maurice Geerard, *Clavis apocryphorum Novi Testamenti*, Corpus Christianorum (Turnhout: Brepols, 1992), 71; Mimouni, "Les Vies de la Vierge," 216–23. Here and elsewhere I use the designation "the Maximus *Life of the Virgin*" not as an assertion of his authorship but instead as shorthand for "the *Life of the Virgin* attributed to Maximus the Confessor."

35 Epiphanius the Monk, *Life of the Virgin* (PG 120.185–8).

36 Stephen J. Shoemaker, "Death and the Maiden: The Early History of the Dormition and Assumption Apocrypha," *St Vladimir's Theological Quarterly* 50 (2006): 59–97, 60–6; Shoemaker, "Georgian *Life of the Virgin*," 320–1.

37 Maximus the Confessor, *Life of the Virgin* 2.

38 Concerning these pseudonymous homilies, see esp. Roberto Caro, *La Homiletica Mariana Griega en el Siglo V*, 3 vols., Marian Library Studies, New Series, 3–5 (Dayton, OH: University of Dayton, 1971–73), vol. 2, 353–9, 380–8, 452–67, 481–522, 533–67, 604–10.

39 Ps.-Dionysius, *On the Divine Names* 3.2 (Beate Regina Suchla, ed., *Corpus Dionysiacum*, 2 vols., vol. 1, *Pseudo-Dionysius Areopagite De divinis nominibus*, Patristische Texte und Studien 33 (Berlin: de Gruyter, 1990), 141); also, PG 3.681C–684A.

40 Gregory of Nyssa, *Homily on the Nativity* (Ernestus Rhein et al., eds., *Gregorii Nysseni Opera*, vol. 10.2, *Gregorii Nysseni Sermones, Pars III* (Leiden: E. J. Brill, 1996), 235–69; the quoted passage is on p. 252), cited at Maximus the Confessor, *Life of the Virgin* 2.

41 Maximus the Confessor, *Life of the Virgin* 62.

42 See esp. Shoemaker, "Georgian *Life of the Virgin*," 320–6.

43 Stephen J. Shoemaker, *Ancient Traditions of the Virgin Mary's Dormition and Assumption*, Oxford Early Christian Studies (Oxford: Oxford University Press, 2002), 46–51; Stephen J. Shoemaker, "Epiphanius of Salamis, the Kollyridians, and the Early Dormition Narratives: The Cult of the Virgin in the Later Fourth Century," *Journal of Early Christian Studies* 16 (2008): 369–99. Concerning the date, see also Stephen J. Shoemaker, "A Peculiar Version of the *Inventio crucis* in the Early Syriac Dormition Traditions," *Studia Patristica* 41 (2006): 75–81, which updates and corrects Shoemaker, *Ancient Traditions of the Virgin Mary's Dormition*, 286–7. See also Richard Bauckham, *The Fate of the Dead: Studies on Jewish and Christian Apocalypses*, Supplements to Novum Testamentum, 93 (Leiden: Brill, 1998), 358–60; van Esbroeck, "Some Earlier Features."

44 Michel van Esbroeck, «Les textes littéraires sur l'assomption avant le Xe siècle,» in *Les actes apocryphes des apôtres*, ed. François Bovon (Geneva: Labor et Fides, 1981), 265–85, 269; Simon C. Mimouni, *Dormition et Assomption de Marie: Histoire des traditions anciennes*, Théologie Historique 98 (Paris: Beauchesne, 1995), 124; Shoemaker, *Ancient Traditions of the Virgin Mary's Dormition*, 51; Shoemaker, "Death and the Maiden," 60–6; Shoemaker, "Georgian *Life of the Virgin*," 320–1. Ps.-John's dependence on the earlier Six Books narrative has been compellingly demonstrated by Maximilian Bonnet, "Die ältesten Schriften von der Himmelfahrt Mariä," *Zeitschrift für Wissenschaftliche Theologie* 23 (1880): 227–47. See also van Esbroeck, "Les textes littéraires," 269–75; Édouard Cothenet, "Marie dans les Apocryphes," in *Maria: études sur la Sainte Vierge*, ed. Hubert Du Manoir de Juaye, 7 vols., vol. 6 (Paris: Beauchesne,

1952), 71–156, 119. Regarding the liturgical usage of the Ps.-John *Transitus*, see Simon C. Mimouni, "La lecture liturgique et les apocryphes du Nouveau Testament: Le cas de la Dormitio grecque du Pseudo-Jean, " *Orientalia Christiana Periodica* 59 (1993): 403–25.

45 For more information regarding this literary tradition, see Shoemaker, *Ancient Traditions of the Virgin Mary's Dormition*, 32–46.

46 See Brian E. Daley, *On the Dormition of Mary: Early Patristic Homilies* (Crestwood, NY: St. Vladimir's Seminary Press, 1998), 14–18; Ps.-Modestus of Jerusalem, *Homily on the Dormition* (PG 86.3280B); Andrew of Crete, *Homily on the Dormition* 2 (PG 97.1060A–1064B).

47 Shoemaker, "Death and the Maiden," 60–4.

48 Daley, *On the Dormition of Mary*, 18–23. See also Kallistos Ware, "'The Earthly Heaven': St John of Damascus on the Assumption of the Theotokos," in *Mary for Earth and Heaven: Essays on Mary and Ecumenism*, ed. William McLoughlin and Jill Pinnock (Leominster, UK: Gracewing, 2002), 355–68, 362, who reaches the same judgment in regard to John's homilies. Regarding Cosmas Vestitor, see esp. Antoine Wenger, *L'Assomption de la T.S. Vierge dans la tradition byzantine du VIe au Xe siècle; études et documents*, Archives de l'Orient chrétien 5 (Paris: Institut français d'études byzantines, 1955), 155–72. Wenger maintains that Cosmas also used a copy of the earliest Greek Dormition narrative, which John of Thessalonica has revised in his homily, but this is not necessarily the case. Only one element of Cosmas' homilies appears to derive from this earliest Greek narrative, namely the existence of a book of mysteries that is given to Mary together with the palm from the Tree of Life. This is in fact a very early element of the Palm traditions not preserved in John of Thessalonica's homily as we have it today. But certain individual manuscripts of John's homily preserve very early elements from the Palm traditions that ultimately were eliminated from the larger manuscript tradition: see, e.g., Shoemaker, *Ancient Traditions of the Virgin Mary's Dormition*, 291 n. 6. It is quite possible that Cosmas somehow utilized a version of John's homily that had preserved the tradition of a book of mysteries together with the palm. Otherwise, if we suppose that Cosmas actually used a version of the earliest Greek narrative in addition to John's revision of it, as Wenger maintains, it is then difficult to explain why the earliest Greek narrative has influenced Cosmas on only this one point and nowhere else. Wenger perhaps did not consider this alternate possibility because he was concerned to demonstrate the antiquity of this early Greek narrative, which is now rather obvious in light of more recent discoveries.

49 Published in Agnes Smith Lewis, *Apocrypha Syriaca*, Studia Sinaitica 11 (London: C. J. Clay and Sons, 1902).

50 One of these manuscripts has been published in William Wright, *Contributions to the Apocryphal Literature of the New Testament* (London: Williams and Norgate, 1865) (*Protevangelium of James* and *Infancy Gospel of Thomas*); and William Wright,

"The Departure of My Lady Mary from This World," *The Journal of Sacred Literature and Biblical Record* 6–7 (1865): 417–448 and 108–160 (the Six Books). The other manuscript is an unpublished sixth-century manuscript in the Göttingen collection that I am preparing for publication.

51 Pier Franco Beatrice, "Traditions apocryphes dans la *Théosopie de Tübingen*," *Apocrypha* 7 (1996): 109–22; Pier Franco Beatrice, "Pagan Wisdom and Christian Theology According to the *Tübingen Theosophy*, " *Journal of Early Christian Studies* 3 (1994): 403–18.

52 γεννήσεως καὶ ἀναλήψεως τῆς ἀχράντου δεσποίνης ἡμῶν θεοτόκου: *Tübingen Theosophy* 4 (Hartmut Erbse, ed., *Theosophorum Graecorum Fragmenta* (Stuttgart: Teubner, 1995), 2–3).

53 Shoemaker, *Ancient Traditions of the Virgin Mary's Dormition*, 67–71.

54 Stephen J. Shoemaker, "The Cult of Fashion: The Earliest *Life of the Virgin* and Constantinople's Marian Relics," *Dumbarton Oaks Papers* 62 (2008): 53–74, esp. 66–74.

55 Ibid., esp. 61–6, 74.

56 See the discussion of this homily in Wenger, *L'Assomption*, 114–27. The text of Theodore's homily has been published in François Combefis, ed., *Historia haeresis Monothelitarum: sanctaeque in eam sextae synodi actorum vindiciae, diversorum item antiqua, ac medii aevi, tum historiae sacrae, tum dogmatica, graeca opuscula*, Graeco–Latine Patrum Bibliothecae novum auctarium 2 (Paris: Antonii Bertier, 1648), cols. 751–88. For the date of the Avar attack I follow here Averil Cameron, "The Virgin's Robe: An Episode in the History of Early Seventh-Century Constantinople," *Byzantion* 49 (1979): 42–56, esp. 43 n. 7; and Alexander Kazhdan, ed., *The Oxford Dictionary of Byzantium*, 3 vols. (New York: Oxford University Press, 1991), s. v. "Theodore Synkellos," vol. 3, 2048. Mango, however, maintains that 623 is the correct date for these raids: Cyril Mango, "The Origins of the Blachernae Shrine at Constantinople," in *Acta XIII Congressus Internationalis Archaeologicae Christianae: Split – Poreč*, ed. Nenad Cambi and Emilio Marin, 3 vols. (Vatican City: Pontificio Istituto di Archeologia Cristiana, 1998) , vol. 2, 61–76, 67–8.

57 Van Esbroeck, ed., *Maxime le Confesseur: Vie de la Vierge*, XXVII–XXVIII (Fr).

58 Shoemaker, "The Cult of Fashion," esp. 56–61.

59 Ibid., 63.

60 Shoemaker, *Ancient Traditions of the Virgin Mary's Dormition*, 78–141.

61 Ibid., 67–71; Shoemaker, "The Cult of Fashion," 63, 66–72.

62 A critical text of this excerpt from the *Euthymiac History* as preserved in John of Damascus, *Homily on the Dormition II* 18, may be found in Bonifaz Kotter, ed., *Die Schriften des Johannes von Damaskos*, 5 vols., Patristische Texte und Studien 7, 12, 17, 22, 29 (Berlin: Walter de Gruyter, 1969–88), vol. 5, 536–9. Regarding the nature of the text and its date, see Wenger, *L'Assomption*, 136–9; Michel van Esbroeck, "Un témoin indirect de l'Histoire Euthymiaque dans une

lecture arabe pour l'Assomption," *Parole de l'Orient* 6–7 (1975–6): 479–91, 480–5; Mimouni, *Dormition et Assomption*, 556–61; Shoemaker, "The Cult of Fashion," 63, 66–72.

63   Maximus the Confessor, *Life of the Virgin* 117.

64   See, e.g., Hans Urs von Balthasar, "Das Scholienwerk des Johannes von Scythopolis, " *Scholastik* 15 (1940): 16–38; Hans Urs von Balthasar, *Cosmic Liturgy: The Universe according to Maximus the Confessor*, trans. Brian E. Daley (San Francisco: Ignatius Press, 2003), 359–87; Louth, *Maximus the Confessor*, 28–32; Shoemaker, *Ancient Traditions of the Virgin Mary's Dormition*, 30; Paul Rorem and John C. Lamoreaux, *John of Scythopolis and the Dionysian Corpus: Annotating the Areopagite*, Oxford Early Christian Studies (Oxford: Clarendon Press, 1998), 199–200.

65   Shoemaker, "A Mother's Passion"; Shoemaker, "The Virgin Mary in the Ministry of Jesus," 458–60. George's Passion homilies have been published in PG 100.1457–1504.

66   Van Esbroeck, ed., *Maxime le Confesseur: Vie de la Vierge*, XIX–XXVII (Fr); Shoemaker, "Georgian *Life of the Virgin*," 313–16; Shoemaker, "The Virgin Mary in the Ministry of Jesus," 460–5. Symeon the Metaphrast's *Life of the Virgin* has been published in Basilius Latyšev, ed., *Menologii anonymi byzantini saeculi X quae supersunt*, 2 vols. (Saint Petersburg: [Akad. nauk], 1912), vol. 2, 347–83. Unfortunately, John the Geometer's *Life of the Virgin* has yet to be published in its entirety, and only its concluding section, which treats the Virgin's Dormition and the traditions of her relics, has been published by Antoine Wenger: Wenger, *L'Assomption*, 364–415. Although van Esbroeck had prepared an edition of this important text that was to appear in the Sources chrétiennes series, its whereabouts are currently unknown, and with his untimely passing, it seems unlikely that an edition will be forthcoming any time in the near future. Michel van Esbroeck himself showed me the completed edition of this text at his home in Louvain-la-Neuve in August 2003, just before his passing. He said that he wanted to compare his translation one more time with the Latin translation by Balthasar Cordier (Bibliotheca Bollandiana 196, f. 59–182v; see ibid., 187–8.) before publishing the text. Efforts to locate the edition among Fr. Michel's various computer files have proven unsuccessful. Presumably, the hard copy of his edition can be found with the rest of his papers and his library, which I understand were taken to the Bollandist library after his death.

67   Maria Vassilaki and Niki Tsironis, "Representations of the Virgin and Their Association with the Passion of Christ," in *Mother of God: Representations of the Virgin in Byzantine Art*, ed. Maria Vassilaki (Milan: Skira, 2000), 453–63, 457; Niki Tsironis, "The Lament of the Virgin Mary from Romanos the Melode to George of Nicomedia" (Ph.D. diss., University of London, 1998), 279, 292. Cf. George L. Papadeas, ed., *ΑΙ ΙΕΡΑΙ ΑΚΟΛΟΥΘΙΑΙ ΤΗΣ*

ΜΕΓΑΛΗΣ ΕΒΔΟΜΑΔΟΣ ΚΑΙ ΤΟΥ ΠΑΣΧΑ/Greek Orthodox Holy Week & Easter Services (South Daytona, Fla.: Patmos Press, 1996), pp. 231–3, 238, 257, 265–6. 293–4, 305–6, 321–2, 340–3, 377, 383, 385, 387–94. See also Shoemaker, "The Virgin Mary in the Ministry of Jesus," 465–7; Shoemaker, "Mother's Passion."

68 See esp. Shoemaker, "The Virgin Mary in the Ministry of Jesus," 444–57.

69 Maximus the Confessor, *Life of the Virgin* 92.

70 Maximus the Confessor, *Life of the Virgin* 98.

71 E.g., R. W. Southern, *The Making of the Middle Ages* (New Haven: Yale University Press, 1953), 231–40; Rachel Fulton, *From Judgment to Passion: Devotion to Christ and the Virgin Mary, 800–1200* (New York: Columbia University Press, 2002), 60–192; Caroline Walker Bynum, *Jesus as Mother: Studies in the Spirituality of the High Middle Ages* (Berkeley: University of California Press, 1982), 16–17,77–81, 85–90, 129–35; Thomas H. Bestul, *Texts of the Passion: Latin Devotional Literature and Medieval Society*, Middle Ages Series (Philadelphia: University of Pennyslvania Press, 1996); Sarah McNamer, *Affective Meditation and the Invention of Medieval Compassion* (Philadelphia: University of Pennsylvania Press, 2010). Regarding the alleged new emphasis on Mary's maternal role in the Christian East in the ninth century, see esp. Ioli Kalavrezou, "Images of the Mother: When the Virgin Mary became the *Meter Theou*," *Dumbarton Oaks Papers* 44 (1990): 165–72; and Henry Maguire, *Art and Eloquence in Byzantium* (Princeton: Princeton University Press, 1981), 91–108.

72 See, e.g., Fulton, *From Judgment to Passion*, esp. 204–43; Miri Rubin, *Mother of God: A History of the Virgin Mary* (New Haven: Yale University Press, 2009), 243–55; McNamer, *Affective Meditation*, 150–73.

73 Maximus the Confessor, *Life of the Virgin* 85.

74 In this regard, see Stephen J. Shoemaker, "Mary at the Cross, East and West: Maternal Compassion and Affective Piety in the Earliest *Life of the Virgin* and the High Middle Ages." *Journal of Theological Studies* 62 (2011): 570–606.

75 Jean Galot, "La plus ancienne affirmation de la corédemption mariale: Le témoignage de Jean le Géomètre," *Recherches de science religieuse* 45 (1957): 187–208; see also Jean Galot, *Marie, mère et corédemptrice* (Paris: Parole et Silence, 2005), 170–3.

76 Regarding Christ's sufferings as the basis of redemption in Anselm's doctrine of the atonement, see *Cur Deus Homo* I.11–15. See also R. W. Southern, *Saint Anselm: A Portrait in a Landscape* (Cambridge: Cambridge University Press, 1990), 225–7; Jaroslav Pelikan, *The Christian Tradition: A History of the Development of Doctrine*, vol. 3, *The Growth of Medieval Theology (600–1300)* (Chicago: University of Chicago Press, 1978), 139–44; Timothy Gorringe, *God's Just Vengeance: Crime, Violence, and the Rhetoric of Salvation*, Cambridge Studies in Ideology and Religion (Cambridge: Cambridge University Press, 1996), 85–108; Stephen Finlan, *Options on Atonement in Christian Thought* (Collegeville, Minn.: Liturgical

Press, 2007), 56–8. By contrast, David Bentley Hart rejects the notion (following Adolf von Harnack in particular) that Christ's suffering is redemptive in Anselm's view: David Bentley Hart, *The Beauty of the Infinite: The Aesthetics of Christian Truth* (Grand Rapids, Mich.: W. B. Eerdmans, 2003), 371. Nevertheless, as Aulén rightly notes, even if this position is expressed more explicitly by Thomas Aquinas, it certainly is present in Anselm's thought: Gustaf Aulén, *Christus Victor*, trans. A. G. Hebert (London: SPCK, 1931), 93–4. In any case, according to those Roman Catholic theologians who favor the idea of Mary's coredemption, this concept is in fact central to the Roman Catholic doctrine of redemption, which is based primarily on Anselm's idea of the atonement. Consequently, such an understanding of Christ's sufferings as the basis of redemption as derived from the thought of Anselm (and Aquinas) is fundamental to their arguments for the Virgin's coredemption: see, e.g., the references in the following note. The foreignness of this Scholastic theology of the atonement to the Greek theological tradition is the essential point here.

77 See, e.g., Galot, *Marie, mère et corédemptrice*, 147–9, 161–3; Mark I. Miravalle, *Mary: Coredemptrix, Mediatrix, Advocate* (Santa Barbara: Queenship Publishing, 1993), 12, 16, 23; William G. Most, "Mary Coredemptrix in Scripture: Cooperation in Redemption," in *Mary: Coredemptrix Mediatrix Advocate: Theological Foundations: Towards a Papal Definition?*, ed. Mark I. Miravalle (Santa Barbara: Queenship Publishing, 1995), 147–71, 157–60; Stefano Maria Manelli, F.F.I., "Mary Coredemptrix in Sacred Scripture," in *Mary: Coredemptrix, Mediatrix, Advocate: Theological Foundations II: Papal, Pneumatological, Ecumenical*, ed. Mark I. Miravalle (Santa Barbara: Queenship Publishing, 1996), 59–104, 65–8, 87, 94; Arthur Burton Calkins, "Pope John Paul II's Teaching on Marian Coredemption," in *Mary: Coredemptrix, Mediatrix, Advocate: Theological Foundations II: Papal, Pneumatological, Ecumenical*, ed. Mark I. Miravalle (Santa Barbara: Queenship Publications, 1996), 113–47, 116, 120, 122, 132; Peter Damian M. Fehlner, F.F.I., "Immaculata Mediatrix: Toward a Dogmatic Definition of the Coredemption," in *Mary: Coredemptrix, Mediatrix, Advocate: Theological Foundations II: Papal, Pneumatological, Ecumenical*, ed. Mark I. Miravalle (Santa Barbara: Queenship Publications, 1996), 259–329, 263, 265, 301–4, 319, 322, 324; Mark I. Miravalle, "Mary Coredemptrix: A Response to 7 Common Objections," in *Mary at the Foot of the Cross II: Acts of the Second International Symposium on Marian Coredemption* (New Bedford, Mass.: Academy of the Immaculate, 2002), 151–92, 167.

78 Philip Trower, "Introduction," in *Mary at the Foot of the Cross: Acts of the International Symposium on Marian Coredemption, Radcliffe College (NR, Leicester, Fosse Way, England)* (New Bedford, Mass.: Academy of the Immaculate, 2001), vii–xiii, ix.

79 Manelli, "Mary Coredemptrix in Sacred Scripture," 65.

80 See, e.g., Vladimir Lossky, "Redemption and Deification," in *In the Image and Likeness of God* (Crestwood, NY: St. Vladimir's Seminary Press, 1985), 97–110, perhaps the single best discussion of Anselm's relation to Greek Patristic thought on this topic. I do not find persuasive David Bentley Hart's attempt to "rehabilitate" Anselm from an Orthodox perspective, although in any case, he argues that Anselm's theory of atonement is widely misunderstood and that in fact Anselm actually restates the position articulated by the Greek Fathers rather than offering a radical new perspective on atonement: see Hart, *Beauty of the Infinite*, 360–72, which is essentially a reprint of David Bentley Hart, "A Gift Exceeding Every Debt: An Eastern Orthodox Appreciation of Anselm's *Cur Deus Homo*," *Pro Ecclesia* 7.3 (1998): 333–48. According to Hart, both the western and eastern theological traditions have as a whole completely misread Anselm, and while his interpretation is refreshing, it does not convince. I find his "renarration" of Anselm's argument problematic, and his assurance that the notion of recapitulation and the importance of the Resurrection are so implicit that they do not need to be voiced is somewhat questionable. Likewise, his reflections on Anselm's concept of God's "honor" are not as contextualized or convincing as are Southern's or Gorringe's (among others).

81 Galot, "La plus ancienne affirmation de la corédemption," 207; Sandro Sticca, *The Planctus Mariae in the Dramatic Tradition of the Middle Ages*, trans. Joseph R. Berrigan (Athens: University of Georgia Press, 1988), 22. See also Peter Damian M. Fehlner, F.F.I., "Opening Address," in *Mary at the Foot of the Cross VIII: Coredemption as Key to a Correct Understanding of Redemption* (New Bedford, Mass.: Academy of the Immaculate, 2008), 1–10, 3, which underscores that Anselm's logic of the atonement is essential to the notion of Marian coredemption.

82 See George S. Gabriel, *Mary: The Untrodden Portal of God*, 2nd rev. ed. (Ridgewood, NJ: Zephyr, 2005), esp. 72–3, where Augustine's doctrine of original sin is also identified (along with Anselm's doctrine of the atonement) as perhaps the more profound complication from an Orthodox point of view.

83 Maximus the Confessor, *Life of the Virgin* 78. There are admittedly other instances where she clearly expects the Resurrection, which makes this passage all the more peculiar. But see also §92, which seems to suggest that it was only after the Resurrection had occurred that she "believed in all the mysteries of his divine economy," and particularly in the Resurrection itself.

84 See, e.g., Bertrand de Margerie, S.J., "The Knowledge of Mary and the Sacrifice of Jesus," in *Mary at the Foot of the Cross: Acts of the International Symposium on Marian Coredemption, Radcliffe College (NR, Leicester, Fosse Way, England)* (New Bedford, Mass.: Academy of the Immaculate, 2000), 31–40; Calkins, "Pope John Paul II's Teaching," 138–9; Fehlner, "Immaculata Mediatrix," 304, 324; Galot, *Marie, mère et corédemptrice*, 168–9.

85 H. E. W. Turner, *The Patristic Doctrine of Redemption: A Study of the Development of Doctrine During the First Five Centuries* (London: Mowbray, 1952), 20–1.

86 For instance, Athanasius in one passage maintains that since death was imposed as a consequence of sin, it was necessary that either humanity or Christ should die: *On the Incarnation,* 7–9. There is, however, no sense here of Anselm's juridical concept of a debt to God that could only be satisfied by God's own ultimate sacrifice; instead, the Son's assumption of mortality through the Incarnation, which remains the primary principle, is the means by which sin and death are undone. Much more importantly, however, as Lossky notes, Athanasius differs markedly from Anselm and the later western tradition in his reliance on a wide range of metaphors for describing the process of salvation, focusing especially on the theme of the triumph of life over death, as opposed to Anselm's narrow reading through the images of sacrifice and redemption: Lossky, "Redemption and Deification," 99–100.

87 See, e.g., John Meyendorff, *Byzantine Theology: Historical Trends and Doctrinal Themes,* 2nd ed. (New York: Fordham University Press, 1979), 160–2; Lossky, "Redemption and Deification"; John S. Romanides, *The Ancestral Sin,* trans. George S. Gabriel (Ridgewood, N.J.: Zephyr, 1998), esp. 17–28; Peter Bouteneff, "Christ and Salvation," in *The Cambridge Companion to Orthodox Christian Theology,* ed. Mary B. Cunningham and Elizabeth Theokritoff (Cambridge: Cambridge University Press, 2008), 93–106; Vladimir Lossky, *Orthodox Theology: An Introduction* (Crestwood, NY: St. Vladimir's Seminary Press, 1978), 110–15. See also Aulén, *Christus Victor,* 16–47; Turner, *Patristic Doctrine of Redemption,* 70–95; Jaroslav Pelikan, *The Christian Tradition: A History of the Development of Doctrine,* vol. 2, *The Spirit of Eastern Christendom (600–1700)* (Chicago: University of Chicago Press, 1974), 137–9; Antony Khrapovitski, *The Dogma of Redemption* (Montreal: Monastery Press, 1979); and Kallistos Ware, *How Are We Saved?: The Understanding of Salvation in the Orthodox Tradition* (Minneapolis: Light & Life Publishing, 1996).

88 See, e.g., Southern, *Making of the Middle Ages,* 234–6; Southern, *Saint Anselm,* 207–11.

89 Gregory of Nyssa, *Catechetical Oration* 22–4; Gregory of Nazianzus, *Homily 45 (Second Homily on Easter)* 22; cf. Bouteneff, "Christ and Salvation," 98; Romanides, *Ancestral Sin,* 100–1.

90 As, e.g., in Maximus the Confessor, *Life of the Virgin* 129.

91 See, e.g., Aulén, *Christus Victor,* 47–55; Turner, *Patristic Doctrine of Redemption,* 61, 94–5; Lossky, "Redemption and Deification," esp. 100.

92 In addition to the passages cited below, see also Maximus the Confessor, *Life of the Virgin* 20, 26, 27, 51, 94, 129.

93 Maximus the Confessor, *Life of the Virgin* 25.

94 Maximus the Confessor, *Life of the Virgin* 28.

95 Maximus the Confessor, *Life of the Virgin* 34.

96 Maximus the Confessor, *Life of the Virgin* 15.

97 E.g., Romanos the Melode's sixth-century hymn on "Mary at the Cross": José Grosdidier de Matons, ed., *Romanos le Mélode: Hymnes*, 5 vols., Sources chrétiennes 99, 110, 114, 128, 283 (Paris: Éditions du Cerf, 1964), vol. 4, 143–87. Also a Syriac lament from the West Syrian liturgy for Holy Saturday dating to the fifth or sixth century: *Breviarium juxta ritum Ecclesiae Antiochenae Syrorum*, 7 vols. (Mosul: Typ. Fratrum Praedicatorum, 1892), vol. 5, 276–7; trans. Sebastian P. Brock, *Bride of Light: Hymns on Mary from the Syriac Churches* (Kottayam: St. Ephrem Ecumenical Research Institute (SEERI), 1994), 108–10. Finally, a brief passage in Jacob of Serug's *Homily on the Dormition*: Paul Bedjan, ed., *S. Martyrii, qui et Sahdona, quae supersunt omnia* (Leipzig: Otto Harrassowitz, 1902), 710–11; trans. Shoemaker, *Ancient Traditions of the Virgin Mary's Dormition*, 409.

98 Maximus the Confessor, *Life of the Virgin* 97, 99.

99 Maximus the Confessor, *Life of the Virgin* 74, 128.

100 Maximus the Confessor, *Life of the Virgin* 117.

101 See, e.g., Maximus the Confessor, *Life of the Virgin* 5.

102 Maximus the Confessor, *Life of the Virgin* 132.

103 Maximus the Confessor, *Life of the Virgin* 109.

104 Maximus the Confessor, *Life of the Virgin* 5, 12, 15.

105 Maximus the Confessor, *Life of the Virgin* 115, 125.

106 E.g., Heb 10.12. See also Lossky, "Redemption and Deification," 99–102; Bouteneff, "Christ and Salvation," 98.

107 Aulén, *Christus Victor*, 16–80, and esp. 8–9, 57–8; Finlan, *Options on Atonement*, 18–52; Lossky, "Redemption and Deification," 99–103; Bouteneff, "Christ and Salvation," 96–9; Turner, *Patristic Doctrine of Redemption*, 47–95; Ware, *How Are We Saved?*, 48–9.

108 Note that while H. E. W. Turner finds evidence of early Church Fathers who focused on the redemptive value of Christ's suffering, in each case these are western Church Fathers: Tertullian, Cyprian, Ambrose, and Augustine. There is no clear evidence of such a focus in the writings of the Greek Fathers. See Turner, *Patristic Doctrine of Redemption*, 100–11. The same is also true of Manfred Hauke, "The Concept of Redemption in the Patristic Tradition," in *Mary at the Foot of the Cross VIII: Coredemption as Key to a Correct Understanding of Redemption* (New Bedford, Mass.: Academy of the Immaculate, 2008), 79–109.

109 Bouteneff, "Christ and Salvation," 98

110 Aulén, *Christus Victor*, 28–35, 41–7; Turner, *Patristic Doctrine of Redemption*, 20–1; Lossky, "Redemption and Deification," 102–3; Ware, *How Are We Saved?*, 48–9.

111 Maximus the Confessor, *Life of the Virgin* 73.

112 Trower, "Introduction," viii; Manelli, "Mary Coredemptrix in Sacred Scripture," 66–9. See also Galot, *Marie, mère et corédemptrice*, 156.

113 Manelli, "Mary Coredemptrix in Sacred Scripture," 68. See also Galot, *Marie, mère et corédemptrice*, 156.

114 Galot, *Marie, mère et corédemptrice*, 161–2.

115 René Laurentin, *Le titre de corédemptrice* (Rome and Paris: Éditions Marianum and Nouvelles éditions latines, 1951), 12–16; cf. Galot, *Marie, mère et corédemptrice*, 145–9.

116 Miravalle, *Mary: Coredemptrix, Mediatrix, Advocate*, 29, emphasis in the original.

117 In addition to the quotation above, see also, e.g., ibid., xvi, 55–6; Arthur Burton Calkins, "The Proposed Marian Dogma: The 'What' and the 'Why'," in *Contemporary Insights on a Fifth Marian Dogma: Mary Coredemptrix, Mediatrix, Advocate, Theological Foundations III*, ed. Mark I. Miravalle (Santa Barbara: Queenship Publishing, 2000), 15–38, 20–31.

118 Mark I. Miravalle, "The Whole Truth About Mary, Ecumenism, and the Year 2000," in *Mary: Coredemptrix, Mediatrix, Advocate: Theological Foundations II: Papal, Pneumatological, Ecumenical*, ed. Mark I. Miravalle (Santa Barbara: Queenship Publishing, 1996), 3–55, 41–2; Manelli, "Mary Coredemptrix in Sacred Scripture," 68.

119 See Miravalle, *Mary: Coredemptrix, Mediatrix, Advocate*, 36–7; Gabriel, *Mary*, 157–68. It is thus surprising to find Gabriel seeming to endorse an idea of Mary as *Mediatrix* from an Eastern Orthodox perspective. One of Gabriel's texts is admittedly especially intriguing: a Theotokarion attributed to Andrew of Crete which states that Mary "receives the fullness of the gifts of God, transporting them to all, to angels and to men." Nevertheless, the translation from Ps.-Modestus of Jerusalem in this book is inaccurate. Cf. Ps.-Modestus of Jerusalem, *Homily on the Dormition* 10 (PG 86.3288).

120 Even in the following passage (discussed already above), which perhaps comes closest to the idea of Mary as *Mediatrix*, it is entirely clear that her role as mediator is connected with her intercession: "Now a second mediator goes forth to the first mediator, a devout human being to the incarnate God, a second offering of our nature to the Father after the first one who was himself sacrificed one time on behalf of all, and she is ever living to intercede on behalf of those who approach God through her." Maximus the Confessor, *Life of the Virgin* 128. The same is also true of Mary's role at the wedding at Cana, where the *Life* says that "the mediator of all good things was a mediator of this miracle also." Maximus the Confessor, *Life of the Virgin* 68. Here again Mary's role as mediator is determined by her intercessions with her son that he do something for the bride and groom about the lack of wine, rather than "*distributing to the People of God* the 'gifts of eternal salvation' obtained from the cross."

121 See, e.g., the reasoning expressed in Fehlner, "Immaculata Mediatrix," 314–15.

122 E.g., Tsironis, "Lament of the Virgin Mary"; Niki Tsironis, "George of Nicomedia: Convention and Originality in the Homily on Good Friday," *Studia Patristica* 33 (1997): 573–77; Niki Tsironis, "Historicity and Poetry in Ninth–Century Homiletics: The Homilies of Patriarch Photius and George

of Nicomedia," in *Preacher and Audience: Studies in Early Christian and Byzantine Homiletics*, ed. Mary B. Cunningham and Pauline Allen, A New History of the Sermon 1 (Leiden: Brill, 1998), 295–316; Vassilaki and Tsironis, "Representations of the Virgin"; Niki Tsironis, "From Poetry to Liturgy: The Cult of the Virgin in the Middle Byzantine Period," in *Images of the Mother of God: Perceptions of the Theotokos in Byzantium*, ed. Maria Vassilaki (Aldershot: Ashgate, 2005), 91–102; Maguire, *Art and Eloquence in Byzantium*, 91–108; Margaret Alexiou, "The Lament of the Virgin in Byzantine Literature and Modern Greek Folk Song," *Byzantine and Modern Greek Studies* 1 (1975): 111–40. See also Kalavrezou, "Images of the Mother, " esp. 169–70; Bertrand Bouvier, *Le mirologue de la Vierge: Chansons et poèmes grecs sur la Passion du Christ*, Bibliotheca Helvetica Romana 16 (Rome: Institut suisse de Rome, 1976).

CHAPTER ONE

BIRTH AND CHILDHOOD

1. The chapter titles in this work are taken from the text itself, with the exception only of this first one, which I have added here for consistency.

2. Jerusalem 148 has დიდებულ, which parallels more closely the biblical text. Jerusalem 108 is illegible and Sinai 68 does not begin until the middle of section 6.

3. Following Jerusalem 148, which reads here ლელსა; the form in the edition, ლელესა, which determines van Esbroeck's awkward translation (la tige non fécondée), is presumably a misprint.

4. Jerusalem 148 has აღმოცენა, which is a better reading. The form in the edition, აღმოთაცენა, does not make much sense and is presumably a misprint.

5. This oblique use of გუწადის for ἐπιθυμοῦμεν is paralleled in the translation of Hippolytus of Rome's *De Antichristo* 3: see Gérard Garitte, ed., *Traités d'Hippolyte sur David et Goliath, sur le Cantique des cantiques et sur l'Antéchrist*, Corpus Scriptorum Christianorum Orientalium 263–264, Scriptores Iberici 15–16 (Louvain: Sécretariat du CorpusSCO, 1965), 75 (Geor) and 56 (Lat); cf. G. Nathanael Bonwetsch et al., eds., *Hippolytus Werke*, 4 vols., Die griechischen christlichen Schriftsteller der ersten drei Jahrhunderte 1, 26, 36, 46 (Leipzig,: J. C. Hinrichs, 1897), vol. 1.2, 6.

6. This translation of მეწირს is determined by its use particularly in Lev 6.30, 19.6, 19.21, 22.23, 22.25, 22.27. See also Davit' Č'ubinovi, *Gruzinsko-russko-frantsuzskiĭ slovar'* (*Dictionnaire géorgien–russe–français*) (Saint Petersburg: V tipografii Imperatorskoĭ Akademīi nauk, 1840), 577a.

7. Gregory of Nyssa, *Homily on the Nativity* (Rhein et al., eds., *Gregorii Nysseni Opera*, vol. 10.2, 252).

8 მოგეცენ is a misprint for მოგეცეს.

9 As van Esbroeck explains, Mary was interpreted as a hiphael participle from אור: i.e., מאירה. So one finds, for instance, in Eusebius of Caesarea, *Onomastica Sacra* (Paul de Lagarde, ed., *Onomastica sacra* (Gottingae: prostat in aedibus A. Rente, 1870), 175).

10 Following here the reading from Jerusalem 108, which seems preferable. Tbilisi A-40 reads "imitators" instead of "friends."

11 ორმეოცამეხუთესა in the apparatus is a misprint: Jerusalem 108 reads ორმეოცამეოთხესა, which seems to be the better reading: it is hard to imagine that this Greek author would have followed the Hebrew numbering of the Psalms rather than the Septuagint.

12 ორქერძოვე is a misprint for ორკერძოვე.

13 Van Esbroeck translates this word as "descente," but this does not seem to be a possibility.

14 Literally the "Entrance into the Temple," as this event is known in the Eastern Christian tradition (εἴσοδος). Nevertheless, "Presentation in the Temple" is perhaps more familiar terminology for this event in English.

15 There is slight variation in the manuscript tradition here. In addition to the text from Tbilisi A-40 that appears in van Esbroeck's edition, Jerusalem 108 reads: ვითარ შუენიერ იყო და ფრიად მრავალფერ სამოსლითა ოქროქსოვილითა შემკულ არსო; and Sinai 68 reads: ვითარ შუენიერ იყო ფრიად და მრავალფერ სამოსლითა ოქროქსოვილითა შემკულ არს. My translation reflects a reconstruction of the text based on the two latter witnesses.

16 Both Jerusalem 108 and Sinai 68 have პირად პირადად instead of პირადად, which appears in van Esbroeck's edition: based also on comparison with the biblical text, one would imagine that the initial პირად fell out either in transmission or in preparing the edition. The word მრავალფერ, translated above as "of many colors", is not used in the Old Georgian versions of the Psalms (although this word too very often means simply "diverse" or "diversely"). Instead, one finds in this verse the expression პირად პირადად შუენიერი, which literally means "with diverse adornment." Obviously this is an effort to translate the range of meaning conveyed by the Septuagint's "πεποικιλμένη." Although one might translate the words as "many-colored," as one usually finds in English translations of this verse, the text's author has organized his reflections here around the theme of adornment, thus necessitating the literalism above.

17 Van Esbroeck's translation of პატივითა as "avec respect à l'intérieur" is puzzling.

18 და is a misprint for სადა.

19 Ps 44.14–15 in Georgian. ფესუედითა ოქროვანითა ("with golden tassels") is a fairly literal translation of ἐν κροσσωτοῖς χρυσοῖς from

the Septuagint. Also, here again we find the words პირად პირადაღ, the standard Georgian translation of περιβεβλημένη πεποικιλμένη, encountered already above with respect to Ps 44.10 (although here without შუენიერი). In this instance, however, I have translated "in many colors" instead of "diversely" in order to better reflect the traditional English translation of this biblical verse.

20 The word here is obscure: ფესოან. While the form is clear in Jerusalem 108, Sinai 68 omits a significant portion of this passage, including this word, quite possibly because a copyist found difficulties with some of the language. Van Esbroeck translates "le couleur," which certainly is a possibility. One finds in Georgian the more regular forms ფეროა, ფერო[ვ]ანი, and ფესანგი, all of which mean "colored," and this could be a related term. Nevertheless, in light of the immediate context, which equates Mary's numerous virtues with the tassels, it seems more likely that this word is somehow related to either ფესუ, which means "fringe," ფესუეანი, "fringed," or ფესუედი, the word for a "fringed garment." In either case, the rhetorical point is clear.

21 The phrase "ladder of her wonders" (კიბესა საკჳრველებათა) is peculiar; nevertheless, it appears in both Tbilisi A-40 and Sinai 68. Jerusalem 108 has instead "ladder of her virtues" (კიბესა სათნოებათასა), which is perhaps a correction.

22 უახლესი should instead read უახლესი, the form clearly attested in Sinai 68. Jerusalem 108 is illegible at this point.

23 პასავითა is a misprint for პასაკითა.

24 მომღურებისა is a misprint for მომღურებისა.

25 გულისხისყოფითა is a misprint for გულისხმისყოფითა.

26 Here we follow the reading of Jerusalem 108, ყოველთა. Tbilisi A-40 and Sinai 68 both read სიტყუათა instead. In his edition, van Esbroeck mistakenly has left სიტყუათა in the text, while at the same time signaling სიტყუათა as a variant reading from Tbilisi A-40 in the apparatus. Nevertheless, in his translation he gives here "de tous," reflecting the reading of Jerusalem 108.

27 This is a difficult passage, although van Esbroeck's restoration does not seem necessary. Sinai 68 has shortened this passage considerably, perhaps because of its difficulties.

28 იქცოდა და ტამარსა should read იქცეოდა ტამარსა.

29 Lit., "speaking well."

30 Both Jerusalem 108 and Sinai 68 have მთაღ here, which seems to have been omitted from van Esbroeck's edition.

31 სიწმისაღ should read სიწმიდისაღ.

32 Note that at this point in the text the items to which Mary is compared suddenly shift their case from terminal to (first) nominative.

33 This reading from Jerusalem 108, განრჩუნზილი (which the edition misprints as განძრჩუნზილი), seems correct and is confirmed by Sinai 68.

34 Instead of რაჲ both Jerusalem 108 and Sinai 68 have რაჲმე, which is the better reading.

35 იყვნნეს should read იყვნეს, as in Jerusalem 108 and Sinai 68.

36 აღგრძნას is a misprint for აგრძნას.

37 იქნების is a misprint for იქმნების.

38 Van Esbroeck translates თჳსეყვნეს as "proposaient," as he does above where the same verb is used to describe Zechariah's relationship with the Virgin. The lexica do not support such a rendering, however. It would appear that the text refers here to the tradition that the prospective guardians came from the tribe of Judah and the household of David. See also the *Gospel of Ps.-Matthew* 8, the *Book of the Nativity of Mary* 8, and Abraham Terian, *The Armenian Gospel of the Infancy: With Three Early Versions of the Protevangelium of James* (Oxford: Oxford University Press, 2008), 17

39 The reading from Jerusalem 108 and Sinai 68, მაშინდელთა, is superior to that of Tbilisi A-40.

40 იწამებოდეს is a misprint for ეწამებოდეს.

41 მეუთხრობელთა should read მიუთხრობელთა.

42 That is, his type in the Hebrew Scriptures, Joseph the son of Jacob.

CHAPTER TWO

THE ANNUNCIATION

1 Here we follow Jerusalem 108, whose superior reading is confirmed by Sinai 68.

2 Reading ზეციით from Jerusalem 108 and Sinai 68 instead of ზეცის, which is presumably a misprint.

3 Jerusalem 108 and Sinai 68 have the more standard form of this verb: შეიწყნარეს.

4 Both Jerusalem 108 and Sinai 68 read here მალლისაჲ, following the biblical citation, as opposed to დლიერისაჲ, which appears in van Esbroeck's edition.

5 მეიმოსნეს is a misprint for შეიმოსნეს.

6 Sinai 68 reads here სხეულნი instead of ხილულნი ("visible"), which seems to correspond better with the preceding indication of incorporeality.

7 საკვველისა is a misprint for საკჳრველისა.

8 განიცადდეს is seemingly a misprint for განიცადეთ, which is the form in both Jerusalem 108 and Sinai 68. The second person plural of the imperative here signals the end of the angel's discourse and a shift to the author's direct address to the audience.

9   Both Jerusalem 108 and Sinai 68 have here the preferred form ესმა; perhaps ისმა in the edition is a typo.

10 წინაასწარმეტყუელმან is a misprint for წინაასწარმეტყუელმან.

11 Van Esbroeck's translation, "qu'il était semence," seems to miss the sense of უთესლო.

12 გამობრდელი is presumably a misprint for გამომბრდელი.

13 Van Esbroeck's edition has here ადამალლონ, which is presumably a misprint (although it is the form that he translates). Both Jerusalem 108 and Sinai 68 have here ადამალლო, which corresponds with the form in the Psalm that is being cited.

14 This citation does not reflect exactly either the LXX or the Georgian version of this Psalm, although it is fairly close to the latter.

15 Van Esbroeck's translation here, "nous a assigné le paradis pour héritage," is a bit peculiar.

16 Apparently the word სიტყუანი was inadvertently omitted from the edition at this point. It is present in both Jerusalem 108 and Sinai 68 and is also signaled in van Esbroeck's translation ("paroles").

17 Van Esbroeck's punctuation confuses this passage somewhat, as is reflected in his translation.

18 განკაცებაჲ is presumably a misprint for განკაცებაღ, the form found in both Jerusalem 108 and Sinai 68.

19 შემუსრნნა should read შემუსრნა, as in Jerusalem 108 and Sinai 68.

20 Although slightly different from the Greek, the passage matches the Georgian version precisely.

21 As van Esbroeck explains, this etymology of the name Israel involves a play on words, substituting אֱנוֹשׁ (νοῦς) for אִישׁ (ἄνθρωπος), according to the etymology אִישׁ רָֽא־אֵל. Such an interpretation can be found, as van Esbroeck notes, in Eusebius of Caesarea, *Onomastica Sacra* (de Lagarde, *Onomastica sacra*, 170).

22 The edition is corrupted by a dittography here: instead of განკაცებულსა, და მის მიერ განკაცებულსა და მის მიერ, the text should simply read განკაცებულსა, და მის მიერ, as witnessed in Jerusalem 108 and also as reflected in van Esbroeck's translation. Note that Sinai 68 is missing a folio at this point.

CHAPTER THREE
THE NATIVITY

1   შემოუქუმელისა is a misprint for გამოუთქუმელისა, which is the form in both Jerusalem 108 and Sinai 68.

2   Following the reading of Jerusalem 108 and Sinai 68.

3 Following the reading of Jerusalem 108 and Sinai 68, which have და დაიმწყსნეს (not და დაიმწყნეს, as van Esbroeck indicates)

4 შეიმოსრნეს should read შეიმუსრნეს.

5 Van Esbroeck misunderstands Joseph as the subject here.

6 Following the reading of Jerusalem 108 and Sinai 68.

7 Reading დიდებაძ instead of დადებაძ; Jerusalem 108 and Sinai 68 both have here only the abbreviation დბძ. Also, van Esbroeck's punctuation here is confusing: ". . . ფერჴნი მისნი დ[ი]დებაძ. აურაცხელსა მას ს[ი]მდაბლესა მისსა ვინძე იტყოდის. . . ." The biblical verse being cited ends with ფერჴნი მისნი, and in both Jerusalem 108 and Sinai 68 there is punctuation following მისნი. Likewise, in his translation van Esbroeck understands აურაცხელსა მას ს[ი]მდაბლესა მისსა as the direct object of ვინძე იტყოდის, further understanding ძლიერებათა უფლისათა as a genitive dependent on ს[ი]მდაბლესა. In this case, however, the მისსა following ს[ი]მდაბლესა does not make sense, and the position of ვინძე იტყოდის also is quite unusual. It would seem that the emended text should instead be punctuated as follows: . . . ფერჴნი მისნი. დიდებაძ აურაცხელსა მას სიმდაბლესა მისსა. ვინძე იტყოდის. . . .

8 სამდაბლესა is a misprint for სიმდაბლესა.

9 სისმენელი is a misprint for სასმენელი.

10 Following the reading of Jerusalem 108 and Sinai 68.

11 შუვაკედილი is a misprint for შუვაკედელი.

12 This passage is more commonly interpreted as a symbol of the Annunciation and conception.

13 იერუსალემ ამდე seems to be a misprint. Jerusalem 108 has იერუსალემად მდე, and Sinai 68 reads იერუსალემად.

14 ძიძასწავებელნი is a misprint for მომასწავებელნი.

15 Van Esbroeck misinterprets პურიათა as a genitive dependent on უფლისაძ, but the only way to make sense of the sentence is to understand the form as a dative, indicating the persuasion of "the Jews" by the Magi and the star.

16 გამოუჩინებითა is a misprint for გამოჩინებითა.

17 შეიწირეს is probably a misprint for შეწირეს, the form in both Jerusalem 108 and Sinai 68.

18 Van Esbroeck's translation, "si jamais tu es dans la pauvreté," is rather peculiar.

19 Following the reading from Jerusalem 108 and Sinai 68: კნინდენ მეორისა წლისა, which corrects van Esbroeck's reading as well as his word division.

20 Following Sinai 68 in reading ჟამისა ყოფილთა საქმეთა. Jerusalem 108 is illegible here.

21 Following the reading of Jerusalem 108 and Sinai 68.

22 Following the reading of Jerusalem 108 and Sinai 68.

23 The reading of Jerusalem 108 and Sinai 68 is superior here: უდარესნი (which corrects a typo in van Esbroeck's edition).

24 Both Jerusalem 108 and Sinai 68 have here ერი instead of ერთ, which is presumably a misprint.

25 Both Jerusalem 108 and Sinai 68 read ცუდ და ცრუ; perhaps the omission of და from the edition is a typo.

26 Following Jerusalem 108 and Sinai 68, which read here გამოეჭჳ; perhaps the form in the edition is a typo.

27 Cf. the account of Herod's horrible death in Josephus, *Antiquities of the Jews* 17.5 and *The Jewish Wars* 1.33.5.

28 საფლოვისი is a misprint for საფლოვისა.

29 The edition omits here თჳს, which appears in both Jerusalem 108 and Sinai 68 and is also reflected in van Esbroeck's translation.

30 Sinai 68 has the standard form of this verb: განწმიდნა. The form in Jerusalem 108 is the same as in the edition.

31 წინასრბოლ is a misprint for წინამსრბოლ.

CHAPTER FOUR

THE PRESENTATION IN THE TEMPLE

1 This sentence is ambiguous: it could also mean "that this is purifying and that the same thing is purified," or "that she is purifying and also is purified (or pure)."

2 Jerusalem 108 and Sinai 68 have ურჩულოებით instead of ურჩულოებასა, which is the form in the edition as well as the biblical text.

3 In this last sentence van Esbroeck seems to miss the pluperfect tense, and thus the passive voice, of the first two verbs, which is crucial to the sense of the passage: the subject and object should in fact be reversed for translation. Also, Tbilisi A-40 reads here instead at the end "not only the first-born child will be holy before the Lord." Nevertheless, this variant is most likely a corruption introduced from the beginning of the following sentence. By contrast, Sinai 68 follows the quotation from the Psalms immediately with the statement "that it is not the case that every first-born child will be holy before the Lord" (i.e., the same text as Jerusalem 108), omitting the more complicated section in between.

4 The reference is not entirely clear, although van Esbroeck suggests the possibility of Isa 6.3.

5 განუდებულ should read განუდებელ, as in Jerusalem 108 and Sinai 68.

6 The use of "Joseph" instead of "his father" is characteristic of the Byzantine text.

7 Following the reading of Jerusalem 108 and Sinai 68.

8 Following the reading of Jerusalem 108 and Sinai 68.

9 ბოროტისმეტუელთა is a misprint for ბოროტისმეტყუელთა.

10 Following here the reading of Jerusalem 108 and Sinai 68, which seems superior.

11 According to early apocryphal traditions, seemingly from the later fourth century, John's mother died when he was still young, and he grew up alone in the desert where his mother had brought him. Here the *Life of the Virgin* seemingly alludes to these traditions concerning John's life in the desert as a child and a young man before he began his ministry. See Serapion of Thmuis, *Life of John the Baptist* (Alphonse Mingana, *Woodbrooke Studies: Christian Documents in Syriac, Arabic, and Garshuni*, 4 vols. (Cambridge: W. Heffer & Sons, 1927–34), vol. 1, 138–287, esp. 242–5).

12 და დამომპოვნებელი is probably the result of a reduplication and should instead read და მომპოვნებელი.

13 აღაარებდეს is a misprint for აღიარებდეს.

14 Van Esbroeck suggests that actually Isaiah should be understood here rather than Jeremiah, although he does suggest Jer 25.15–16 as a possible reference, but this is not clear. Instead, he concludes that Isa 19.20–21 is most likely the passage intended. Nevertheless, Jer 22.26 seems a more likely possibility, particularly since the passage from Isaiah makes no reference to the mother: "I will hurl you and the mother who bore you into another country, where you were not born . . ." (Jer 22.26, NRSV). In a note following the index to his translation, van Esbroeck suggests instead that the reference is to a passage from the "Life of Jeremiah" in the recension of *The Lives of the Prophets* attributed to Dorotheus, which is also a possibility: van Esbroeck, *Maxime le Confesseur: Vie de la Vierge*, 140 (Fr). The passage in question refers to the collapse of the idols of Egypt "through a savior, a child born of a virgin, in a manger. Wherefore even to this day they revere a virgin giving birth and, placing an infant in a manger, they worship." *The Lives of the Prophets* 2.8–9 (Theodor Schermann, *Prophetarum vitae fabulosae* (Lipsiae: in aedibus B. G. Teubneri, 1907), 45, lines 6–10; trans. James H. Charlesworth, ed., *The Old Testament Pseudepigrapha*, 2 vols. (Garden City, N.Y.: Doubleday, 1983), vol. 2, 387).

15 გვსწავეს should read გვსწავიეს.

16 წარგინებად is a misprint for წარდგინებად.

17 Literally "the soul," as in Matt 2.20.

18 მიჟხნისა is a misprint for სიმჟნისა, the form in both Jerusalem 108 and Sinai 68.

19 ქადაგებეს should read ქადაგებდეს.

20 The author mistakenly assumes that Pilate was governor of Judea at the same time when Archelaus was ruling. But Archelaus' rule ended in 6 CE, whereas Pilate's began in 26 CE. The first Roman governor of Judea, Coponius, only came into power in 6 CE. Van Esbroeck suggests that perhaps this mistake is the result of a misreading of Luke 2.2., but it is hard to see how that would be the source. Presumably, the author has somehow confused Herod Archelaus with his brother Herod Antipas, who was ruling when Pilate was governor. Although the author below identifies "the son of the other Herod" as the one who according to tradition was involved with Pilate in the trial of Jesus, the similarity of these two brothers' names no doubt contributed to such confusion.

21 Following the reading here of Jerusalem 108 and Sinai 68, which corresponds more closely with the biblical text.

22 The text has actually confused Hyrcanus II and Aristobulus II here, mistakenly identifying Hyrcanus II as the seditious younger brother of Aristobulus II. I have corrected the text accordingly in the translation.

23 Aristobulus successfully led an insurrection against his brother, only to be deposed when the Romans assumed control of Palestine in 63 BCE. Pompey preferred Hyrcanus and reappointed him as high priest and "ethnarch" (rather than king) but as a subordinate to the Roman authorities without any real political power.

24 Here again, Archelaus has apparently been confused with Antipas, as noted above. Antipas is nevertheless distinguished here as "the son of the other Herod," presumably Herod the Great, and also as "Herod the tetrarch": these refer to the same individual.

25 Van Esbroeck mistakenly identifies Luke 2.52 as the reference.

26 Van Esbroeck translates "more perfect and more constant" instead as "d'inachevé et de non affermi." While this also makes some sense here, at least as van Esbroeck interprets the sentence, it would require reading უსრულე and უმტკიცო instead of უსრულეს and უმტკიცეს, which are the forms in the MSS. Also, the genitive forms that follow would be rather curious.

27 Following here the reading of Jerusalem 108 and Sinai 68, პირმეტყუელებისა. Van Esbroeck's indication of Jerusalem 108's reading is a misprint.

28 ვქორინები should read ვროჩინები, as in Jerusalem 108 and Sinai 68 (and the Old Georgian gospels).

29 I.e., *The Infancy Gospel of Thomas*, which in Greek originally had the title Παιδικὰ τοῦ κυρίου ἡμῶν Ἰησοῦ Χριστοῦ.

30 Both Jerusalem 108 and Sinai 68 have here და მაღლითა, which perhaps has fallen out of the Tbilisi manuscript.

31 Following here the reading of Jerusalem 108 and Sinai 68.

32 Both Jerusalem 108 and Sinai 68 have here არამედ, which does not appear
    in van Esbroeck's edition but is indicated in the translation. One would
    imagine that the word also was present in the Tbilisi manuscript but was
    accidentally omitted from the edition.
33 The edition should read here ქამსა განცხადებულად.

CHAPTER FIVE
THE REVELATION (OR THE EPIPHANY)

1   Van Esbroeck's translation seems to miss the sense here: "Tels sont les grands
    mystères que criait le célèbre témoin."
2   The form იესუებსსა, dative singular of the adjective form of Jesus' name,
    is a little unusual here, but the sense seems to be that these two disciples
    switched from being disciples of John to join with Jesus' followers.
3   Van Esbroeck translates სამოსლისა შეცვალებულისა as "vêtement
    de fortune," which is a bit unusual. შეცვალებული generally means
    "dead," according to Sarjvelaże et al., Altgeorgisch–deutsches Wörterbuch, 1396, but
    it could also be a passive participle from შეცვალებაი, which would mean
    "changed." It is thus somewhat difficult to translate these words: "deathly
    garb" or "changed clothing" are possibilities, but in any case the reference to
    John's manner of dress as reported in the gospels is clear: "Now John wore a
    garment of camel's hair, and a leather girdle around his waist; and his food
    was locusts and wild honey" (Matt 3.4).
4   შეუთქს is an irregular form of the third person singular iterative from
    შედგომა: see Ilia Abulaże, ძველი ქართული ენის ლექსიკონი
    (Dzveli K'art'uli enis Lek'sikoni [Dictionary of the Old Georgian Language]) (Tbilisi:
    Mec'niereba, 1973), 490b; cf. also Joseph Molitor, Glossarium Ibericum in quattuor
    Evangelia et Actus Apostolorum antiquioris versionis etiam textus Chanmeti et Haemeti
    complectens, 2 vols., Corpus Scriptorum Christianorum Orientalium 228
    and 237, Subsidia 20–21 (Louvain: Secrétariat du CorpusSCO, 1962),
    vol. 2, 324. Van Esbroeck translates this passage as "car le chevalier vient et
    introduit le roi qui suit," which conveys the sense of the passage but seems
    to misunderstand the second verb. See also the identical rhetorical structure
    in §18 above.
5   Van Esbroeck translates rather oddly, "parce que non seulement il clamait la
    purification."
6   დე is a misprint for მე.
7   დაშეერთებული is a misprint for შეერთებული და.
8   Van Esbroeck translates თუალდებით somewhat literally as "à l'œil," but
    თუალ(თ)დებაი generally means "hypocrisy," "falseness," or "prejudice,"
    which seems to be the sense here. Likewise, van Esbroeck translates

მიმადლებით as "par grâce"; nevertheless, მიმადლებად can also mean "for hire," which makes better sense in this context (and which also suggests quite the opposite of the French expression "à l'œil").

9 Van Esbroeck translates მბრძოლსა მას ბოროტსა as "dans un combat agressif." Nevertheless, this would require reading მბრძოლობასა instead of მბრძოლსა, and "aggressive" does not seem within the range of meaning for ბოროტი.

10 Van Esbroeck translates "les premiers pour leur agrément," which, while not impossible, seems to miss the sense of the remarks that follow.

11 Van Esbroeck translates სტუმარი as "hôte," which is among the meanings indicated in Čʻubinovi, *Gruzinsko-russko-frantsūzskīĭ slovarʻ*. Nevertheless, other more recent dictionaries are agreed in identifying this term as instead referring to a guest.

12 The word ვინაიცა usually means "whence" and thus is a bit odd here. Nevertheless, I have followed van Esbroeck's interpretation above. Moreover, one finds such usage of this word with the meaning "wherever" elsewhere in the text, most notably below in §98, §109, §110, and by Jerusalem 108 in §127.

13 Literally "to hunt," but the context seems to make "to fish" more appropriate.

14 The Jerusalem manuscript reads instead "paralyzed."

15 Van Esbroeck translates rather strangely here, "de s'en aller chez lui."

16 განყიდეს is a misprint for განყიდენ.

17 Following here the reading from Jerusalem 108 and Sinai 68.

18 განწყსნა is a misprint for განმწვსნა. Van Esbroeck translates as "il commença sa pastorale," but the above is clearly correct.

CHAPTER SIX

ON THE PASSION

1 Van Esbroeck translates this passage instead as follows: "C'est pourquoi lorsque le repas, le grand mystère se déroulait, elle se sacrifiait elle-même comme le prête et elle était sacrifiée, elle offrait et elle était offerte." Thus he would understand the Virgin as somehow sacrificing herself and being sacrificed at the Last Supper. The interpretation is not impossible since, as van Esbroeck notes, there are not indications of gender at this point in the text, as is very often the case in Georgian. Nevertheless, for reasons that I have explained elsewhere, it seems far more likely that the text should be understood as referring to Jesus in this role, as I have translated above. Such language describing Christ as both sacrificer and sacrifice is quite common in the Christian tradition, deriving primarily from Heb 9–10. Shoemaker, "The Virgin Mary in the Ministry of Jesus," 447–9.

2 Van Esbroeck translates "ni ne se dérobait en quelque endroit," but this would presumably seem to require reading the verb as some form of მირიდებაჲ rather than from მიდრ(ე)კა. The form in the edition is clearly indicated in the manuscripts.

3 თანამვალნი should read თანამავლნი. Also, it is somewhat difficult to translate ლმობიერად here, particularly in light of its range of meanings. It is tempting to link it with დაუტევეს later in the sentence, in which case one would translate "who bitterly abandoned him." Yet its position in the text seems to associate it instead specifically with თანამავლნი, and so I have attempted to translate it. Although it can mean "bitterly" or "painfully," it can also mean, as Sarjvelaże and Fähnrich indicate, "mitfühlend," as I have tried to render the term here: see Sarjvelaże et al., *Altgeorgisch–deutsches Wörterbuch*, 592.

4 Van Esbroeck's translation, "imitatrice inflexible," is curious.

5 მჭუნვარე is a misprint for მჭმუნვარე.

6 Van Esbroeck suggests in regard to the latter reference that the text has apparently rendered δύσχρηστος as "Christ."

7 Van Esbroeck translates here "la victoire de son fils et Seigneur," but this would require reading მარჯუებაჲ instead of მარჯუენე, which is the form found in the manuscripts.

8 კაცისმკელვლობაჲ is a misprint for კაცისმკლველობაჲ.

9 Or possibly "handwork."

10 Van Esbroeck incorrectly translates აღსძ(უ)არცუეს as "les tueurs ont jeté les sorts."

11 Following here the reading of Jerusalem 108 and Sinai 68.

12 ჯერით is a misprint for ჯერეთ, the form in Sinai 68 and Jerusalem 108.

13 Jerusalem 108 manuscript has მისთა, which seems to be the better reading.

14 აღრახეს is a misprint for აღრაცხეს.

15 The edition here has ნუგეშინისმცელ სადამე. მე არა ვკოვე, but the following word division seems more likely and is much closer to the Psalm being cited: ნუგეშინისმცემლსა, და მე არა ვკოვე. The second მე is presumably a misprint, and it is not present in Sinai 68. The reading of Jerusalem 108 here follows a variant rendering of this verse: ნუგეშინისმცემლ ჩენდა, და მე არა ვკოვე, which also lacks the reduplicated მე of the edition.

16 Following the reading of Jerusalem 108 and Sinai 68.

17 This variant occurs in the writings of various Church Fathers: see Joseph Ziegler, ed., *Ieremias, Baruch, Threni, Epistula Ieremiae*, Septuaginta: Vetus Testamentum Graecum auctoritate Societatis Litterarum Gottingensis editum 15 (Göttingen: Vandenhoeck & Ruprecht, 1957), 155.

18 ურაცხელნი is a misprint for ურიცხელნი.

19 Van Esbroeck's translation here, "et la garde stricte ils la donnèrent aux soldats," seems to miss the sense of უდებყვეს.

20 It should of course not be overlooked that, according to the gospels, the following acts were done not by the Jews but by the Romans.

21 ნარწყვთა is a misprint for ნერწყვთა.

22 არა should read instead არს, the form in Sinai 68, which makes the sense of this passage much clearer than in van Esbroeck's translation. Jerusalem 108 is illegible here.

23 Following the reading of Jerusalem 108 and Sinai 68; the latter has the verb form მოიჴსნეს.

24 უკუნაჲკნელ should read უკუანაჲსკნელ, the form in Sinai 68; Jerusalem 108 is difficult to read but appears to have the same form.

25 სწყალობდენ is probably a misprint. Jeru. 108 is illegible here, but Sinai 68 clearly shows სწყალობდეს.

26 Van Esbroeck translates შთაუწუთინა as "se coagula," although it is not clear how he arrives at this meaning. The meaning "to settle as a thick/dense matter after becoming separated from its liquid part (e.g., curds from whey)" is given for ჩაწვება in S. J. Harrell et al., *Georgian–English Dictionary* (Springfield, VA: Dunwoody Press, 2002), 871. Likewise one finds "(*dregs*) will precipitate, fall to the bottom" in Rayfield, *A Comprehensive Georgian–English Dictionary*, vol. 2, 1547, although here the meaning "(*milk*) will thicken" is limited to the Kakhetian dialect. Yet it would appear that the form is a causative deriving from შთაწუეთება, meaning "to drip" or "to drip into," according to Sarjvelaże et al., *Altgeorgisch–deutsches Wörterbuch*, 1422. On the use of -ინ- to indicate the causative, see Kita Tschenkéli, *Einführung in die georgische Sprache*, 2 vols. (Zürich: Amirami Verlag, 1958), vol. 1, 334–41; Heinz Fähnrich, *Grammatik der altgeorgischen Sprache* (Hamburg: Helmut Buske, 1994), 205–6; George Hewitt, *Georgian: A Learner's Grammar* (London: Routledge, 1996), 349–55.

27 Van Esbroeck's translation seems to miss some of the sense here: "ses yeux et sa pensée étaient attentifs grâce à l'amour de son roi et de son fils."

28 მჳარი should instead read მყარი, the form in Jerusalem 108 and Sinai 68.

29 მისდა should read მის და.

30 Van Esbroeck's edition has here კნინოდენ წინაგებითა, which he translates as "avec un peu de chance." Nevertheless, I am unable to find any lexical entry for a term related to the form წინაგებითა. Jerusalem 108, however, clearly has წანაგებითა instead of წინაგებითა (as well as the better reading კნინოდენითა instead of კნინოდენ). There is no relevant entry for წანაგებითა in either Sarjvelaże et al., *Altgeorgisch–deutsches Wörterbuch*, or E. Cherkesi, *Georgian–English Dictionary* (Oxford: Printed for the Trustees of the Marjory Wardrop Fund, University of Oxford, 1950), but Čʻubinovi, *Gruzinsko–russko–frant͡suzskiĭ slovarʻ*, Richard Meckelein, *Georgisch–deutsches Wörterbuch*, Lehrbücher des Seminars für orientalische sprachen zu Berlin XXXII (Berlin, Leipzig,: W. de Gruyter & Co., 1928), Kita Tschenkéli and Yolanda Marchev, *Georgisch–deutsches Wörterbuch*, 3 vols. (Zürich: Amirami,

1965), and Rayfield, *A Comprehensive Georgian–English Dictionary*, all indicate the word წანაგები with the general meaning of "loss." I have followed this reading in the translation above. The phrase in question is absent, however, from Sinai 68.

31 წალებითა is a misprint for წათებითა; it is not clear how van Esbroeck derives "torches" from either form.

32 Sinai 68 has the more usual spelling, მდღუარი; Jerusalem 108 is illegible here.

33 Van Esbroeck's edition has here შეტყყეს (from შეტყუება?), which does not seem to make much sense. Sinai 68 has instead შეხჯეს, from შეხუეჯა, which fits perfectly, and thus we have translated above. Jerusalem 108 unfortunately is illegible at this point.

34 Sinai 68 has the more standard spelling, განზავებად; Jerusalem 108 is illegible here.

35 ადგილუბანს should read ადგილობანს.

36 The final phrase, "and saw everything that took place," appears in both Jerusalem 108 and Sinai 68, but not in Tbilisi A-40.

CHAPTER SEVEN

ON THE RESURRECTION

1 Literally, "from the beginning" (დასაბამით გან); but cf. 1 Cor 15.20 ("first fruits" = ἀπαρχὴ)

2 გულისმოდგინებითა should read გულსმოდგინებითა.

3 მენელსაცხებელთასა should read მენელსაცხებლეთასა.

4 Van Esbroeck's translation here seems to miss the mark on several points: "les évangélistes ont écrit cela à la cause de la condescendance et du témoignage oculaire de la sainte reine." The equivalent passages in George of Nicomedia's *Homily 9: On the Immaculate Virgin's Vigil at the Tomb* (PG 100, 1497C) and Symeon the Metaphrast's *Life of the Virgin* 36 (Latyšev, ed., *Menologii anonymi byzantini*, vol. 2, 371) offer the same explanation: that the evangelists left out this information because a mother's testimony was likely to be suspect, while George additionally explains that it might be seen as an effort to further glorify the Virgin.

5 Van Esbroeck's translation of დედებითურთ as "avec gloire" seems to have misread this word as დიდებულებითურთ.

6 მოუწთომელი is a misprint for მიუწთომელი.

7 თანაილუწა should be თანა ილუწა.

8 Literally, "her goings": სლვანი მისნი. Van Esbroeck translates: "ses courses méditatives."

193

9 Reading ღმრთივშუენიერთა from Sinai 68 and Jerusalem 108 instead of ღმრთისმშუენიერთა.

10 მოლუაწედ და is a misprint and should read მოლუაწე და.

11 Following here both Jerusalem 108 and Sinai 68, which read მათ instead of მის.

12 Reading მათ from Jerusalem 108 and Sinai 68 instead of მას. Also, van Esbroeck's reading of the verbal forms here as plural is not correct.

13 The word ვინაა usually means "whence" and thus is a bit odd here. Nevertheless, I have followed van Esbroeck's interpretation above. Moreover, one finds similar usage of the related form ვინააცა with the meaning "wherever" elsewhere in the text, most notably above in §68 and below in §109, §110, and by Jerusalem 108 in §127.

14 თანა მოციქულ should read instead თანამოციქულ, as indicated in manuscripts. Van Esbroeck translates "et elles deviennent apôtres avec lui." Nevertheless, there is no object for თანა in the manuscripts. Of course, the meaning is the same in either case.

15 Here we follow Jerusalem 108 and Sinai 68 in reading და მისა მისისა, და მისა მიმართ ყოველთა მათ instead of და მისა მისისა, და მისა მიმართ, და ყოველთა მათ, which appears in the edition. The third და is seemingly a mistake, and it confuses the sense here.

16 Instead of "the success of their preaching," van Esbroeck translates "sa prédication auprès des païens," but this would necessitate reading either წარმართითობაჲ or წარმართთა instead of წარმართებაჲ; furthermore, in this case the grammar would be rather awkward as well.

17 This tradition is from the earliest versions of the "Six Books" Dormition apocryphon, an early Christian account of the end of Mary's life (dating to the mid-fourth century if not possibly even earlier) that the author uses here as well as in the following section. See Wright, "The Departure of My Lady Mary," 417–48 and 108–60, ܡܐ-ܝܐ (Syr) and 143 (Eng); Smith Lewis, *Apocrypha Syriaca*, ܝܘ-ܠܘ (Syr) and 38 (Eng).

18 რქისანი is a misprint, as is also the footnote indicating that Jerusalem 108 reads რქინისანი. Both Jerusalem 108 and Sinai 68 read რკინისანი, as is reflected in the translation. რკინაჲ can also mean "axe" or "sword."

19 Reading უმტკიცესდა და უძლიერეს from Jerusalem 108 and Sinai 68 (and correcting a typo in the edition).

20 Reading დიდებული ითქუა შენ თჳს, ქალაქო ღმრთისაო from Jerusalem 108 and Sinai 68. Presumably ითქუა has fallen out from the text in the edition.

21 Reading უსჯულოებათა from Jerusalem 108 and Sinai 68 (the ჯ in the edition is seemingly a typo).

22 ღმრთისბრძოლი is a misprint for ღმრთისმბრძოლი.

23 The form ნადრეკნი is the same in all of the manuscripts, although this form does not appear in the lexica. Clearly it is related to დრეკა, "to bend," and დრეკაჲ / მოდრეკაჲ, "bending," as indicated by the context. Van Esbroeck notes a parallel tradition from Andrew of Crete's *Homily on the Dormition I* (PG 97, 1073A): "There marble slabs, laid out as a floor, resounded far and wide under the bending knees of the holy body [κατακλίσεις τῶν ἱερῶν γονάτων]" (trans. Daley, *On the Dormition of Mary*, 104). According to van Esbroeck, the phrase from the *Life of the Virgin* is also repeated in John the Geometer's *Life of the Virgin*, but unfortunately this section has not yet been edited.

CHAPTER EIGHT

THE DORMITION

1 The word used here, მიცვალებაჲ, literally means "translation" (i.e., *transitus*), but more commonly it is used as a euphemism meaning "death." I have adopted the traditional theological term "Dormition" as a translation, but it should be noted that, as so often, these other meanings lurk in the background of this now conventional term, which is itself a theologically laden euphemism for Mary's death.

2 The syntax here is a bit unusual, but the translation of John 8.56 in the Adishi Gospels offers an important early parallel for similar use of სწადოდა in this manner. Based on the early traditions of Mary's Dormition, Mary's desire to see John, rather than vice versa, seems more likely here.

3 Van Esbroeck's edition has here დაჲ იგი, which he translates as "leur sœur." Nevertheless, both Jerusalem 148 and Sinai 68 read წმიდაჲ იგი, which makes much better sense, and accordingly one suspects a typo. Jerusalem 108 is not clearly legible at this point.

4 Van Esbroeck's edition has here ღამე, but Jerusalem 148 and Sinai 68 both have ღამედ, which seems to be a slightly better reading. Jerusalem 108 is not legible.

5 Literally "soul," as in John 10.11.

6 Ps.-Dionysius, *On the Divine Names* 3.2 (Suchla, ed., *Corpus Dionysiacum*, vol. 1, 141); also, PG 3, 681C-684A.

7 მოცუმელი is a misprint for მოცემული.

8 The form here, გამოშჩნდით (გამოსჩნდით in Sinai 68), is rather unusual. Although van Esbroeck translates the term as "vous a élus," the ending -ით seems to indicate either a first or second person plural form, most likely derived somehow from გამორჩევა, as van Esbroeck seems to have correctly supposed. The use of this same term in the Georgian translation of

Hippolytus of Rome's *De Antichristo* to translate ἐκηρύχθητε (or ἐκλήθητε in some manuscripts) confirms the translation above: see Garitte, ed., *Traités d'Hippolyte*, 90 (Geor) and 67 (Lat); cf. Bonwetsch et al., eds., *Hippolytus Werke*, vol. 1.2, 20. Although Garitte translates გამოშჩნდით as "apparuistis," no doubt understanding the form as derived from გამოჩენა, in both instances the meaning "to call" rather than "to appear" suits the context much better, and this meaning is further determined through comparison with the original Greek of *De Antichristo*. See also a similar usage of გამოშჩნდით with the meaning "you have been called" in Akaki Šaniże, სინური მრავალთავი 864 წლისა *(Sinuri mravalt'avi 864 çlisa [The Sinai Homilary of the Year 864])*, Żveli k'art'uli enis kat'edris šromebi 5 (Tbilisi: T'bilisis Stalinis saxelobis saxelmcip'o universitetis gamomc'emloba, 1959), 117, line 35.

9 In Greek the title of this chapter is Τίς ἡ τῆς εὐχῆς δύναμις καὶ περὶ τοῦ μακαρίου Ἱεροθέου καὶ περὶ εὐλαβείας καὶ συγγραφῆς θεολογικῆς: Ps.-Dionysius, *On the Divine Names* 3 (Suchla, ed., *Corpus Dionysiacum*, vol. 1, 138); also, PG 3, 680A. The passage in question occurs, as signaled already above, at *On the Divine Names* 3.2 (Suchla, ed., *Corpus Dionysiacum*, vol. 1, 141; also PG 3, 681C–684A). See also the English translation in Pseudo-Dionysius, *Pseudo-Dionysius: The Complete Works*, trans. Colm Luibhéid and Paul Rorem, Classics of Western Spirituality (New York: Paulist Press, 1987), 70.

10 *On the Divine Names* is in fact addressed to Timothy: see Suchla, ed., *Corpus Dionysiacum*, vol. 1, 107; also PG 3, 586A

11 დააჳსენა is a misprint for და აჳსენა.

12 გამოთქუმელითა is a misprint for გამოუთქუმელითა.

13 The text is a bit unusual here. მადლი and დიდებაჲ are in the first nominative case, and as such they seem to need some sort of verb that is lacking here. Nevertheless, it would appear that this is some sort of exclamation of praise. There is a similar construction in one of the folios in the Graz collection, MS 2058C, verso b, lines 4–5: ხოლო ღმერთსა ჩუენსა მადლი და დიდებაჲ აწ და მარადის და უკუნითი უკუნისამდე. ამენ. *Thesaurus Indogermanischer Text- und Sprachmaterialien (TITUS)* ([cited 9 Mar 2010]); available from http://titus.fkidg1.uni-frankfurt.de/texte/etcs/cauc/ageo/tmin/2058c/2058c.htm.

14 The citation that follows does not seem to appear anywhere in the Dionysiac corpus but most likely is rather free elaboration on *On the Divine Names* 3.2.

15 შესხაჲ is a misprint for შესხმაჲ.

16 Van Esbroeck mistakenly reads the verb here as a plural form, and thus understands the subject incorrectly. The passage refers back, as van Esbroeck rightly notes, to Mary's words at the end of §107, where she speaks these words after having witnessed the arrival of the apostles but before her son's arrival.

17 The word here ვინაჲცა, which usually means "whence," is a bit odd for the context. Nevertheless, the form is clear in Jerusalem 108, Jerusalem 148, and

Sinai 68. I have followed van Esbroeck's interpretation above, which seems to be the best solution. Note also a similar use of this term yet again in the following sentence, as well as above in §68 and §98 and below at the end of §110 and by Jerusalem 108 in §127.

18 This translation of შეიწირეს is determined by similar use in Lev 6.30, 19.6, 19.21, 22.23, 22.25, 22.27; cf. Deut 33.11; Dan 9.17. See also Č'ubinovi, *Gruzinsko–russko–frantsuzskiĭ slovar'*, 577a.

19 An unusual word: მჴარუჳკრეს. The form is identical in all three manuscripts that I have examined. Literally, this seems to mean "to take by the shoulder." Nevertheless, Sarjvelaże et al., *Altgeorgisch–deutsches Wörterbuch*, 882b, gives the word მჴარჳკრობით, with the meaning "in a row, shoulder to shoulder." Inasmuch as the lexicon's example involves the context of groups singing "shoulder to shoulder," perhaps we should understand a similar meaning here, since singing also is the context.

20 Van Esbroeck translates here "conduisirent," understanding the verb განიყვანეს as a form of განყვანება, which means "to lead forth," and we have followed this reading in the translation above. Nevertheless, it is quite possible that the form may derive from განყოფა, which means, among other things, "to divide" or "to share." As much is certainly suggested by a nearly identical passage in John the Geometer's *Life of the Virgin*, which uses the Greek verb μερίζω: Καὶ οὕτω λοιπὸν μερίζονται τὴν παρθένον μαθηταὶ καὶ διδάσκαλος, ἐπίγεια καὶ οὐράνια. . . . Wenger, *L'Assomption*, 380. In this case, however, one would presumably expect the more regular form, განიყვნეს. Nevertheless, the form განიყვანეს is clear in Sinai 68, although Jerusalem 108 is damaged at this point, and the photograph of Jerusalem 148 is too blurry to read clearly. Note as well that here ქუეუანამან is a misprint for ქუეყანამან.

21 Again ვინაცა, which usually means "whence," is a bit odd for the context. I have also followed van Esbroeck's interpretation above, which seems the best solution. Van Esbroeck further suggests here that the author reveals an awareness that there were differences of opinion concerning the ultimate fate of Mary's body. I am not able to read the two Jerusalem manuscripts here, and the Sinai manuscript has the following reading, which is not especially helpful: რომელსა იგი ეგულებოდა. შემდგომად მიცვალებაჲ ანუ ვინაცა ენებოს ჯესა და ღმერთსა მისსა. Note also the similar use of this term above in §68, §98, and §109, and by Jerusalem 108 in §127 below.

22 Van Esbroeck has here "sortirent," which does not seem correct for გარემოადგეს.

23 The phrase here is rather peculiar: და შეხოლოუდგა სარწმუნოებასა საქმეცა. Van Esbroeck translates "si seulement l'action suivait la foi," but I think that the above is a more plausible interpretation.

24 The verbal form here would appear to be a singular aorist: გარემოეცვა. Nevertheless, an important parallel is afforded by the Georgian translation of Ps 70.10, where მოეცვა is used to translate φυλάσσοντες. Moreover, such meaning is further signaled by the equivalent passage in Symeon the Metaphrast's *Life of the Virgin* 41: ἀγγέλων ὥσπερ εἰκὸς προθεόντων, περιθεόντων, ἐφεπομένων (Latyšev, ed., *Menologii anonymi byzantini*, vol. 2, 375).

25 ფრთხებითა is a misreading. The Sinai and Jerusalem manuscripts have here ფრთეებითა. Moreover, this form once again is supported by the equivalent passage from Symeon the Metaphrast's *Life of the Virgin* 41: ἀγγελικαῖς ἐπισκιαζόντων ταῖς πτέρυξι (ibid.), as well as John the Geometer's *Life of the Virgin* 31: περισκιαζόντων ταῖς πτέρυξι (Wenger, *L'Assomption*, 386).

26 The Mcxeta version of the Old Testament has equivalent phrasing in these two verses: ერმან ცოფმან და არაბრძენმან and ნათესავი ესე წარწყმედისაჲ მზრახვალი არს და არა არს მათ თანა მეცნიერებაჲ. *Thesaurus Indogermanischer Text- und Sprachmaterialien (TITUS)* ([cited 11 August 2009]); available from http://titus.uni-frankfurt.de/texte/etcs/cauc/ageo/at/mcat/mcat.htm.

27 While the terminal form of the *Nomen actionis* more commonly has an object in the genitive, here the dative is used.

28 შემდგომადცა is a misprint for შედგმადცა.

29 შიშსა should read შიშისა.

30 Van Esbroeck's edition has ჭურვილთა, which is presumably a misprint. The Jerusalem manuscripts have ჭუ[ვ]ოლთა, as translated above, while the Sinai manuscript has ჭირთა, which would translate as "suffering" or "woe."

31 ადგილოით in van Esbroeck's edition is presumably a misprint. The Sinai and Jerusalem manuscripts have instead ადგილო, which also corresponds to the Georgian biblical translations.

32 Here again ვინაჲცა with the meaning "wherever, somewhere" instead of "whence."

33 Here again the author seems to show an awareness of differing opinions that had come to circulate regarding the ultimate fate of the Virgin's body. See Shoemaker, *Ancient Traditions of the Virgin Mary's Dormition*, 142–204.

34 დაჰკრძალოს is a misprint for დაჰკრძალეს.

35 Van Esbroeck's edition has here უჩუნნა ყოველნი, with a note that Jerusalem 108 adds თჳსნი. He translates this as "montra toutes ses (plaies)," noting that Tbilisi A-40 omits "ses," while both Tbilisi A-40 and Jerusalem 108 omit "plaies." One might suspect from this that Jerusalem 148 includes the word for "plaies," since this manuscript is extant in this section, although van Esbroeck does not indicate this in his edition of the Georgian. Yet in actual fact, the word for "wounds," presumably წყლულნი, is not present

in any manuscript. Jerusalem 108 and Jerusalem 148 both read უჩუნ[ნ]ა ჴელნი თჳსნი, while Sinai 68 has უჩუნა ჴელნი. Likewise, none of these three manuscripts has ყოველნი.

36 Literally "the airs."

37 Following Jerusalem 148, which reads here გამოთქუას ჯეროვნად კეთილთა მსთა სიმრავლე.

38 Or possibly "brought this gift home to the faithful people": სახედ could be the terminal form of either სახჱ or სახლი. Perhaps it reflects the words τίνα τρόπον, present in Symeon the Metaphrast's *Life of the Virgin*, which may have been doubly translated as ვითარ სახედ. Van Esbroeck's translation seems to omit this word, possibly with the latter interpretation in mind.

39 Van Esbroeck's edition has here ეწესა, as does Sinai 68 as well. Nevertheless, both Jerusalem manuscripts have the reading დაეწესა, which seems to be the more standard form.

40 Van Esbroeck translates აჴოცნა as "pardonna clairement," but this does not seem to be within the range of meaning for this verb. Generally it is used to mean "to destroy" or "to kill." The object of the verb seems to be Aspar and Ardaburius, whereas van Esbroeck appears to understand Galbios and Candidos as the object, and thus must find a somewhat different meaning. Aspar and Ardaburius were in fact both Arian Christians who were executed by Leo in 471: see, e.g., Kazhdan, ed., *The Oxford Dictionary of Byzantium*, vol. 1, 210–11, "Aspar". The contrast with Galbius and Candidus introduced in the following sentence certainly suggests this as well.

41 Literally "goodness" or "the good."

42 See the similar statement in Symeon the Metaphrast's *Life of the Virgin* 45 (Latyšev, ed., *Menologii anonymi byzantini*, vol. 2, 378): πλὴν ἀλλὰ τὴν ἐκείνης ψυχὴν χωρίον ἂν εἶπες τὸ μὲν νῦν ἔχον ἀφεγγές, εὔχρηστον μέντοι πρὸς ὑποδοχὴν φωτὸς καὶ ἀκριβῶς ἐπιτήδειον.

43 Although the word here is სახლი, which generally means "house," both Theodore Synkellos and Symeon the Metaphrast have here οἴκημα, which makes a great deal more sense. One would imagine that this was the Greek word that Euthymius aimed to translate with სახლი. See Theodore Syncellus, *Homily on the Virgin's Robe* (François Combefis, ed., *Historia haeresis Monothelitarum*, 762A); and Symeon the Metaphrast, *Life of the Virgin* 46 (Latyšev, ed., *Menologii anonymi byzantini*, vol. 2, 378).

44 The term მობარკე commonly indicates some sort of tribute, as does the verbal phrase მობარკე-ყოფა: e.g., Sarjvelaże and Fähnrich give "tributpflichtig machen" as the meaning of მობარკე-ყოფა (Sarjvelaże et al., *Altgeorgisch–deutsches Wörterbuch*, 817). Nevertheless, მობარკე can also mean "strebsam" or "eifrig," according to Sarjvelaże and Fähnrich, and both the context and comparison with the Greek suggests instead the idea that they were zealous or fervent in their request. Symeon the Metaphrast, for instance,

has here καὶ ἔτι ἐκθύμως ἐκάλουν: *Life of the Virgin* 46 (Latyšev, ed., *Menologii anonymi byzantini*, vol. 2, 378).

45 Van Esbroeck has here მიცაიცნობეს, presumably for მიერცა აცნობეს, a reading also found in the Sinai manuscript. Both Jerusalem manuscripts have the reading მერმეცა აცნობეს, as he signals in the apparatus (with the misprint აცნობღეს).

46 Van Esbroeck oddly mistranslates იტყოდა as "eurent entendu" and mistranslates ბრძენნი as "les Grecs": this would be ბერძენნი instead of ბრძენნი, which is the form in the edition and in the manuscripts.

47 The verb here, თავსჰჯცო, is most peculiar. Van Esbroeck translates it as "nous avons supporté," which seems rather likely, given the context. Perhaps it should be understood as some derivation of a verb თავს-ცემა, although such a form is both aberrant and otherwise unattested. Theodore Synkellos' *Homily on the Virgin's Robe* is vaguely similar here, as the two men explain that they have undertaken the journey to Jerusalem only for divine veneration, to glorify and celebrate the holy mysteries: μὴ δὴ κρύψῃς ἀφ' ἡμῶν, ἱερώτατον γύναιον. διὰ μόνην γὰρ καὶ ἡμεῖς τὴν τοῦ θείου προσκύνησιν, καὶ τοῦ θαυμάζειν καὶ δοξάζειν τὰ θεῖα μυστήρια τὴν ἐπὶ τὴν Ἰερουσαλὴμ πορείαν ποιούμεθα. Combefis, ed., *Historia haeresis Monothelitarum*, 762E. Symeon the Metaphrast's *Life of the Virgin* is slightly different, however, and thus is not especially helpful: the two men are said to ask the woman to tell them the truth, if for no other reason, in consideration of the difficulty of their journey: αἰδεσθεῖσαν εἰ μή τι ἕτερον, ἀλλὰ κόπον γε τοσαύτης ὁδοιπορίας. *Life of the Virgin* 47 (Latyšev, ed., *Menologii anonymi byzantini*, vol. 2, 379).

48 Although დედაკაცისა ქალწულისა is a singular form, clearly the attribute is meant to apply to both women.

49 მომარხვემი is a misprint for მმარხვემი.

50 The Sinai and Jerusalem manuscripts have here "Jerusalem" instead of "Israel," which perhaps reflects the words spoken by the two men in the following section.

51 The punctuation in van Esbroeck's edition is incorrect here, and this error introduces some slight problems with his translation. Van Esbroeck translates as follows: "Sois assurée que personne à Jérusalem n'entendra de nous cette histoire en témoignage. Nous te confions à la sainte Théotokos elle-même, . . ." Nevertheless, the text should be punctuated as follows: გულსავსე იყავ ვითარმედ არავინ იერუსალჱმს ესმეს ჩუენ განსიტყუაჲ ესჱ: მოწამედ მოგცემთ თავადსა მას წმიდასა ღმრთისმშობელსა. This makes clear that მოწამედ belongs with the verb მოგცემთ, yielding the translation above. This interpretation of the text is also indicated by Symeon the Metaphrast's *Life of the Virgin* 49 (Latyšev, ed., *Menologii anonymi byzantini*, vol. 2, 380), which reads: αὐτήν σοι μάρτυρα τούτου τὴν Θεοτόκον προσάγομεν.

52 The Georgian is again საბლსა, but Theodore Synkellos also has here οἴκημα: Theodore Synkellos, *Homily on the Virgin's Robe* (Combefis, ed., *Historia haeresis Monothelitarum*, 766B). Symeon the Metaphrast's *Life of the Virgin* is slightly different here.

53 The Sinai and Jerusalem manuscripts do not include the second და that appears in van Esbroeck's edition, reading instead თანააქუნდა მათ მიერ. Perhaps this is a misprint.

54 Instead of "earth," van Esbroeck translates "le matin," although it is not clear why.

55 Van Esbroeck's edition has here საშუელებელადი, which does not appear to be a recognizable form. The Sinai and Jerusalem manuscripts, however, all have the form საშუებლად, which we have translated above.

56 Van Esbroeck's "trésor" is a mistranslation.

57 Van Esbroeck does not appear to translate fully სანატრელ იყვნეს ყოველთა მიერ, giving only "les bienheureux," which is not sufficient.

58 Van Esbroeck fails to translate სადიდებელად წმიდისა ღმრთისმშობელისა.

59 სიდიდრედ is a misprint for სიმდიდრედ.

60 According to Theodore Synkellos' *Homily on the Virgin's Robe*, in the process of nursing Mary's garment had become stained with drops of her breast milk that were still visible in his day (Combefis, ed., *Historia haeresis Monothelitarum*, 771D–E). Although this detail is absent from the Georgian text, it almost certainly was present in the Greek original, as indicated by the mention of visible drops of her breast milk on this garment in both John the Geometer, *Life of the Virgin* 43 (Wenger, *L'Assomption*, 394–5), and Symeon the Metaphrast, *Life of the Virgin* 53 (Latyšev, ed., *Menologii anonymi byzantini*, vol. 2, 383). Since both of these *Lives* depend on the Maximus *Life of the Virgin*, they almost certainly have borrowed this motif from their common source. For more on the dependence of these two *vitae* on the Maximus *Life*, see van Esbroeck, ed., *Maxime le Confesseur: Vie de la Vierge*, xix–xxix (Fr); Shoemaker, "Georgian Life of the Virgin"; Shoemaker, "The Virgin Mary in the Ministry," 441–67; and with respect to this point specifically, Shoemaker, "The Cult of Fashion," 58, 64–65.

CHAPTER NINE
CONCLUSION

1 Following here the reading of Jerusalem 108, Jerusalem 148, and Sinai 68.

2 The remainder of this section bears a close relation to parts of the Akathist hymn.

3 საუტევნელისაჲ is a misprint for დაუტევნელისაჲ.

4 დამტებ[ვ]ელი does not appear in the lexica, but clearly it is related to ტება, as reflected in the translation above.

5 From this point on the text in Sinai 68 has greatly condensed and modified the conclusion, and thus it generally is not useful for comparison.

6 This translation of შეიწიროს is determined by its use particularly in Lev 6.30, 19.6, 19.21, 22.23, 22.25, 22.27. See also Č'ubinovi, *Gruzinsko-russko-frantsūzskīĭ slovar'*, 577a.

7 Reading გეგედრები, the form found in Jerusalem 108 and Jerusalem 148, instead of შეგედრები.

8 შემკობით should read შემკობილ, as in Jerusalem 108 and Jerusalem 148.

9 Following the reading of Jerusalem 108 here.

10 Although van Esbroeck's edition (and translation) has here მზისაჲთა, "the sun," this cannot be the correct reading. Jerusalem 108 is illegible here, but Jerusalem 148 reads მამისაჲთა, which surely is correct.

11 Van Esbroeck translates "venue" here, and while this is a possibility, "assistance" seems more appropriate. The idea seems to be the Trinity working in concert.

12 In his edition and translation, van Esbroeck decides for the reading of Jerusalem 108, but the reading of the Tbilisi manuscript (which is also the reading of Jerusalem 148) seems preferable, and so I have translated above. Jerusalem 108 has ვინაჲცა, here used again in the sense of "somewhere, wherever," as seen above in §68, §98, §109 and §110.

13 შთაამტკიცოს is presumably a misprint for დაამტკიცოს, the reading in Jerusalem 108 and 148.

14 Following here the reading of Jerusalem 108 and 148. Also, მომართ should read მიმართ.

15 The three angelic groups belonging to the highest order, according to Ps.-Dionysius, *On the Celestial Hierarchy*, with which the author is likely familiar in light of the previous reference to *On the Divine Names*.

16 Reading here წუენდა instead of ჩემდა. The form is abbreviated in Jerusalem 108, and the photograph of Jerusalem 148 is blurred here. Nevertheless, Jerusalem 108 also appears to have the verb in the first person plural, although it is difficult to read. Also, the plural is more consistent with other forms in the text at this point.

17 Van Esbroeck reads here პავლისა, which yields the following translation: "Maintenant le second intercesseur est parti chez Paul l'intermédiaire, un être humain revêtu de Dieu aupès de Dieu incarné. . . ." Nevertheless, პირველისა is almost certainly the correct reading. Although Jerusalem 148 is illegible here, Jerusalem 108 reads plisა, an abbreviated form that van Esbroeck later interprets as პირველისა (instead of პავლისა) only

a few lines below. Van Esbroeck's reading is rather difficult to comprehend, and he is forced to attempt an explanation in a footnote, where he also notes that his reading disagrees with John the Geometrician's *Life*. Consequently the reading adopted above is much preferable.

18 მოლუაწებითა should read მოლუაწებათა.

19 Van Esbroeck seems to miss the sense of this passage by dividing the sentence into two sentences, which creates grammatical difficulties. This requires him to understand მეოხებანი as a verbal form, which does not seem possible.

20 Here again van Esbroeck seems to misread the manuscripts: his edition prints at this point წინასწარმეტყუელობისანი, which yields the translation, "les demandes des prophètes," which does not make a great deal of sense (and it should be noted that წინასწარმეტყუელობისანი means not "of the prophets" but instead "of prophecy"). Nevertheless, both Jerusalem 108 and 148 read here წყლ[ო]ბისანი, which is almost certainly an abbreviation for წყალობისანი. The punctuation in Jerusalem 108 indicates that the omission was between the characters ყ and ლ. Moreover, this reading certainly makes more sense of the passage than the one proposed by van Esbroeck.

21 Van Esbroeck translates დაცვანი as "jeûnes," but it is not clear why.

22 შუვაქედელი should read შუაკედელი.

23 და is absent from the edition but present in Jerusalem 148. Jerusalem 108 is not legible here, but the conjunction seems to be required.

24 მროლომან is a misprint for მხოლომან.

25 საძუელებად is a misprint for დაძუელებად.

26 კაცთა განხდლუენო should read კაცთა გან დლუენო.

27 Here I follow the reading of the Tbilisi manuscript and Jerusalem 148.

28 მოასწავე შენ is a misreading of მოასწავებენ.

29 სულიერით is a misprint for სულიერითა.

APPENDIX
A GUIDE TO LITURGICAL READING

1 Also the Feast of the Nativity, but especially of David and James the Brother of the Lord. Note that these commemorations are given according to the liturgical calendar of early medieval Palestine.

2 The Feast of the Holy Innocents

3 The Feast of the Annunciation to Joachim and Anna

4 The Feast of Joseph and Nicodemus

5 The Feast of the Apostle James, Son of Zebedee

6   The Feast of the Virgin at the Time of Christ's Presentation in the Temple
7   The Feast of the Birth of John the Baptist
8   The Feast of the Deposition of the Virgin's Garment at Blachernai
9   The Feast of the Archangel Gabriel
10 The Feast of Mary of Magdala
11 The Dormition of Anna, the Mother of Mary
12 The Feast of the Virgin in the village of Bethor; Vigil of the Dormition
13 The Feast of the Exaltation of the Virgin
14 The Feast of the Girdle at Chalkoprateia
15 The Feast of the Apostles Philip and Thomas
16 The Nativity of the Virgin
17 The Feast of the Dedication of the Virgin's Tomb in Gethsemane
18 The Feast of the Presentation of the Virgin in the Temple

INDEX OF NAMES AND SUBJECTS

INDEX OF NAMES AND SUBJECTS

Hierotheus, 133–34

Hyrcanus II, 86, 188 nn 22–23

Incense, 49, 56, 131, 137, 140, 144, 146, 147, 150

India, 126, 142

Infancy Gospel of Thomas (*The Infancy of Christ*), 15, 17–18, 89

Irenaeus of Lyons, 27

Isaac, 59

Isaiah, 47, 52, 76, 157

Israel, 59–60, 62–63, 67–68, 76–79, 82–86, 93, 138, 145

Jacob, 53, 62, 64, 67

James the brother of the Lord, 23, 97, 125

James the Greater (son of Zebedee), 95, 97–98, 124

Jeremiah, 83, 107, 187 n 14

Jerusalem, 4, 10, 18, 20, 23, 48, 64, 66–68, 70–71, 75, 77, 84–88, 92, 100, 116, 120–22, 125–26, 133, 135–37

Jesus Christ, Ascension, 23, 98, 120–22, 154; baptism, 15, 89–90, 92, 94–95, 97, 98, 120; burial, 23, 101, 112–16, 118, 140–41, 152; childhood and youth, ignorance concerning, 89–91; Crucifixion, 24–34, 81, 87, 98–99, 101, 103–15, 117–18, 122, 129, 134, 139, 152, 154; family, relationship with, 88–89, 95–96, 109–10; female followers, 96–99, 102, 117–18; hypostatic union, 51, 53, 94; Incarnation, 27–29, 31–35, 40, 45, 47, 57, 79, 86, 115, 119; lack of fleshly body, 80; lack of human mind, 80; miracles, 15, 53, 71, 80–81, 89, 91, 95–101, 126–28; resurrection appearances to Mary, 120; second coming, 74, 121,

152; Transfiguration, 135 *See also* redemption

Jews, 42, 49, 59, 62, 67–69, 72, 78, 85–88, 91, 93, 101–2, 104, 106–8, 113–15, 118, 120, 123–26, 135, 192 n 20; attack on Mary's funeral procession, 137–39; attack on Mary's house, 126–28; in the Galbius and Candidus legend, 143–47 *See also* Israel

Joachim, father of Mary, 38–39

Joanna, 98

John of Damascus, 12; *Homilies on the Dormition*, 17, 21

John of Scythopolis, 21

John of Thessalonica, *Homily on the Dormition*, 14, 16–17

John Moschus, 8–9

John the Almsgiver, 8–9

John the Apostle, 23, 59, 92, 95, 97–98, 109–10, 117, 120, 122–25, 131–32, 135, 137, 140, 156

John the Baptist, 47, 49, 56, 64, 70–71, 82, 92–95, 98, 100, 187 n 11

John the Geometer, *Life of the Virgin*, 21, 25–27, 29, 34–35, 173 n 66, 195 n 23, 197 n 20, 198 n 25, 201 n 60, 203 n 17

Ps.-John the Theologian, *Transitus Mariae*, 14, 16–17

Jordan River, 92, 94, 98, 100

Joseph, 38, 48, 50, 55, 60, 61, 63–64, 70–71, 78, 81–86, 88–89, 96–97, 117, 125; daughters of, 48, 64, 97; sons of, 64, 97

Joseph of Arimathea, 23, 113–16, 153

Judah, 38, 62–63, 67–68, 86

Judas, 47, 102, 115

Jude, son of Joseph, 97

Judea, 62–63, 66, 68, 71, 73, 83–87, 92, 98–99, 122

Index of Names and Subjects

INDEX OF BIBLICAL CITATIONS
AND REFERENCES
(INCLUDING THE *PROTEVANGELIUM OF JAMES*)